WHO CAN YOU TRUST?

THE THRILLER IN FILM AND TELEVISION

EDITED BY JAMES BELL

A BFI COMPENDIUM

BFI
21 Stephen Street
London W1T 1LN

www.bfi.org.uk

First published 2017

ISBN 978-1-912292-00-4

© 2017 BFI

Typeset in Caecilia and Monod Brun
Designed by chrisbrawndesign.com
Printed in England by Colt Press
Image retouching DawkinsColour

Back cover: *Les Diaboliques* (1955)

Inside front cover: *M* (1931)

Inside back cover: *The Silence of the Lambs* (1991)

This page: *The Conversation* (1974)

Introduction: *The Third Man* (1949)

CONTENTS

INTRODUCTION

BY JAMES BELL

We all want to trust in others, in the lives we build, in the social order that surrounds us, in our selves. But experience teaches us to be cautious, for the world is a place of danger and deception, and the illusion of security can give way to chaos in an instant. Such is the lesson of the thriller.

When we speak of watching a thriller, we tend to describe the experience in physical terms; we might say we were 'on the edge of our seat', or describe the effect as 'nail-biting'. That we do so is because in any great thriller, we're made to experience vicariously what the hero or heroine feels when they're wrenched from their everyday world into a disorientating nightmare. For in the thriller, whether seen through the eyes of a hardboiled gumshoe or an imperilled innocent, a world-weary spy or the president of the United States, there's always a sense that – unlike the cartoonish heroes of an action movie or the monstrous villains of a horror film – the protagonist's predicament is a relatable one. We're right there with them in this world, where we may find ourselves caught in a web of political conspiracy, on the run from foreign agents, among cops on the trail of a serial killer, living in fear of a loved one, or even doubting our own sanity. Always, we're forced to ask ourselves how we would act in the situation. Where would we turn? What would we do? Who could we trust?

The best thrillers get our minds racing as well as our pulses, and encoded within the adrenalin-rush has always been an expression of societal fears. The thriller reflects the anxieties of the age, whether that's in the British films made in the post-war years, with their realisation of the country's diminished place in the world; the tales of domestic suspense told in the same period, when husbands returned from the war bearing terrible secrets; the Cold War thrillers made when the Cuban Missile Crisis was freshly burned on the collective memory; or the paranoid conspiracy dramas made around the time that Watergate shattered illusions of the nobility of the presidency.

The chapters that follow trace the story of the thriller through the critical prism of trust. We learn how filmmakers of the silent age developed the language of suspense through editing – compressing or extending our impression of time, revealing or withholding information to craft suspense – and prompted audiences to ask if they could even trust the screen itself. We see how the espionage and detective fictions of the early 20th century fused with the growing interest in psychology to enrich and deepen the mysteries of the thriller, in stories often centred on women and adapted from novels by women crime writers. We meet such formative masters of suspense as Alfred Hitchcock, Fritz Lang and Henri-Georges Clouzot, later thriller specialists such as Alan J. Pakula, Claude Chabrol and John Frankenheimer, as well as more recent innovators like Jordan Peele, David Fincher and Jane Campion. And we explore such archetypal figures as the world-weary spy and the psychopathic stranger.

The chapters are grouped into three main sections: 'Can You Trust the System?' explores those thrillers which centre on the organisations and structures that govern, influence or protect us, from politicians abusing their power and police departments mired in corruption to the movie studios and cinema itself. 'Can You Trust Others?' spans those thrillers in which the danger is closer to home and has a face, from serial killers to femmes fatales and murderous spouses, and also explores how the thriller has reflected issues of racism and homophobia. Lastly, 'Can You Trust Yourself?' probes those thrillers in which the protagonists come to question their own mind or resourcefulness, from breathless chase narratives in which innocents-on-the-run are forced to rely on their wits to survive, to daring erotic thrillers in which the following of desires can turn deadly.

So watch who you trust and remember, just because you're paranoid, it doesn't mean they're not after you.

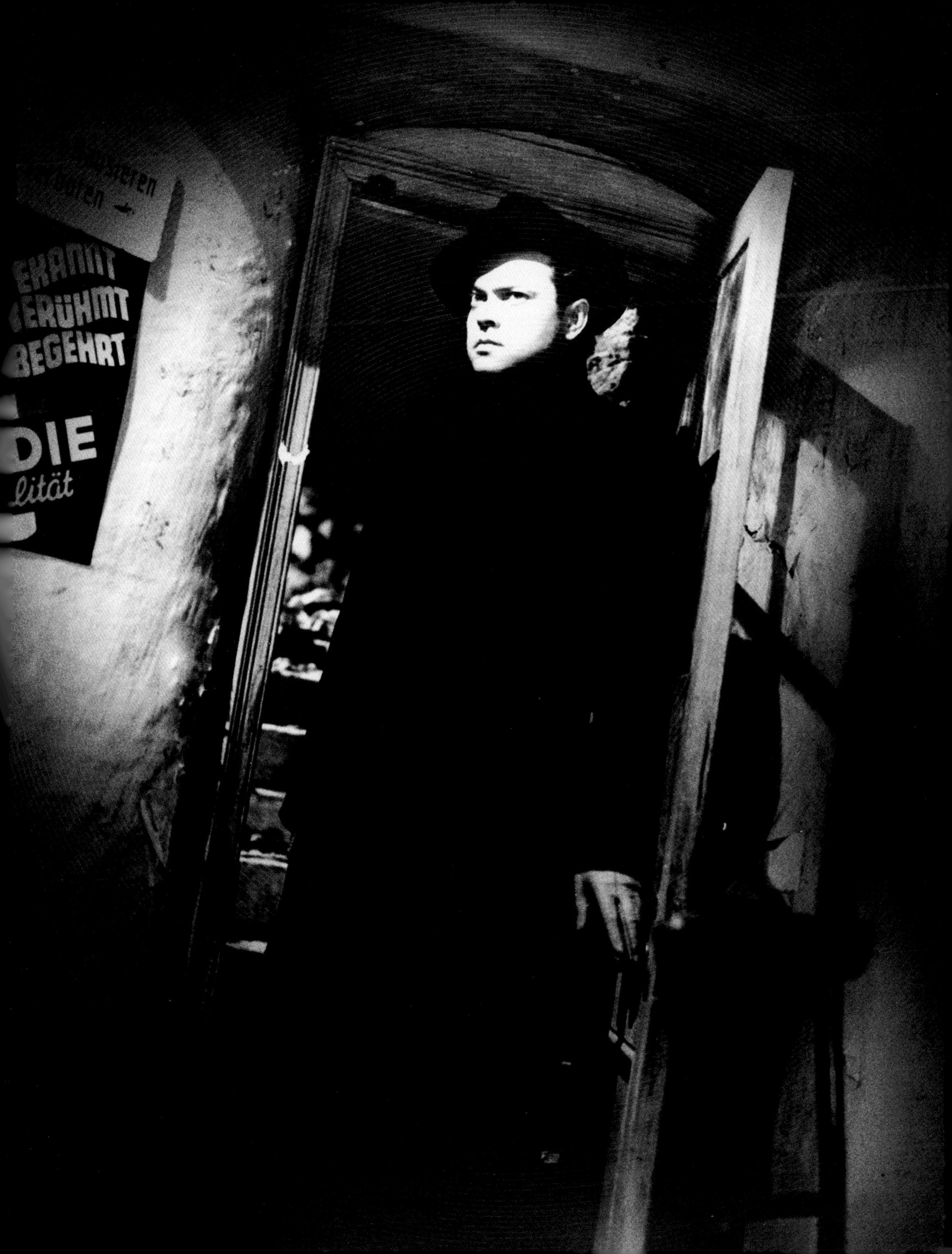
EKANNT
ERÜHMT
BEGEHRT
DIE
lität

CAN
YOU
TRUST
THE
SYSTEM?

CAN YOU TRUST THE GOVERNMENT?

THE AMERICAN POLITICAL CONSPIRACY THRILLER

BY RICHARD T. KELLY

(Opposite)
Dustin Hoffman and
Robert Redford as
investigative journalists
Carl Bernstein and Bob
Woodward in *All the
President's Men* (1976).

Closing his farewell address to parliament as prime minister in 2007, Tony Blair seized the moment to mount a defence of politics as a vocation. "If it is on occasions the place of low skulduggery," Blair contended, "it is more often the place for the pursuit of noble causes." Where politics has inspired thrilling movies, though, it's mainly that sense of skulduggery that has interested filmmakers and audiences alike – both groups inclined to suspicion of the powers-that-be, believing, as did the great Victorian historian Lord Acton, in "the certainty of corruption by authority".

Thus, in the modern political thriller the usual villain is corrupt government, its corridors of power purposely darkened so as to conceal malfeasance from public scrutiny. The ur-plot will involve one law-abiding citizen stumbling on a stray insight into this nefarious world, resolving then to expose the truth, but having to learn fast against a ruthless, Hydra-headed adversary. As such the genre relies heavily on the exciting tropes of the detective and the fugitive – elements that might be expected to work against a plausible depiction of real-life politics. Still, filmmakers can be consoled that in the political world, famously, truth is often stranger than fiction.

It was in American cinema *circa* 1960 that the political thriller found its definition, after some

eventful years in which the US had redirected energies from the defeat of Nazism to the countering of Soviet communism. In 1947 the US established its Central Intelligence Agency (CIA) for covert Cold War work overseas; but that 'covert' element would soon stoke public concern about secrecy at the heart of Washington DC. American citizens had already heard it alleged that their government was rotten with communist spies – this from the House Un-American Activities Committee (HUAC) and from Senator Joseph McCarthy. In 1958 the wealthy confectioner Robert Welch founded The John Birch Society, whose keen membership believed in an 'international communist conspiracy' so pervasive that President Eisenhower was part of it.

The US did have fair reason to fear and abhor communism. It had gone to war in Korea in 1950 on the side of the South against the communist North as backed by Stalin and Mao. In the conflict many US POWs were brutalised by Chinese captors, and some returned with stories of attempted 'brainwashing' – psychological tortures designed to turn a soldier to the other side. This seemingly implausible notion was latched on to by Richard Condon for his 1959 novel *The Manchurian Candidate*, in which a US war veteran comes home mentally reprogrammed by the Chinese to act as

the 'sleeper' assassin of a presidential candidate.

A certain American tendency to "heated exaggeration, suspiciousness and conspiratorial fantasy" was proposed by historian Richard Hofstadter in a seminal 1963 lecture entitled 'The Paranoid Style in American Politics'; and one could surely see the group-psychology grounds for a conservative fear of an alien enemy, inimical to American democracy. But this paranoia was ratcheted up some way if one could believe that the enemy came not from without but within.

Leaving office in 1961 Eisenhower issued a stunning critique of what he felt to be overly cosy relations between Pentagon defence procurers and America's huge arms industry: he argued that Americans would have to guard against the "unwarranted influence" of a "military-industrial complex". Eisenhower's Republicans had lost the White House to John F. Kennedy, outflanked by Kennedy's made-up claims of a shortfall ('missile gap') in US defence spending. But Kennedy took office acting like he meant what he said, further making good on a pledge to act against Fidel Castro's Cuba. The action Kennedy took, however – an invasion at the Bay of Pigs, directed by the CIA – was a disastrous failure that led to a nuclear stand-off with the Soviets the following year. Still, American rightists, having denounced Eisenhower, now found a Democrat at least attempting what they had lobbied for. Kennedy was generating rich material for filmmakers, if they cared to pay attention.

The Kennedy presidency – coupled with the emergence from live TV of director John Frankenheimer – galvanised the political thriller. In 1962 Frankenheimer filmed *The Manchurian Candidate* with a bold, twisty brilliance, its standout performance coming from Angela Lansbury as the queen-bee conspirator Eleanor Iselin, who masterminds the movie's assassination plot so that her husband, a red-baiting US senator, might inherit the presidency. Mrs Iselin, though, is actually KGB: a red infiltrator of America's anti-communist movement. By this ingenious stroke *The Manchurian Candidate* suggested that Americans should beware the kind of foghorn patriot who insists the country is going to hell in a handcart, since said patriot might secretly be doing the steering.

Kennedy enjoyed Frankenheimer's film, and they became friendly enough for the president to encourage the director in another project. Journalists Fletcher Knebel and Charles Bailey had written a thriller called *Seven Days in May* in which the US military's joint chiefs of staff, incensed by their president's nuclear disarmament treaty with the Soviets, plot a *coup d'état*. Knebel based his chief plotter, General Scott, on General Edwin Walker, an ardent rightist who complained of "little men" in the White House and whom Kennedy relieved of his command in Germany for distributing John Birch Society pamphlets to his troops. In Frankenheimer's taut 1964 film version Burt Lancaster plays Scott with a coldly furious eloquence, while Kirk Douglas essays a rare good-guy turn as the colonel who rumbles the plot. The movies, then, could still depict one honest individual fishing out a few bad apples. But what if the rot was wider? Kennedy, who disliked his own joint chiefs, might have appreciated Frankenheimer's film; but he didn't live to see it.

The killing of Kennedy in broad Dallas daylight was a nightmarish turn in American history, worsened when his alleged assassin Lee Harvey Oswald was shot dead in custody before live TV cameras. Within a week *Life* magazine printed frame stills of the president's murder as captured on 8mm by camera buff Abraham Zapruder; and something peculiar in the motion of Kennedy's head when the fatal bullet hit caused many to puzzle over the precise timing and provenance of the shots. Ten months later the Warren Commission ruled that Oswald – a one-time defector to the USSR who had taken a shot at Edwin Walker earlier that year – was solely responsible. In his epic *Oswald's Tale* (1995) novelist Norman Mailer would come to the same conclusion, albeit "gloomily" – believing that artists "must prefer conspiracy to a lonely protagonist" if only for the imaginative possibilities. But a lot of ordinary Americans were now feeling imaginative too. Journalist Christopher Hitchens would argue that "modern American conspiracy theory" began with the Warren findings.

Still, it seemed to require another constitutional crisis – Watergate, *circa* 1972 – to refocus American film on political intrigue. The White House of Richard Nixon, paranoid, corrupt, and desirous of a second term, had formed a Special Investigations Unit ('The Plumbers') for dirty jobs, headed by CIA veteran Howard Hunt. A bungled operation to burgle Democratic headquarters in Washington's Watergate complex would be Nixon's undoing. The televising of subsequent select committee hearings in 1973 broadcast Nixon's criminality to the country and threw up lines – what did the president know, and when did he know it? – worthy of a top-dollar screenwriter.

Watergate – also the Zapruder film, and

Antonioni's *Blow-Up* (1966) – created the frame for Francis Coppola's modishly brilliant *The Conversation* (1974), in which surveillance expert Harry Caul (Gene Hackman) – already a recessive, neurotic sort – is unbalanced further by the fear that his work has made him an accomplice to a killing

Such was the climate in which filmmakers now revisited the monstrous possibilities of Kennedy's murder. Dalton Trumbo – once a keen Stalinist, jailed and blacklisted for refusing to testify before HUAC – scripted *Executive Action* (1973), positing that the assassination was plotted by Texan oilmen, overseen by a veteran CIA presence and executed by soldiers of fortune. As a thriller, though, the movie was stodgy, its plausibility hampered by the stagy shoehorning of all the conspirators into one room for the sake of lengthy explanatory dialogues.

More compelling – because it came at the Kennedy mythology from an oblique angle – was Alan J. Pakula's *The Parallax View* (1974). Journalist

(Above)
Hawkish General Scott (Burt Lancaster, right) plots a *coup d'état* in Frankenheimer's *Seven Days in May* (1964), co-starring Kirk Douglas.

(Above)
Robert Redford plays a CIA operative who is endangered after he stumbles on a secret plot in *Three Days of the Condor* (1975).

(Opposite)
Warren Beatty (right) plays a man targeted by a sinister organisation after he witnesses an assassination in *The Parallax View* (1974).

Joe Frady (Warren Beatty) is one bystander in a throng when presidential candidate Charles Carroll is shot dead, and he's disinclined to dispute what he saw until his colleague Lee Carter (Paula Prentiss) seeks him out in distress, insistent that someone is systematically rubbing out eyewitnesses. We, and the sceptical Frady, next see Carter on a mortuary slab, whereupon Frady realises he must go undercover, and there finds an enigmatic organisation that recruits political assassins. Brilliantly shot by Gordon Willis, *The Parallax View* makes America's august icons of state (flags, monuments, anthems) pregnant with menace. In a final pessimistic twist it proposes that, under harsh lights, a crusading hero might even be mistaken for a 'deranged loner'. What it fails to do – perhaps purposely – is help us understand the real malefactor, and the reason why it did its evil.

Robert Redford – like Beatty, a liberal-minded leading man – got in on the game with Sydney Pollack's *Three Days of the Condor* (1975), playing a bookish CIA desk worker named Joe Turner who nips out for lunch one day and returns to find his officemates slain. Turner has to go on the run, fight off trained killers, and figure out what he was working on that made him a target. It turns out he had handled material exposing a rogue plot within the CIA to invade the Middle East. ("This whole damn thing was about oil!" he exclaims when the penny drops.) At *Condor*'s climax Turner challenges CIA Director Higgins (Cliff Robertson), who is briskly sure the plot would have served the interests of the American people. Of Turner's acerbic quip that the people should have been asked for their views, Higgins is dismissive: "Ask 'em when there's no heat in their homes and they're cold… They won't want us to ask 'em. They'll just want us to get it for 'em." This statement of bad-guy realpolitik – the secret state only does what the people secretly, selfishly, wish it to – would become a genre staple.

Turner's revenge on Higgins is to tell his story to the *New York Times*, the fourth estate acting as the last bastion of democracy. Redford doubled down on this proposition by next working with Pakula on *All the President's Men* (1976), the story of how *Washington Post* reporters Bob Woodward and Carl Bernstein broke the Watergate scandal. As a thriller the picture was a harder sell than its bestselling source suggested. Audiences knew how it ended, and its villains – Nixon's 'Plumbers' – lacked the stagy malevolence we expect from the genre. ("These are not very bright guys, and things got out of hand," is what Woodward hears from

his anonymous informer, 'Deep Throat'.) And yet Pakula again showed himself to be a gifted director of suspense. The picture has a carefully 'factual' feel – real dates and names, authentically hesitant voices on phone lines, authentic-looking locations even when (as with the *Post* newsroom) built on a Burbank soundstage. Pakula's great achievement is that no physical threat to the reporters' investigations ever materialises, and yet the tension we feel for their possible fate is exquisite.

As Nixon retired in disgrace, the canonised air around Kennedy persisted. But at the end of the 1970s his assassination was revisited on film with a blackly cynical spin: a sense that

the self-aggrandising desire of the Kennedy clan to found a dynasty – remorselessly driven by its patriarch, JFK's father Joseph P. Kennedy – might now be interrogated. On this theme Richard Condon had penned another of his juicy *roman à clef* fictions, *Winter Kills*; and in William Richert's 1979 film Jeff Bridges plays the spoiled scion of the Keegan family, brother of a slain president, who is drawn into his own belated investigation of the killing only to uncover the prodigious corruption of his own kin – most eminently his father, 'Pa Keegan' (John Huston).

The American public had looked askance at the Kennedys since the 'Chappaquiddick

---

ANATOMY OF A SCENE

ALL THE PRESIDENT'S MEN (1976)

1. In his riveting first face-to-face encounter with source 'Deep Throat' in a car park, journalist Bob Woodward admits the story has stalled.

2. "All we've got are pieces." he says. But Deep Throat tells him to "Forget the myths that the media has created about the White House."

3. "The truth is these are not very bright guys, and things got out of hand." He then advises Woodward he should "Follow the money".

4. It's the breakthrough the story needed. "You tell me what you know, and I'll confirm," he says. "I'll keep you in the right direction…".

(Top)
The paranoia of the
Watergate era is felt in
Francis Ford Coppola's
The Conversation (1974),
starring Gene Hackman
as a surveillance expert.

(Above)
The 'Chappaquiddick
incident' of 1969 was
riffed on in Brian De
Palma's *Blow Out* (1981),
starring John Travolta
as a movie soundman.

incident' of 1969 when Senator Edward Kennedy
was found culpable for the death by drowning
of Mary Jo Kopechne after a car crash, a sorry
episode that ended his presidential ambitions.
In 1981 Brian De Palma made a fiendish splice of
Chappaquiddick with the Zapruder film for his
thriller *Blow Out*, in which a soundman for slasher
films (John Travolta), out late one night gathering
wild-track effects by a river, happens to record a
car with a burst tyre plunging into the water. The
driver, it turns out, was presidential contender
McRyan, but he had died in the accident, and
so had the young lady who was with him. Only
on reviewing the tapes does our hero suspect
the real story is even dirtier than it seems.

Come 1991, though, the Kennedy integrity
– and the theory that JFK had been grievously
conspired against at a high level – found a new
cinematic champion in Oliver Stone, his *JFK*
fictionalising the investigation into the events of
Dallas mounted by New Orleans DA Jim Garrison
(Kevin Costner). Stone employed technical sorcery
of a kind that Frankenheimer might have dreamed
of for his *Seven Days in May*; and, as with that
movie, Stone's tale was one of *coup d'état* – except
that Stone believed he was telling the God's
honest truth: that Kennedy's murder was plotted
by the CIA (angry that the president made them
carry the can for the Bay of Pigs debacle) and
senior military (apparently believing, on slender
evidence, that Kennedy didn't intend to make war
in Vietnam); with sympathetic assistance, too,
from the Mafia, anti-Castro Cubans and the FBI.
Such a byzantine thesis risked the same failings
as *Executive Action;* and, sure enough, Stone had to
resort to a terrible ten-minute monologue scene
where Costner's Garrison listens admiringly while
ex-military insider Mr X (Donald Sutherland,
modelled on conspiracy theorist L. Fletcher Prouty)
gabbles the whole thing out, off the record.

Whether or not Americans now felt
themselves to be "children of a slain father-leader",
(as Stone has Costner's Garrison describe them),
they did appear to have a sharpened suspicion
of the powers behind the throne. Wolfgang
Petersen's *In the Line of Fire* (1993) made clever use
of Kennedy, as Clint Eastwood's veteran secret
service man – "JFK's favourite agent", haunted by
Dallas – is targeted by John Malkovich's ex-CIA
hit-man Leary, who desires to see him "standing
over the grave of another dead president". Leary's
real motive, though, is to show the world how
he was made into a monster by the Agency.
("Do you have any *idea* what I've done for God
and country?" he fulminates.) Eastwood saves

(Above)
The famous amateur
'Zapruder film' of
John F. Kennedy's
1963 killing, as
recreated in Oliver
Stone's JFK (1991).

the day, of course, but again the audience is encouraged to feel that their elected leaders are temporary, and surprisingly vulnerable; while the secret state endures and has no scruple.

Throughout the 1980s the White House was Republican again, occupied by the staunchly anti-Soviet Ronald Reagan and ex-Texas oilman and CIA director George H.W. Bush. The political thrillers of this era found richly disturbing material in a number of covert government operations against leftist regimes in Central America: scandalous conduct that attained critical mass in 1986 when it was revealed that Admiral John Poindexter of the National Security Council had channelled proceeds from proscribed arms sales to Iran in order to fund *contra* fighters against Nicaragua's socialist junta. The scandal was smartly prefigured by Roger Spottiswoode's *Under Fire* (1983), and given a popular reshaping by Philip Noyce's film of Tom Clancy's *Clear and Present Danger* (1994), in which a US president authorises a covert invasion of Colombia by US special forces and is only thwarted by one honest CIA man (Harrison Ford).

Bill Clinton's occupancy of the Oval Office from 1992-2000 inspired Hollywood to a run of thrillers driven by character flaws (sexual indiscretions, usually) on the part of a fictional president: Clint Eastwood's *Absolute Power* (1997) epitomised the trend. But the broader concerns political thrillers sought to reflect were public anxieties over the intrusive surveillance powers of the National Security Agency, and the menace of Islamist terror crystallised by Al-Qaeda's attempted truck-bombing of the World Trade Center in 1993. Tony Scott's *Enemy of the State* (1998) was a hectic thriller starring Jon Voight as the NSA baddie who blithely has an interfering congressman killed, and Will Smith as the fugitive-detective hero. Edward Zwick's *The Siege* (1998), meanwhile, imagined New York under concerted Islamist attack and resorting to martial law: Bruce Willis took the Burt Lancaster role of the bullet-headed general with authoritarian ideas above his station.

Al-Qaeda, of course, finally achieved its 'spectacular' ambitions for real on the dreadful day of September 11 2001. The most rapid fictional response was on TV: the serial *24* (2001-10) in which Jack Bauer, agent of a fictional CIA Counter Terrorist Unit, foiled plots in real time, by any means necessary, in a crunchy remedy for America's new unease. After 9/11 President George W. Bush would be accused of abuses of power (from unauthorised wiretapping to abuse of terror suspects detained at Guantánamo Bay) done in the name of defending the American people; and the 2003 invasion of Iraq to topple Saddam Hussein was decried by many as a war of choice made by the military-industrial complex. In 2004 Jonathan Demme felt moved to remake *The Manchurian Candidate*: this time the plotters weren't communists but, in Demme's

(Below, top)
The post-9/11 terrorist threat was reflected in *24* (2001-10), starring Kiefer Sutherland as CIA agent Jack Bauer.

(Below, bottom)
Islamic terrorism provides the background threat in *Homeland* (2011-), with Claire Danes as CIA agent Carrie Mathison.

words, "the multinational corporations who profit from war". Gavin Hood's *Rendition* (2007) dramatised the grim return of torture to the armoury of US counter-terror techniques.

The political thriller's problem was now, perhaps, one of familiarity: the genre – for all its commendable boldness in telling complex stories, critical of governments and corporations – had taught audiences too well just how bad things might be. This problem dogged *Syriana* (2005), adapted by writer-director Stephen Gaghan from a book by ex-CIA case worker Robert Baer. The movie concerns a fictional oil-producing Gulf state where the incoming emir begins to tilt his favours away from Texas toward China. The usual American suspects conspire to stop this happening in Gaghan's superbly multi-stranded yet strangely conventional plot; and bleeding heart lawyer Jeffrey Wright is scolded by Texan oilman Tim Blake Nelson for sounding squeamish about the underhand pursuit of competitive advantage ("Corruption keeps us safe and warm. Corruption is why you and I are prancing around in here instead of fighting over scraps of meat out in the streets!")

Just as cynicism seemed to have become a default, the Showtime TV series *Homeland* (2011-) was a thoughtful attempt to dramatise the idea that America's fight against Al-Qaeda and Daesh had integrity, its drama arising from the turbulent mindset of CIA agent Carrie Mathison (Claire Danes). The short-lived AMC series *Rubicon* (2010), visually indebted to Pakula's 1970s thrillers, also proposed that US intelligence contained some honourable people suffering under the burden of protecting the public from secretly orchestrated wickedness. As Adam Kirsch wrote in the *New Republic*, "This is emphatically a post-9/11 vision, in which it is not the government's power that frightens, but its impotence."

The lens of the political thriller must turn again following the election of President Trump, another of history's wealthy demagogues posturing as a tribune of the common man, whose clammy embrace of Putin's Russia might inspire another crack at *The Manchurian Candidate*. But if they are to avoid formula, politically aware filmmakers will need to be as adept at dramatising the 'tough choices' of people in power as they have been at conjuring up dastardly conspiracies. In real politics 'us and them' can be another form of dangerous delusion – or, as Senator Silas Radcliffe puts it in Henry Adams's great 1880 novel *Democracy*, "No representative government can long be much better or much worse than the society it represents."

CAN YOU TRUST EUROPE?
THE EUROPEAN POLITICAL THRILLER

BY ANDY WILLIS

Yves Montand (left) in Costa-Gavras's 'State of Siege' (1972)

The late 1960s were a period of social turmoil across Europe. Political activism was rife on university campuses, in the factories and on the streets. France's colonial war in Algeria, the USA and its allies' escalating involvement in Vietnam, the student uprisings in Paris in May '68 and the Soviet Union's military intervention in Czechoslovakia's Prague Spring of the same year – all fuelled the volatile mood of the times and shook the certainties of the old order.

In European cinema, this spirit was felt in a stream of political thrillers. The breakthrough was Z (1969), the gripping third feature by Costa-Gavras, the son of a Greek political activist who had left Greece for Paris when he found his opportunities to attend university were limited due to his father's left-wing affiliations. Though Z was based on a 1966 novel by Greek writer Vassilis Vassilikos, its release in 1969 chimed with the times. The film's political, campaigning nature was apparent from a statement that appeared on screen at the beginning: "Any similarity to actual events or persons living or dead is not coincidental. It is intentional."

Inspired by the assassination of Greek politician Grigoris Lambrakis in 1963, and shot with restless urgency by Raoul Coutard, Z focuses on the investigation that follows the killing of a charismatic politician who had been leading the opposition to a dictatorial government – an investigation that exposes layers of corruption and lies.

Costa-Gavras and Yves Montand would together work on another two landmark political thrillers of the early 1970s, *The Confession* (1970) and *State of Siege* (1972). *The Confession* reflected the dismay many on the left had begun to feel towards the Soviet Communist Party after the USSR's intervention in the Prague Spring. It was adapted from a book by Artur London, which recounted how, as a former resistance fighter turned Czech Communist official, he was tortured into confessing to trumped-up charges and sentenced to life in prison. The opening informs the audience through dialogue and the use of images associated with both the resistance in France and the Spanish Civil War (such as propaganda posters and Robert Capa's famous photograph of the falling soldier), that even veterans of these conflicts, heroes of the left, were not safe from the vicissitudes of Soviet communism. Montand was fully committed to his role as London, losing weight and remaining distanced from his co-workers throughout the shoot, and Costa-Gavras heightens the film's claustrophobic intensity through tight framing of Montand's emaciated and brutalised body.

State of Siege, meanwhile, reflected growing mistrust at US interventions overseas. Montand plays a CIA operative covertly advising a pro-US Latin American government on torture practices, who is kidnapped by guerillas modelled on the Uruguayan Tupamaros.

Following this, Costa-Gavras turned his attention to collaboration during the German occupation of France in *Special Section* (1975), and later made a number of politically engaged films in the US, such as *Missing* (1982), *Betrayed* (1988) and *Music Box* (1989).

The Years of Lead

Few European countries felt as volatile during the late 60s and 70s as Italy, where terrorism from both left- and right-wing factions was especially brutal, a period known as the 'Years of Lead'. One Italian director whose work caught the prevailing mood was Francesco Rosi, who by the mid-1960s had already built an international reputation based on a series of politicised films that explored corruption within Italian society, including *Salvatore Giuliano* (1962) and *Hands over the City* (1963). These works introduced Rosi's distinctive *cine-inchieste* style, one centred on characters undertaking investigations – often exposing political corruption – and utilising flashbacks to reveal crucial events. The 1970s saw Rosi make a series of brilliant investigative thrillers that offered critiques of the establishment within Italy: the Palme d'Or-winning *The Mattei Affair* (1972), about the mysterious murder of an oil magnate after World War II; *Lucky Luciano* (1974), about the infamous gangster; and *Illustrious Corpses* (1976), starring Lino Ventura as a detective investigating the murders of several supreme court judges, and exposing a conspiracy at the highest level in the process.

Like Rosi, director Elio Petri developed a close working collaboration with actor Gian Maria Volontè, in films including *We Still Kill the Old Way* (1967), *The Working Class Goes to Heaven* (aka *Lulu the Tool*, 1971) and *Todo modo* (1976). Volontè's presence is perhaps best utilised by Petri in his ultra-stylish exploration of Italian police corruption *Investigation of a Citizen Above Suspicion* (1970), in which the actor plays a police inspector who murders his mistress, then investigates the scene of the crime himself.

There were also Italian thrillers that reflected the tumult of the time in a less literal manner. In the late 1960s and early 1970s the Italian industry produced a series of highly stylised murder mysteries known collectively as *gialli* after the yellow covers of the crime novels from which many were adapted. The *giallo* found real success at the box office with Dario Argento's *The Bird with the Crystal Plumage* (1970). Most *gialli* focused on crime and psycho-sexual murder, but some

Francesco Rosi's 'Illustrious Corpses' (1976)

found ways to comment directly on the unrest of the time. One was Lucio Fulci's *Don't Torture a Duckling* (1972), a film that took the *giallo* format and used it to create a meditation on what Fulci saw as the corrupting influence of the Catholic Church on Italy's rural south.

This setting had already proved an effective backdrop for a discussion of political corruption in Damiano Damiani's 1968 adaptation of Leonardo Sciascia's novel *The Day of the Owl*, which exposed the collaboration of local politicians and the Mafia to such an extent that the production was threatened when shooting in Sicily. Damiani made a series of thrillers in the 1970s that explored corruption within Italy's political institutions and their involvement with the Mafia, including *Confessions of a Police Captain* (1971) and *How to Kill a Judge* (1974), the latter extending its critique to include the negative influence of the media. These films were key entries in what became known as the *poliziotteschi* sub-genre – tough, violent thrillers set in an unforgiving milieu of criminals and cops. Other key *poliziotteschi* included Carlo Lizzani's *Bandits in Milan* (1968), which used *cinéma vérité*-like techniques to explore the world of organised crime; Umberto Lenzi's ultra-violent kidnap shocker *Almost Human* (1974); and Fernando Di Leo's underworld drama *Milan Caliber 9* (1971).

Autumn in Germany

As in Italy, political tensions led to very real violence in West Germany in the 1970s, with groups such as The Red Army Faction (popularly known in its early years as the Baader-Meinhof Group), whose activities peaked in 1977 with the 'German Autumn' (a term lifted from the portmanteau

Costa-Gavras's breakthrough third feature, the hugely influential thriller 'Z' (1969)

1977 film *Germany in Autumn*, whose contributors included Rainer Werner Fassbinder, Alexander Kluge and Edgar Reitz). A number of German filmmakers concerned themselves with the state's responses to these actions, and how they encroached on the lives of ordinary people. A standout was Volker Schlöndorff and Margarethe von Trotta's *The Lost Honour of Katharina Blum* (1975), adapted from a celebrated novel by Heinrich Böll about a young woman (played by Angela Winkler), who sleeps with a young radical involved with the Red Army Faction, and is thereafter put under surveillance by the police. The tabloid press are led to her door, and subject her to a brutal, misogynistic character assassination. As with Z, the film sets out its position in an opening statement: "All characters and events are fictitious.

Similarities with some journalistic practices are neither intentional or the result of chance, but inevitable."

Winkler also played the wife of Bruno Ganz's central character Hoffman in Reinhard Hauff's *Knife in the Head* (1978), another film that explores the impact of terrorist activities on ordinary people, and the state's response to them. Hoffman gets caught up in a violent situation not of his making and is injured, resulting in memory loss. Was he really involved in any political activity or is the state simply implying he was to justify its actions? The film suggests that he, like West Germany, has to rethink how society should operate.

Spain after Franco
Strict censorship under the dictatorship of General Franco meant that until

the second half of the 1970s Spanish filmmakers tended to work in more obliquely allegorical modes than others in Europe. One rare example of a Spanish political thriller from this period is José Luis Borau's *B Must Die* (1974), which, though shot in English with American actors, can be read as commenting on Spain's internal politics through its setting in a fictitious, repressive South American dictatorship.

Following Franco's death in 1975 and the lifting of censorship two years later, Spanish filmmakers turned increasingly to thriller modes. Juan Antonio Bardem, long an opponent of the dictatorship and a member of the Spanish Communist Party, portrayed the recent murders of a group of left-wing labour lawyers by a right-wing death squad in the taut, documentary-style *Seven Days in January* (1979). Eloy de la Iglesia, another director with links to the country's Communist Party, made a series of startling films that blended melodrama with elements of the political thriller. This cycle began in 1978 with *The Deputy*, about a gay Communist Party candidate who realises that his relationship with a young juvenile delinquent leaves him open to blackmail from the forces of the right, still active in the shadows. De la Iglesia followed this with a series of juvenile delinquent films, including *Navajeros* (1980), *El Pico* (1983) and *El Pico II* (1984).

The tensions between the Spanish government and Basque separatists, meanwhile, were covered by Italian director Gillo Pontecorvo – who had made his name as a political filmmaker with *The Battle of Algiers* in 1966 – in the Spanish-Italian co-production *Operación Ogro* (1979), which recreated the ETA assassination of Admiral Carrero Blanco in 1973.

CAN YOU TRUST THE BRITISH?

THRILLERS IN THE AGE OF POST-WAR DECLINE

BY PHILIP KEMP

"There are bad times just around the corner,"
sang Noel Coward in 1952. "There are dark
clouds hurtling through the sky / And it's no use
whining / About a silver lining / For we know
from experience that they won't roll by."

Seven years after the end of the war, and
one year after a general election in which the
Tories, despite winning fewer votes than Labour,
scooped a majority of seats with the backing of
the Ulster Unionists (starting to sound familiar?),
the heroic World War II myth of gallant little
Britain was wearing thin and the mood of glum
pessimism lampooned by Coward seemed set to
last. Following the hasty, ill-thought-out retreat
from India (and the mass slaughter consequent
on Partition), with British forces wearily battling
insurgencies in Kenya, Malaya and Aden, and
independence movements fermenting in colony
after colony, the British Empire was visibly
crumbling. The drab austerity of rationing still
hung over the country (in 1949's *Passport to Pimlico*
the open-air lunch marking the reabsorption
of the briefly Burgundian enclave into the UK
features a ration-book on every plate); and anyone
hoping to escape the delights of powdered egg
and snoek piquante with a gourmet trip abroad
would have been restricted to purchasing a
munificent £25 worth of foreign currency.

One side-effect of this downbeat national
mood was a growing mistrust of political
aspirations, and indeed of political authority
in all its forms, something reflected – even if in
sometimes muted tones – in the films of the
period. Roy Boulting's *Seven Days to Noon* (1950)
anticipates the founding of CND seven years
later. An idealistic scientist, Professor Willingdon
(Barry Jones), purloins an atomic device from the
research lab where he works and threatens to
destroy himself and London unless the British
government renounces nuclear weapons. The
film finally chickens out of following up its
implications – by the end Willingdon has become
little more than a dangerous madman who has to
be destroyed – but before this his views are treated
with some respect, and terrorism and government
actions are shown as mirroring one another.

In 1952 Ealing released two films rather
outside its usual cosy domestic image. Thorold
Dickinson's *Secret People*, though set in the 1930s,
reflected the political unease of the post-war
period. A refugee from a fascist state (Valentina
Cortese) living in England is drawn into a plot to
assassinate the dictator of her country during
his visit to London. The plan goes disastrously
wrong, but the bumbling intervention of the British
authorities only makes things worse, and the film

ends indecisively, quoting Auden: "We must love one another or die." And Basil Dearden's *The Gentle Gunman* attempted, rather clumsily, to tackle IRA terrorism, with John Mills and Dirk Bogarde improbably cast as Irish brothers. Historical factors were elided – no mention, for example, of the Black and Tans – and the ending collapsed into farce.

Two other films tried, in their very different ways, to tackle the Irish Question. Frank Launder's *I See a Dark Stranger* (1946) starred Deborah Kerr, of all people, as a passionate Irish nationalist who becomes a spy for the Germans until she learns the error of her ways from Brit intelligence officer Trevor Howard. Carol Reed's *Odd Man Out* (1947) had James Mason as a wounded IRA man on the run in Northern Ireland after a bank robbery goes wrong. All five of these films, though ultimately backing away from their political implications – often in order to placate the censor – contrive to suggest, however tentatively, that the official British government line on political activism isn't necessarily the only valid viewpoint.

Criminals, too, sometimes come in for relatively sympathetic treatment in British films of this period – something that the tighter pre-war British censorship would probably never have allowed. One reason might be that hitherto respectable British citizens, exasperated by the restrictions of rationing, found themselves breaking the law by dabbling in the black market for luxuries such as steak or nylons. Trevor Howard stars again in Alberto Cavalcanti's *They Made Me a Fugitive* (1947); this time as an ex-RAF officer who, once demobbed, finds post-war civilian life lacking in the purpose he knew in the war. (This aligns him with Freddie Page in Terence Rattigan's *The Deep Blue Sea*, filmed by Anatole Litvak in 1955 and played there by Kenneth More; the role was reprised by Tom Hiddleston in Terence Davies's 2011 adaptation.) He drinks too much and drifts into crime, joining a gang who deal in smuggled goods, but retains some principles, refusing to deal in drugs. "I may be a crook but I'm not that kind of crook," he tells his girlfriend. For this he gets framed for manslaughter by his associates and sentenced to 15 years in jail, but breaks out to revenge himself and clear his name. OK, it's not quite *I Am a Fugitive from a Chain Gang* (1932), but Cavalcanti's film exerts something of the same empathetic pull.

That same year, in Robert Hamer's *It Always Rains on Sunday*, it's escaped jailbird Tommy Swann (John McCallum) who represents dangerous excitement to Googie Withers's East End wife. He was briefly her lover; now she's stuck in a

(Opposite)
James Mason as an IRA man on the run after a bank robbery gone wrong, in Carol Reed's *Odd Man Out* (1947).

(Above)
Political unrest in Ireland was also tackled in Frank Launder's *I See a Dark Stranger* (1946), starring Deborah Kerr.

(Below)
The sympathetic view of criminals in *It Always Rains on Sunday* (1947) reflected the feeling of many at the time.

dull, stolid marriage. His re-intrusion into her life threatens her stability but at the same time reawakens in her an intensity of emotion that she'd long forgotten or suppressed. At the end of the film he's recaptured and she's safe, respectable once more; but her 'safety' closes in on her like the slamming of a prison door. In David MacDonald's *Good-Time Girl* (1947) a cruelly repressive reform school pushes minor delinquent Jean Kent further down the slope towards serious crime. And while Roy Boulting's *Brighton Rock* (1947) opens with a disclaimer that the pre-war seaside town it depicts, "another Brighton of… crime and violence and gang warfare", is "now happily no more", viewers at the time would have had little trouble recognising the spivs, gangsters and wide-boys of contemporary urban Britain, regularly denounced in the popular press of the period.

A decade later, in Seth Holt's directorial debut *Nowhere to Go* (1958, co-written by Holt and Kenneth Tynan), the criminal has become a near-existential figure who seems to carry the inevitability of his own downfall with him. Paul Gregory, a Canadian con-artist (George Nader), cheats an elderly widow (silent movie star Bessie Love) out of her late husband's coin collection. Given a longer jail-term than he anticipated, he breaks out, accidentally kills his former partner-in-crime (Bernard Lee, a few years pre-'M') after an altercation and goes on the run with a sympathetic young woman (Maggie Smith in her first major screen role). Critic Jeff Stafford commended the film's "mood of desolation and overwhelming loneliness", and Paul Beeson's cinematography makes London look as *noir* as it's ever been.

But *Night and the City* (1950) must surely qualify as the archetypal British *noir* title. Directed by the American Jules Dassin, fleeing the Hollywood blacklist and en route to France to make *Rififi* (1955) and from there to Greece (*Never on Sunday, Topkapi*), it stars Richard Widmark as American grifter Harry Fabian, determined to "be somebody", with plans to make his fortune as a wrestling promoter. Harry is dishonest, manipulative, self-destructive and he steals money from his long-suffering girlfriend (Gene Tierney), but there's something perversely admirable about his sheer persistence; Dassin gives us a view of London's sordid underworld all the more acerbic for coming from an outsider. "Perhaps no *noir* city is quite so hellish, so imbued with the stench of mortality, as the London depicted in *Night and the City*", wrote Paul Arthur in the booklet to the Criterion Blu-ray and DVD release. Another refugee from McCarthyism, Joseph Losey, turned an even colder outsider's eye on the crumbling British complacencies of the post-war era – the critic Raymond Durgnat found in his work "a (highly sublimated) moral pessimism". *Time Without Pity* (1957) skewers the rigidity of the British legal system, presenting an argument against capital punishment as powerful as J. Lee Thompson's *Yield to the Night* (1956, based on the Ruth Ellis case); in *Blind Date* (1959) a police inspector (Stanley Baker) is pressured from above to pin a murder on a young Dutch artist (Hardy Kruger); and in *The Damned* (1961) Oliver Reed's band of thugs are innocence itself compared with the government scientists carrying out experiments on children in their nuclear lab.

By the early 60s police thrillers were getting tougher, less avuncular, heralding the advent of *Z Cars* on television (even though cosy old *Dixon of Dock Green* would chunter on until 1976). Val Guest's *Hell Is a City* (1960) – the city for once is Manchester, not London – has Stanley Baker on best clenched-jawed form as a seasoned cop

(Opposite, top left)
Stanley Baker in Val Guest's *Hell Is a City* (1960), shot largely on location in Manchester.

(Opposite, top right)
London is a gritty *noir* underworld in *Night and the City* (1950), with Richard Widmark.

(Opposite, bottom left)
Diana Dors faces capital punishment in J. Lee Thompson's powerful *Yield to the Night* (1956).

(Opposite, bottom right)
Earl Cameron and Susan Shaw in Basil Dearden's *Pool of London* (1951).

THE THIRD MAN (1949)

1. Holly Martins has come to Vienna to meet Harry Lime, only to be told that Harry has died. But one night, he spots a man hiding in the shadows.

2. "What kind of a spy do you think you are?" Holly asks the man. "Cat got your tongue? Step out into the light and let's have a look at you".

3. The noise awakens a local, who turns on her bedroom light, and in one of the great entrances in all cinema, the figure is revealed as Harry.

4. A car passes between them, and in that instant, Harry flees, leaving Holly to chase his shadow as he races away into the Vienna night.

(Above)
Trevor Howard (right)
in *They Made Me a
Fugitive* (1947), which
caught Britain's mood
of post-war malaise.

grimly determined to track down a brutal escaped
con he helped to put away. Shooting largely on
location, Guest creates a near-documentary
sense of downbeat realism, and the action's
driven by Stanley Black's jazz-based score.
The city is shown as seedy and decrepit, the
surrounding moors as scoured and windswept;
this is a Britain with little comfort to offer.

Basil Dearden, often written off along with his
producer partner Michael Relph as the workhorse
team of the Ealing stable, slipped trenchant
criticisms of British society into several of his
films. "They're kindly, good-natured people, most
of them – easy-going," Bob (David Farrar) tells his
young German bride in *Frieda* (1947), bringing her
to his little home-town in southern England. But
what Frieda (Mai Zetterling) encounters is hostility
and whispered prejudice that eventually drive her
to attempt suicide. Caribbean merchant seaman
Johnny (Earl Cameron) in *Pool of London* (1951), the
first British film to hint – cautiously – at a romance
between a black man and a white woman, finds
plenty of Londoners ready to judge him on his skin
colour alone. And *Victim* (1961) not only liberated

Dirk Bogarde (much to his relief) from matinee-idol status but, by showing how the law left gay men helplessly vulnerable to blackmail, famously fed into the campaign to decriminalise homosexuality.

Charles Crichton's *Against the Wind* (1948) crosses genre boundaries, combining war movie, spy movie and thriller elements. It did poorly at the box office, being ahead of its time; audiences weren't yet ready for a film that took such a sceptical, downbeat view of Britain's war effort. An SOE group, training to infiltrate occupied Belgium on a sabotage mission, are sent over to rescue one of their number who's been captured. Their amateurish efforts end up with several of them dead and very little accomplished; the final bleak image is of a gate idly swinging in the wind. Something of the same post-war malaise that afflicted Trevor Howard's character in *They Made Me a Fugitive* also motivates the ex-naval officers in Dearden's *The Ship That Died of Shame* (1955), who gang together to fit up a navy gunboat as a smuggling vessel for bringing over "life's little luxuries people are short of". Starting with wine and chocolate, they soon graduate to more profitable but far less innocuous cargo. War service, it seems, has fitted them for little but antisocial activities.

Two exceptionally bitter views of the heroic British wartime myth came in Anthony Asquith's *Orders to Kill* (1958) and Jack Lee's *A Circle of Deception* (1960). In Asquith's film an American ex-bomber pilot, Gene Summers (Paul Massie), is sent to London to be trained to infiltrate the French Resistance and eliminate a traitor. (The trainer, here as in *Against the Wind*, is played by James Robertson Justice, bluffly cynical.) In France Gene is told the suspect is a quiet middle-aged man, Marcel Lafitte (Leslie French); he strikes up a friendship with Lafitte and becomes increasingly doubtful that he's the informer. But he's persuaded to go through with it, and strangles the man with his bare hands. Lafitte is subsequently proved innocent, and after the war Gene's handed the task of presenting a medal to the dead man's widow. Lee's film is, if anything, even darker. Towards the end of the war the British OSS want to pass some false information to the Germans. They choose a Canadian officer, Capt Raine (Bradford Dillman), and send him into occupied France believing the information he bears is genuine, while at the same time ensuring he'll be captured and interrogated by the Gestapo; their logic is that information extracted under torture is much more likely to be credited. Raine duly cracks under the torture. He survives the war, but

is a broken man both mentally and physically.

Under the Labour government elected in 1945, the trade unions had gained unprecedented power. Though the lot of the working class was immeasurably improved, British filmmakers – many of whom will have tussled with the notoriously bolshy Association of Cinematograph and Allied Technicians (ACTT) – didn't always see union power as an unreservedly good thing. Alexander Mackendrick's *The Man in the White Suit* (1951) is a comedy, of course, but when at the film's climax the idealistic young scientist played by Alec Guinness is pursued through the dark streets of a Northern industrial town by a lynch-mob of bosses and workers set on destroying him, it edges close to thriller territory. Still, it's almost benevolent in comparison with Guy Green's *The Angry Silence* (1960), surely the most virulently anti-union film ever made in Britain. Richard Attenborough plays a factory worker who refuses to join an unofficial strike, and gets cold-shouldered by his fellow-workers. Worse follows: his son is bullied and smeared with tar at school, and he himself is beaten up in the

(Above)
Britain's pretentions to world-power status were spoofed in *Our Man in Havana* (1959), starring Alec Guiness.

street and loses an eye. The workers are shown as ignorant, sheeplike and credulous, and the whole affair is orchestrated by a saturnine outsider who arrives by train from London, and is evidently meant as a Communist Party apparatchik.

Britain's fading pretensions to influential world-power status were gleefully spoofed in the last of Carol Reed's collaborations with Graham Greene, *Our Man in Havana* (1959). Alec Guinness at his most self-effacing plays Jim Wormold, a vacuum-cleaner salesman in the Cuban capital who's recruited by Hawthorne (Noel Coward), a British spymaster, to gather secret information. Unable to come up with any, he sends blueprints of vacuum-cleaner designs purporting to be elaborate super-weapons. A highpoint is our first view of Hawthorne, beside whom James Bond would appear the last word in unobtrusiveness, striding though the sunlit streets of Havana in a dark suit and carrying a rolled umbrella, followed by a small mariachi band delightedly serenading him.

Ten years earlier, and with rather more subtlety, Greene and Reed had hinted at Britain's precarious place in the post-war world in their joint masterpiece *The Third Man* (1949). Though the two main characters – Orson Welles's Harry Lime

and Joseph Cotten's deluded Holly Martins – are both American, it's Trevor Howard's short-fused military policeman, Major Calloway ("Calloway, not Callaghan!" he snaps at Martins. "I'm English, not Irish!"), who's key to the action, showing Martins the crippled children who've been dosed with Lime's adulterated penicillin, and persuading him to stay in Vienna and betray his erstwhile friend. But it's significant that Calloway, for all his professionalism, can only trap Lime with the help of the naive Martins – who, let's not forget, writes sub-Zane Grey cowboy novels. A quiet comment, perhaps, on Britain's post-1945 dependence on the less politically sophisticated United States?

Briefly jump ahead three decades, and the implications of that dependence have become painfully evident. In John Mackenzie's *The Long Good Friday* (1980), cockney gangster Harold Shand (Bob Hoskins) needs the co-operation of a bunch of American mob-bosses for help in expanding his London crime empire. But he's incurred the enmity of the IRA, and that's enough to make the Yanks pull out. Without them Harold's left exposed, and the Irish gunmen move in for the kill. Can Britain ever hope to stand alone again? An all too relevant thought for our times...

CAN YOU TRUST THE ESTABLISHMENT?
THE BRITISH CONSPIRACY THRILLER

BY MARK DUGUID

Trust, not suspicion, is our natural state. Any parent knows that a young child is wonderfully, terrifyingly trusting, secure in the conviction that her parents will protect her as she explores her environment. Letting go of that instinctive trust – learning to fear – is a crucial part of survival in a world of perils. Children's stories like *Little Red Riding Hood* are central to that education: they teach us to question our trust.

Adult conspiracy stories, of course, go much further, warning us that all trust is misplaced. The psychiatrist might call such narratives pathological: paranoia, is after all, a clinical diagnosis of mental illness. But in a volatile world, in which democracy – where it exists at all – is fragile, paranoia may be entirely rational: just because you're paranoid, it doesn't mean that they're not out to get you.

Certainly, the fear that fuelled 1940s *film noir* was real, imported by European émigrés like Fritz Lang, who knew all too well what emerging totalitarianism looked and felt like. But it was a Brit who, in projecting his own abundant personal anxieties on to celluloid, arguably did most to induce fear and unease among cinema audiences in America and well beyond in the middle years of the 20th century.

Alfred Hitchcock was the first true cinematic champion of Britain's own paranoid tendency. While his own paranoia would find full expression across the Atlantic, his mid-30s British films are striking in the way they express the unease of a Europe sliding again towards war. The cycle beginning with *The Man Who Knew Too Much* (1934) and taking in adaptations of John Buchan's *The Thirty-Nine Steps* (1935) and Joseph Conrad's *The Secret Agent* (filmed as *Sabotage*, 1936), as

Alberto Cavalcanti's 'Went the Day Well?' (1942)

well as the trans-European eve-of-war classic *The Lady Vanishes* (1937), established a cinematic language of conspiracy that anticipates *noir*.

As war arrived, fears of German spies among us were expressed in such films as *The Next of Kin* (1942) and *Went the Day Well?* (1942), which, alongside their familiar propaganda messages (walls have ears; beware of strangers asking questions) carried warnings about the dangers of blind trust in those in positions of authority or with high social status (the quisling in *Went the Day Well?* turns out to be the village squire). This reproach to ordinary Britons' class deference was poignant and justified, given lingering aristocratic sympathies with Nazism even after 1939.

As World War gave way to Cold War, anxiety only intensified. Britain had exchanged one adversary for another, but in the nuclear age the stakes were infinitely higher. Now, though, the enemy was both within and without. Britain's pursuit for the bomb involved an act of unparalleled subterfuge on its own people, and the

formidable intelligence apparatus built during the war against Hitler was now dedicated to monitoring not just the new Soviet threat but any signs of internal dissent. Big Brother was watching us.

The ur-text of British paranoid fiction, George Orwell's *Nineteen Eighty-Four* (published in 1949) imagines a nuclear war as the precursor to the state's capture by the authoritarian IngSoc. Nigel Kneale's potent television adaptation (BBC, 1954) established the template for a series of dystopian dramas imagining a Britain under the yoke of totalitarianism – and signalled that the conspiracy genre had a new natural home: television. It launched a strain of fiction that would extrapolate contemporary concerns to a dystopian near-future (or, sometimes, an alternative present). Like Orwell's novel (originally titled *Nineteen Forty-Eight*), Kneale's drama reflected 1940s Britain, with pervasive markers of austerity and, crucially, a structure of power that was mapped on to existing class hierarchies.

By the late 1960s it was increasingly clear to both the traditional left and the emerging hippy counterculture that, despite a Labour government, truly radical social and political change faced a foe more implacable than the police or parliament alone. The term 'Establishment' became ubiquitous. This shadowy, polymorphous nexus of politicians, civil service, royalty, aristocracy, judiciary, church, police, military, intelligence services, media barons and business leaders who collectively maintain and enforce the existing political order in their own interests, gained currency from the mid-50s, but became ubiquitous in the 60s. In one shape or another, the Establishment would be the ne-plus-ultra of TV villains.

One of the most iconic visions of Establishment power was *The Prisoner* (ITV, 1967-68), which retrofitted the 1960s spy adventure for the counterculture. Eccentric and highly stylised, it was utterly of its time and somehow outside of it, combining zeitgeist concerns (identity, individualism, technology, altered consciousness, concealed networks of power) and hip Edwardiana with an idiosyncratic and unfashionably earnest performance from Patrick McGoohan, an unlikely countercultural hero. While it resisted clear messages, *The Prisoner* clearly marched to the anti-Establishment drum. Its fantastical, superficially genteel setting, 'the Village', is in reality a ruthless internment camp for rogue intelligence agents, applying sophisticated methods of surveillance, psychological conditioning and torture in order to isolate, interrogate and realign its inmates – all, apparently, with authorisation from the very top.

Dystopias in the 1970s reflected the extent to which collapsing political consensus and apparently intractable social and economic problems were prompting some in the Establishment to grow impatient with democracy. Just as in the 1930s, it was a time for some to muse (usually but not always idly) about the attractions of 'benevolent dictatorship'. One unusually detailed answer unfolded over the 13 episodes of *The Guardians* (1971), set in a near-future Britain where social and economic freefall has led to a quasi-fascist dictatorship. The prime minister (a puppet of military and security forces) justifies his legitimacy by observing that "democracy is a form of group suicide". As its title suggests, *1990* (1977) was more explicitly Orwellian, evoking a bureaucratic dictatorship characterised by restrictions on freedom of information and the press, overseen by the oppressive Public Control Department. Like Orwell's, its model was more Stalin's Russia than Hitler's Germany, with an emphasis on surveillance, limits to free movement and petty privations as well as the elevation of the bureaucrat class and (revealingly in the 1970s) trade unionists.

For some, the 1980s showed signs that the dystopian nightmare was becoming reality. Margaret Thatcher's election in 1979 heralded a sharp rightward turn and a renewed suspicion of 'subversive' elements among left-

Bob Peck in 'Edge of Darkness' (1985)

wing protest movements. The 'enemy within' – Thatcher's term for striking miners – expressed a new language of paranoia on the part of the state: proof that conspiracy thinking was no longer the province only of the left. A new vocabulary of official secrecy, D Notices and injunctions, prosecutions of whistle-blowing civil servants and attempts to silence investigative journalists fostered fears of an increasingly clandestine 'secret state' and the rolling back of civil liberties. Such anxieties demanded a more realistic expression, with a clearly defined present-day setting.

Bird of Prey (1982) and *In the Secret State* (1985) explored the dawn of the computer age, with its vast scope for fraud, surveillance and 'counter-subversion'. Both dramas presented archetypes of super-patriotism operating at the heart of the state but prepared to undermine both government and citizenry to pursue their visions of a greater Britain. *A Very British Coup* (Channel 4, 1988) went still further, with the forces of the Establishment conspiring with US intelligence to frustrate and ultimately overthrow an elected left-wing government bent on nuclear disarmament. From a novel by Labour MP Chris Mullin, it was inspired by the belief (later corroborated by official papers) that the security forces had worked to undermine the Wilson governments of the 1960s and 70s. From the opposite side of the political divide, though no less cynical in its portrait of Establishment corruption, came *House of Cards* (1990) and its sequels *To Play the King* (1992) and *The Final Cut* (1995). Adapted from a novel by Tory apparatchik Michael Dobbs, the series drew on Shakespeare's *Richard III* and *Macbeth* in charting the political ascent of the ruthless and utterly

David Morrissey and John Sym in Paul Abbott's 'State of Play' (2003)

unscrupulous Francis Urquhart.

Nuclear power – civilian and military – was the driving force of *Edge of Darkness* (BBC, 1985), probably the definitive UK conspiracy drama. Troy Kennedy Martin's richly ambitious script blended key 1980s concerns – state secrecy, a global capitalism grown beyond scrutiny or accountability, looming environmental catastrophe, the Reagan administration's 'Star Wars' defence system and its dreams of a winnable nuclear war in Europe – in a troubling but deeply satisfying package with strong mythic undertones. *Defence of the Realm*, a rare conspiracy thriller for cinemas also released in 1985, explored similar themes, with a journalist investigating a ministerial sex scandal exposing the cover-up of a near-catastrophic nuclear accident.

But among the most contentious dramas of the period were those that focused on covert state activity in Northern Ireland. The mid-80s exposure of an illegal 'shoot to kill' policy by the Royal Ulster Constabulary inspired Ken Loach's feature *Hidden Agenda* (1990), which fell victim to a British media backlash even as it won international

awards. The Peter Kosminsky-directed drama-documentary *Shoot to Kill* (1990), meanwhile, was withheld from broadcast in Northern Ireland by Ulster TV, saw producers Yorkshire TV sued for libel by RUC Chief Constable Sir John Herman and was subsequently blocked from public screening or video release by ITV.

Undeterred, Kosminsky would return to the drama documentary form to investigate contemporary political reality, becoming a leading interrogator of New Labour in 2002's *The Project* (a fictionalised but intensely researched account of the Blair/Mandelson capture of the party); *The Government Inspector* (2005), which probed the events surrounding the death of UN weapons inspector Dr David Kelly; and *Britz* (2007), which weighed the radicalising effects of British foreign policy in the Islamic world on young Muslims at home.

Kosminsky, not unreasonably, would reject the 'conspiracy drama' label. Others, though, have enthusiastically embraced it. The ten-series run of *Spooks* (2002-11) dug deep into the heart of the Establishment, unearthing a

seemingly limitless supply of intrigue, inter-agency rivalry and treason. Paul Abbott's *State of Play* (2003), meanwhile, served up a wholly fictional response to the New Labour era in a satisfying conspiracy thriller package that worked in the international oil trade, political corruption, murder and sexual intrigue.

More recent years have seen an unstoppable rush of TV dramas – and a new wave of big-screen counterparts – fuelled as much by the conspiracy-generating machine that is the internet as by the chronic global instability ushered in by the most epic conspiracy of our era: 9/11. From Britain alone, the wave of Jihadi terrorism helped inspire such dramas as *The Hamburg Cell* (2004), *Yasmin* (2004), *The State Within* (2006), *United 93* (2006), *Chris Ryan's Strike Back* (2010), *The Honourable Woman* (2014) and Kosminsky's *The State* (2017). But other fictions have stepped back from realism to imagine conspiracy on a truly epic scale. The iconoclastic, blackly comic *Utopia* (2013-14), pitched squarely at youth audiences, spun out from cryptic messages buried in a cult graphic novel to a global conspiracy to conquer overpopulation through mass sterilisation.

But where, in the end, does all this intrigue leave us? More cynical about power and those who wield it, perhaps. But the bombardment of revelations – real or fictional – may also induce weary resignation, a conspiracy fatigue. Conspiracy narratives have lost none of their intoxicating appeal, but they have lost their capacity to shock. Evidence of real-world conspiracies is greeted with the same detached fascination as fictional ones. It may well be that, for our Establishment overlords, like other 21st-century plotters, the safest place to hide is in plain sight.

CAN YOU TRUST THE POLICE?

WATCHING THE DETECTIVES: THE COP THRILLER

BY JAKE ARNOTT

Dashiell Hammett had already written one novel and many stories with an unnamed protagonist called simply the 'Continental Op' before he baptised the primary archetype of the *noir* detective, Sam Spade, in his 1929 novel *The Maltese Falcon*. Perhaps he was thinking of Dickens's Inspector Bucket, the first fictional police detective in English Literature, who makes his appearance in *Bleak House* (1853). Hammett's nomenclature certainly creates a sharp counterpoint to his Dickensian precursor. Bucket and Spade: both are implements of rudimentary excavation. The former might carefully dredge and sift, collect evidence and eventually hold the solution to a complex yet containable problem; the latter hacks away into the matter, digging deeper but risking revealing merely a gaping hole in our understanding.

Mystery is order, *noir* is chaos. *Noir* is not sustained by some impeccable logic the way that mystery is, nor does it put its trust in a process of investigation that might inexorably re-establish a comfortable status quo. As the 'Golden Age' of mystery – the Agatha Christie school with its clever puzzles and urbane sleuths – gave way to this more anarchic genre, it required a tool of the trade with an edge. And this incisive instrument was not merely the protagonist but the creator of

this dark new narrative, one who might uncover the detectives themselves as part of the problem.

Two earlier screen versions were made before John Huston's seminal film *The Maltese Falcon* (1941) had Humphrey Bogart embody the cynical and world-weary Spade. Hammett's work was massively influential, particularly on Raymond Chandler, who praised the creation of Spade, insisting, "Down these mean streets a man must go who is not himself mean, who is neither tarnished nor afraid". But Hammett knew a reality beyond this naive dictum, that the detective is inevitably a tarnished creature. The author had worked for the Pinkerton agency, which sent him to Montana in 1917 to spy on striking miners. There he was offered $5,000 to kill a leading trade union activist who was later lynched by vigilantes. "Hammett saw that the actions of the guards and the guarded," writes his biographer Diane Johnson, "of the detective and the man he's stalking, are reflexes of a single sensibility, on the fringe where murderers and thieves live." It was such experiences that made him a lifelong Marxist. And though Spade isn't exactly corrupt, he is morally ambiguous, volatile and far more dangerous than his reliable offspring Philip Marlowe. Spade is a vision of what was to come.

The 1940s *film noir* boom often dispensed with

a detective figure altogether. The horrors of war and the sense of disorder and dislocation insisted upon a narrative of collective guilt rather than a simple whodunit. Set against the black market and a bombed-out cityscape, the 'spiv cycle' of British cinema, portraying dissolute characters on the fringes of the underworld, lasted until the end of the decade. Then Basil Dearden's *The Blue Lamp* (1950) offered an optimistic vision of police procedure, culminating in the martyrdom of PC George Dixon (Jack Warner), gunned down by neurotic young spiv Tom Riley (Dirk Bogarde). Although Dearden would go on to make notable thrillers dealing with social issues (racism in *Sapphire*, 1959; male homosexuality in *Victim*, 1961) the spirit of his scrupulous British bobby would haunt the culture for years to come.

Fritz Lang's expressionistic *The Big Heat* (1953) lifted the lid on American police corruption, as straight-arrow homicide cop Dave Bannion (Glenn Ford) investigates the crooked dealings in his own department. Playing an upstanding family man, Ford makes for a wholesome, rather inert, Bucket-like detective. It is Gloria Grahame's gang moll who really moves the action along as she takes revenge on her abusers. Order is restored, if a little too hastily. The lid is replaced but it doesn't quite fit anymore.

Other films opened up the subject – *Shield for Murder* (1954) and *Rogue Cop* (1954) – but it was Orson Welles's classic *noir Touch of Evil* (1958) that blew the theme wide open. His obese, self-loathing Hank Quinlan makes for a plausible monster, intent on framing suspects his famous 'intuition' has convinced him to be guilty. While the political point is clear ("A policeman's job is only easy in a police state," declares Charlton Heston's Mexican detective Vargas), a sense of moral corruption clouds the piece and Quinlan remains essentially unknowable. Marlene Dietrich's brothel madame utters the last words in the perfect *noir* eulogy: "He was some kind of a man. What does it matter what you say about people?"

In Britain, meanwhile, a narrative of honest certainty still attached itself to our police force. The constable sacrificed in *The Blue Lamp* had been miraculously resurrected into a television series *Dixon of Dock Green* (1955-76) and for more than two decades projected the probity of our guardians of the law. But reality would eventually blur that impeccable image as movements for political change in the 1960s inevitably found themselves up against the law, often with very direct consequences.

The real-life detective sergeant Harry Challenor had been well practised in 'fitting-up'

(Left)
Humphrey Bogart as the morally ambiguous Sam Spade in John Huston's 1941 film of *The Maltese Falcon*.

(Below)
As seen in *Dixon of Dock Green* (1955-76), the honest copper character was a staple of post-war British film and TV.

suspected racketeers in Soho for years, but when he planted a brick on a demonstrator he arrested in 1963, his methods backfired. His victim was a member of the National Council for Civil Liberties who brought a successful case against the officer and further instances of his corrupt practices were uncovered. This led to the first police inquiry into its own ranks and the 1964 Police Act.

Joe Orton used Challenor as a model for the psychotic Inspector Truscott in his stage play *Loot* (1966) and his keen ear captures the idiosyncratic verbal style of his inspiration. Truscott's line, "You're nicked, my fucking beauty," is a direct quote from Challenor and although the play was written as an absurd farce, Orton was always insistent on the crucial realism of his subject. "Everyone else thinks the play is a fantasy," he said. "Of course, the police know that it's true." Unfortunately Silvio Narizzano's film version *Loot* (1970) is a complete travesty, with Richard Attenborough playing Truscott for

cheap laughs, but the Challenor case had already inspired David Greene's *The Strange Affair* (1968). Here rookie cop Peter Strange (Michael York) is caught up in the machinations of a tough and jaded Scotland Yard detective and, amid mod couture and pop-art imagery, Swinging London is brightly depicted in all its dodgy glory.

By now radical politics, civil rights and social permissiveness had all worn away at the notion of detective as moral protector, but with the 1970s came an inevitable backlash. Don Siegel's *Dirty Harry* (1971) and William Friedkin's *The French Connection* (1971) were both a brutal reaction to lefty notions of law enforcement, featuring tough cops with ruthless methods and cartoon nomenclature. 'Dirty' Harry Callahan (Clint Eastwood) presents a straightforward right-wing fantasy figure, breaking free from the straitjacket of the liberal establishment with periodic bursts of explosive violence. Amid the lurid deviance of San Francisco and constantly hampered by far-fetched legal technicalities that protect the wrongdoer, Callahan's authoritarian dogma is forcefully direct: that the greatest threat to the public is their own civil liberty. But in Friedkin's film, 'Popeye' Doyle (Gene Hackman) and 'Cloudy' Russo (Roy Scheider) deliver a more complex and perplexing double act.

Based on a legendary transatlantic drugs bust by an NYPD special narcotics unit, the film digs at authenticity while shovelling over an underlying truth. Shot in semi-documentary style with handheld camera work and minimal lighting, it was cinematically impressive and highly influential. The actors spent time with the actual detectives on the case and so Hackman and Scheider improvise *vérité* dialogue as they rampage through the streets, beating up drug dealers on the way. We witness the shakedowns, the use of

---

ANATOMY OF A SCENE
THE FRENCH CONNECTION (1971)

1 Tough detective Popeye Doyle begins a bar-room shakedown: "Popeye's here. Get your hands on your heads and stand by the wall!"

2 As the various men in the bar do as they're asked, the camera cuts to floor level, revealing the vials of illegal drugs they have just dropped.

3 Popeye gathers up the drugs and drops them into a cocktail shaker, pouring over a glass of beer. "Anybody want a milkshake?", he asks.

4 Proving he's not a man to be messed around, Popeye dumps the sodden contents on the counter, before rounding up two suspects.

(Above)
Al Pacino plays an idealistic cop who finds he works in a corrupt police force in Sidney Lumet's *Serpico* (1973).

(Below)
The job has taken its toll on the detective played by Sean Connery in Lumet's *The Offence* (1972).

violence, the casual racism and misogyny, all a means to a holy grail-like end of the capture of 50 kilograms of heroin, smuggled to New York from Marseille (the 'French Connection' of the title). But the real cops weren't merely hard-nosed in their methods, they were part of the most corrupt law enforcement agency in American history. A year after the film was released it was discovered that all of the French Connection heroin, with a street value of around $50 million, had been checked out from a police evidence store by a crooked narcotics officer and replaced with flour and corn starch.

By now the Knapp Commission had been set to investigate the NYPD, just as Robert Mark was appointed to clean up the Met in London. Police corruption was a hot topic, the time was right for some proper spadework and one director was up to the task of exhuming both American and British experiences of the phenomenon.

A consummate chronicler of New York, Sidney Lumet had been examining the paradoxes of criminal justice since his first feature *12 Angry Men* (1957) and his less flashy social realist style was perfect for the groundbreaking *Serpico* (1973) – another true story but this time a little closer to the facts. We see Frank Serpico (Al Pacino) go from rookie patrolman to hippie-like undercover detective, an honest cop who refuses to take bribes within a police culture constantly on the take. A portrait of idealism

that came at the height of radical criminology, Serpico dares to offer a solution: "Take all that energy, see? Put it into straight police work, we'd have the city cleaned up in a week." Wounded in a drugs bust and presented as something of a bearded hipster-saint by the end of the film, we are left with a note of downbeat optimism.

This is undercut by Lumet's previous film *The Offence* (1972), a viscerally disturbing work set in an unnamed British suburb. The American director manages to envision an utterly convincing English *noir* set amid new-build housing estates and drab concrete shopping centres. Here Detective Sergeant Johnson (Sean Connery), haunted by crimes he has witnessed over the years, finally cracks and beats to death a suspected child killer in his custody who taunts, "Nothing I have done can be worse than the thoughts in your head." Lumet interrogates a corruption of the very soul that can come with the awful realities of law enforcement. At one point Johnson recites a litany of horrors, full of revulsion for these terrible acts yet unable to escape their seductive power.

Lumet returns to familiar territory with *Prince of the City* (1981). NYPD narcotics officer Danny Cielo (Treat Williams) exposes corruption in his own department in a sprawling epic that suits the complexity of its subject. Unlike Serpico, Cielo is compromised, having taken bribes for years, and conflicted as to what and how much he is prepared

to admit to. Playing a double game, he begins to lose touch with reality. "I was on the street and undercover for ten years," he pleads. "I don't know what the truth is anymore." Cielo was based on real detective Robert Leuci, and there are references to the Knapp Commission and the French Connection heroin theft, but such realist references only make for a bewildering hall of mirrors.

"It's all coming apart," complains cop and murderer Mike Brennan (Nick Nolte) in Lumet's final film on police corruption *Q&A* (1990), "I want it to be the way it used to be. I mean, you lose control of this fucking jungle, you're finished." Lumet's thorough investigation into the theme leaves us with a necessary lack of certainty, a reminder that we should be ever-vigilant of how our laws are enforced. From this we go to the sheer nihilism of Abel Ferrara's *Bad Lieutenant* (1992), which charts the descent of an unnamed officer (Harvey Keitel) into utter degradation. The Bad Lieutenant yearns for redemption and this curious desire for absolution is echoed in *Prince of the City*, where a character observes, "They're cops, in their hearts they want to admit their guilt. That's the way cops are."

Since the early 1990s, some diversity has appeared in the corruption narrative with black protagonists in *Deep Cover* (1992) and *Training Day* (2001). And a retro form emerged, with history refocused through a glass darkly in American films

(Above)
Denzel Washington as the corrupt cop guiding rookie Ethan Hawke into the job in *Training Day* (2001).

(Top)
The labyrinthine character of police corruption is well served by long-form TV dramas like *The Wire* (2002-08).

(Above)
The BBC's *Line of Duty* (2012-) depicts a fictional police anti-corruption unit in an unidentified British city.

such as *Mulholland Falls* (1996) and *L.A.Confidential* (1997) and British TV dramas *Our Friends in the North* (1996) and the 1970s-set *Red Riding* trilogy (2009), adapted from the novels by David Peace.

But by the end of the 20th century there was a return to the certainties of mystery with the serial-killer narrative dominating the crime genre. With it came the perverse reassurance of horror: that we can locate and isolate evil amid the chaos. With psychological profiling, DNA analysis and all the modern magic of forensics, an individual criminal type is investigated rather than any collective problem. Wrongdoing seems containable once more, as the specimen jar becomes the new bucket. And the compulsive public appetite for gruesome murder demands a detective more troubled than troubling.

The riots in England in 2011 and the unrest in Ferguson, Missouri, in 2014, however, once more brought to the surface the precarious nature of policing by consent. There will always be a need to unearth that troubled relationship between the guards and the guarded where detective and criminal can occupy the same sensibility.

Currently the long-form television drama seems best suited to address the labyrinthine character of police corruption. In the US there has been *The Shield* (2002-08), set in Los Angeles, and based on a corrupt anti-gang unit; in the UK *Line of Duty* (2012-) depicts a fictional AC-12 anti-corruption unit operating in an unidentified city. The sexism, racism and homophobia of these worlds are now tempered by officers who are female, black and ethnic minority, and gay, and all quite capable of being as bad as their white male counterparts. *The Wire* (2002-08) has been most successful of all in revealing corruption – in its case as it affects every institution across the city of Baltimore. Underfunded and without proper supervision, the police quickly become compromised. And organised crime inevitably becomes part of a capitalist system. "You follow drugs, you get drug addicts and drug dealers," explains an officer in the Major Crimes Unit in *The Wire*. "You follow the money and you don't know where the fuck it's going to take you."

"You cops don't own the world," announces a mobster in *Prince of the City*, "but you get to shake it a little." And it's all too easy to simply blame the cops – or even the villains for that matter. We all risk being complicit in some way. Few of us could walk down any mean street truly untarnished or unafraid. As NYPD detective Robert Leuci asserted: "There is no cop born, ever, that changed the street. But the street has changed every single cop."

CAN YOU TRUST THE STATE?
THE SPANISH LANGUAGE THRILLER

BY MAR DIESTRO-DÓPIDO

Since the turn of the millennium the thriller has become, along with horror, Spain's most exportable genre, best suited to illuminating the darker corners of recent Spanish history. What many of these thrillers have in common is a need to interrogate official histories and to explore the moral ambiguities of political strife by way of characters working in state institutions such as Franco's secret service and national police, or members of the Basque terrorist organisation ETA. Examples include Miguel Courtois's *El lobo* (2004), based on the true story of a secret-service agent who managed to infiltrate ETA.

The cornerstone of this recent flowering was the abundance of police thrillers made in the 1950s and 1960s. One of the key figures in this era was Miguel Iglesias, whose unscrupulous characters were showcased in titles such as *Muerte en primavera* (1965), *El fugitive de Amberes* (1955) and most notably *El cerco* (1955). The death of Franco in 1975 caused these generally straightforwardly *noirish* films to assume more complex guises in the late 70s and 80s, in the hands of directors such as Imanol Uribe, whose gripping *La muerte de Mikel* (1984) relates the life of a gay member of ETA. Homosexuality is also a crucial ingredient of Eloy de la Iglesia's *The Deputy* (1978). Vicente Aranda's 1982 *Murder in the Central Committee* investigates the killing of the leader of the Spanish Communist Party; while in 1986, Pedro Almodóvar directed his most thriller-like film, the hyper-stylised *Matador*.

By 1989, with Spain now in the EU, shifts were occurring; Fernando Trueba's *Twisted Obsession*, with Jeff Goldblum and Miranda Richardson, hinted at the internationalism to come, and Pedro Olea's historical thriller *El Maestro de*

Marshland (2014)

esgrima (1992) gave the genre a sleek feel, far removed from the lo-fi aesthetic of the 80s *movida*. Moving deeper into the 90s, the Spanish thriller underwent a kind of generational renewal, best exemplified by Chilean-born but Spain-based Alejandro Amenábar, whose scabrous *Tesis* (1996) and masterful psychological thriller *Open Your Eyes* (1997) established him internationally.

But it's the noughties when the Spanish thriller really became an international phenomenon, with titles such as *Intacto* (2001) *La caja 507* (2002), *Alatriste* (2006) and Juan Antonio Bayona's psychological horror-thriller *The Orphanage* (2007). Nacho Vigalondo shook up genre expectations with his mind- and time-bending *Timecrimes* (2007), Gonzalo López-Gallego created a stir with *The King of the Mountain* (2008), Alex de la Iglesia made the English-language *The Oxford Murders* (2008), and psychological thrillers arrived in the form of *Julia's Eyes* (Guillém Morales, 2010) and the oppressively claustrophobic *Buried* (Rodrigo Cortés, 2010), with Ryan Reynolds.

By the second decade the focus was back on the policier, most notably in Alberto Rodríguez Librero's outstanding *Marshland* (2014), set in 1980, in which the discovery of the

bodies of two young women reveals the misogyny and violence overlooked by the local Andalucian community.

Turning to Latin America, the cornerstones of Argentine thrillers include Jorge Cedrón's *Operación masacre* (1973) and Luis Puenzo's Oscar winner *The Official Version* (1984). In Gustavo Mosquera's *Moebius* (1996), set in contemporary Buenos Aires, the aptly named UM-86 subway disappears under mysterious circumstances – 1986 was the year the 'Full stop law' was passed, granting amnesty to those accused of political violence during the dictatorship. In the noughties Argentinian thrillers became more imbued with social realism, exemplified by Fabián Bielinsky's petty thieves negotiating the economic crisis in *Nine Queens* (2000) and the outstanding *El aura* (2005), both starring Ricardo Darín. In 2009 Juan José Campanella's Oscar winner *The Secret in Their Eyes* was a massive international success, once more focusing on crimes committed during the dictatorship.

Chile's best-known thrillers are those directed by Pablo Larraín, who brilliantly rethinks not only his country's history but also genre conventions, from *Post Mortem* (2010) to *Neruda* (2016). Since 2015, Colombia's most successful work in the thriller genre has been on TV, with the fast-paced *Narcos*. And, in Mexico, *Amores perros* (2000) made Alejandro González Iñárritu an international figure. But I'll round off this brisk survey with one of Mexico's thriller jewels, *The Castle of Purity* (1972) by Arturo Ripstein. The film is based on the true story of a patriarch who locked up his wife and three children in an attempt to guard them from 'contamination' by the outside world. In its portrayal of a masculine, policing, violent world, it seems to distil the very essence of the thriller itself.

CAN YOU TRUST FOREIGN POWERS?

LIVING WITH THE BOMB: THE COLD WAR THRILLER

BY ROBERT HANKS

(Opposite)
Richard Burton in
Martin Ritt's adaptation
of John le Carré's
*The Spy Who Came in
from the Cold* (1965).

In Graham Swift's 1983 novel *Waterland* – remembered with fondness largely for its digressions on eels and beer in the Fens around East Anglia – the narrator, a history teacher at a South London school, has to deal with a pupil, Price, who wears corpse-white make-up and leads a group of pupils called the Holocaust Club, whose slogan is "Fear is here!" Price disrupts history lessons because, he says, the only important thing about history is that it's got to the point where it's probably about to end.

At the time, I thought Price didn't fit into the book at all – his hysteria about the possibility of annihilation was overdrawn, unrealistic. Now, though, at a point in history when the men with the two worst haircuts in the world seem poised to unleash a holocaust on the Korean peninsular, I read the book differently. History scraped through for a few more years, but what does that prove? The only thing that strikes me as unrealistic about Price is that a 15-year-old could see things so clearly. For more than 40 years, from the first Soviet atomic test in 1949 until the collapse of the Soviet Union in 1991, two superpowers stood ready to launch nuclear weapons at one another – pretty soon, enough of them to destroy every living thing many times over; through much of this time, though they didn't confront one another openly, they jostled and scratched for superiority through spies and proxy wars, geeing each other up to the point of open warfare. Why weren't we all making ourselves up as corpses? Why weren't we running around and screaming about fear every minute of every day?

That was the context for Cold War thrillers. (I'm limiting myself to Anglo-American examples, to cinema rather than television, and to thrillers made during the Cold War itself – otherwise, the whole thing would, and I use the word advisedly, mushroom.) The thing at stake in the Cold War was, at bottom, beneath the political manoeuvring, the possibility that the world was about to end; but this was something nobody liked to contemplate – it was the unthinkable, as in *Thinking About the Unthinkable* (1962), the book in which the American strategist Herman Kahn put his doctrine of winnable nuclear war in front of the public. Thrillers need to be grounded in reality, but with a mixture of comforting fiction. And so the world's situation is sometimes perceived most clearly by squinting at films that weren't grounded in reality at all: at the apocalyptic science-fiction of *The Thing from Another World* (1951), Byron Haskin's *The War of the Worlds* (1953) and *Invasion of the Body Snatchers* (1956). Or perhaps the situation is mapped out in Henri-Georges Clouzot's *The Wages of Fear* (1953):

wasn't the whole world speeding down a dirt road with a load of nitroglycerine in the back?

Even thrillers that seemed to be about the Cold War often managed to be about something else. When James Bond is up against Russian assassins, as in *From Russia with Love* (1963), it is because they are being manipulated by the supervillains of Spectre; when atomic bombs come into the picture, as in *Goldfinger* (1964) or *Thunderball* (1965), they are in the hands of Spectre; and later, atom bombs are abandoned for fantasy devices, ray guns and nerve gases. By the mid-70s, and *The Spy Who Loved Me*, the West and the Soviets are working hand in hand (and other things in other things) to stop nuclear war breaking out – Cubby Broccoli worried about jolting that nitro, maybe.

Some films did manage to call things by their proper names, though, and to treat them with due seriousness. In *Seven Days to Noon* (John and Roy Boulting, 1950), a nuclear scientist tries to blackmail the British government into abandoning its nuclear weapons programme by stealing a warhead and threatening to detonate it in central London (this was seven years before the founding of the Campaign for Nuclear Disarmament). But since disaster is finally averted, annihilation is glimpsed at a remove – through the pinball machine on which a youth is playing in a bar, labelled Atomic Racer and decorated with a picture of a giant mushroom cloud; in images of a lifeless London, as the authorities mount an evacuation; and in the nocturnal sequence in which Professor Willingdon's landlady is kept awake by his pacing overhead. His footsteps are a kind of pre-echo of the rhythmic radio signal which in *On the Beach* (Stanley Kramer, 1959) apparently indicates the possibility of a lone survivor of nuclear holocaust, but which turns out to be caused by a Coke bottle caught on the string of a blind, knocking against a radio transmitter: a memorable image of the vanity of human wishes.

Atomic explosions remained vanishingly rare in films, though there is a notable exception in the fiery mushroom cloud that opens Sam Fuller's *Hell and High Water* (1954) and continues to roil all the way through the credits. This bang, in theory explained by the plot (hardbitten navy veteran Richard Widmark and hot-bodied science prodigy Bella Darvi on a creaky secondhand submarine in pursuit of a Red Chinese freighter), is repeated at the film's end. Even apocalypse palls quickly, though: the second time around it feels tame. And the science is all wrong, the bomb set off by an airplane crashing, when the truth is that an atom bomb is a complex mechanism – not

so much a bottle of nitroglycerine as a clock, and you can't start a clock by throwing it at the wall. Likewise, the briefcase-size warhead in *Seven Days to Noon* wasn't technically feasible, and the demonic conflagration that ends *Kiss Me Deadly* (1955), supposedly set off by some highly radioactive isotope, makes little scientific sense; but then Robert Aldrich's apocalypse is better thought about in biblical terms.

Diffidence, or tact, about the end of everything lasted well into the 60s; but the Cuban Missile Crisis was followed by a small flurry of thrillers based on the possibility of an accidental nuclear war. *Fail Safe* (1964) and *The Bedford Incident* (1965) were both overshadowed by *Dr. Strangelove or: How I Learned to Stop Worrying and Love the Bomb* (1964), which is too droll and fantastic to satisfy the criteria for a thriller, though it gives me the willies every time. All are in black and white, to emphasise their seriousness. But *Fail Safe* is a moving and alarming film, with its opening dream sequence of a tormented bull in a corrida, and its assumption that we are not led by madmen, or not many of them (some of the military have been trained into madness). Henry Fonda's American president and the unseen Soviet premier on the other end of the hotline both seem to be intelligent, honourable men; but intelligence and decency turn out to have little meaning in a system built around fear and aggression. Even the Dr Strangelove figure, a political scientist apparently based on Herman Kahn, is reasonable rather than insane, and not entirely repulsive (the casting of Walter Matthau confuses the spectator's sympathies).

The director of *Fail Safe* was Sidney Lumet; like his policiers, it is a story of human fallibility and

attempting to live decently in a fallen world. To convince the USSR that Moscow has been bombed through technical error, not as a stratagem, the president agrees to launch a nuclear strike on New York City too, sacrificing one metropolis for the world. The film ends with a brief panorama of Manhattan life – shops, cabs, parks, sidewalks, children playing, a flight of pigeons – before the moment of detonation. No explosion: silence, and a rapid series of crash-zooms on to freeze-frames, as though time has stopped.

The Bedford Incident (directed by James B. Harris, Kubrick's producer on the films before *Strangelove*) similarly breaks away from cinematic convention at the end: a Soviet submarine having been provoked into firing a nuclear torpedo at the USS *Bedford* (commander: hardbitten Richard Widmark, channelling captains Ahab, Bligh and Queeg), the film freezes momentarily on members of the crew and on Sidney Poitier's visiting journalist; then the film melts, as though the explosion has blasted away the idea that this is fiction, or only fiction. Or as though cameras cannot bear very much reality.

Spy games

A war in which action was forbidden – the nitro in the truck again – had instead to be fought by invisible means, through stealth, disguise, lies, bribery, seduction and betrayal. In the 1950s and 60s the air was thick with secrets and spies: atom bombs were followed by H-bombs, then Sputnik and the space race; the Rosenbergs, Klaus Fuchs, the Portland spy ring, George Blake, Philby, Burgess and McLean. Soon, naturally, the cinemas were filled with spies, with kidnapped scientists and smuggled microfilm, with defectors and border patrols.

Some of the best spy films of the era float free of the geopolitical context: *North by Northwest* (1959) – one of innumerable thrillers to adopt smuggled microfilm as its macguffin – is ostensibly about Soviet spies, but it is hard to think that the perfection of its construction and the density of its wit and feeling would have been noticeably diminished if they had been old Nazis or emissaries of Ruritania. In Sam Fuller's *Pickup on South Street* (1953), two-bit pickpocket Richard Widmark (again) lifts a purse containing

(Above)
Berlin also provided the
Cold War background
in Carol Reed's *The
Man Between* (1953),
with James Mason
and Hildegaard Neff.

microfilm (again) destined for communist agents;
but this is a story of love (mixed with a bit of
sexualised violence) among the low-lifes; and
while Fuller worked a lot of contempt for 'Reds'
into the dialogue, it betrays little awareness of
what Reds are or what they think. "What do I know
about commies?" Thelma Ritter's down-at-heel
informer tells the spy who's turned up to grill
her: "Nothin'. I know one thing. I just don't like
them." In France, it was dubbed into a story about
drugs; again, I cannot imagine much being lost.

Other films embraced the new geopolitics,
though, creating a subgenre of frontier thrillers,
about people caught between borders or on
the wrong side of them, or flitting between the
zones into which European cities were divided:
Vienna in *The Third Man* (1949), Berlin in *The Man
Between* (1953) – both directed by Carol Reed – and
UN-administered Trieste in Henry Hathaway's
Diplomatic Courier (1952), a more straightforward
caper, shorn of the romantic fatalism of Reed's
films. Nunnally Johnson's *Night People* (1954) is an
underrated example of the subgenre, a picture of
life in pre-Wall Berlin with a didactic streak that if

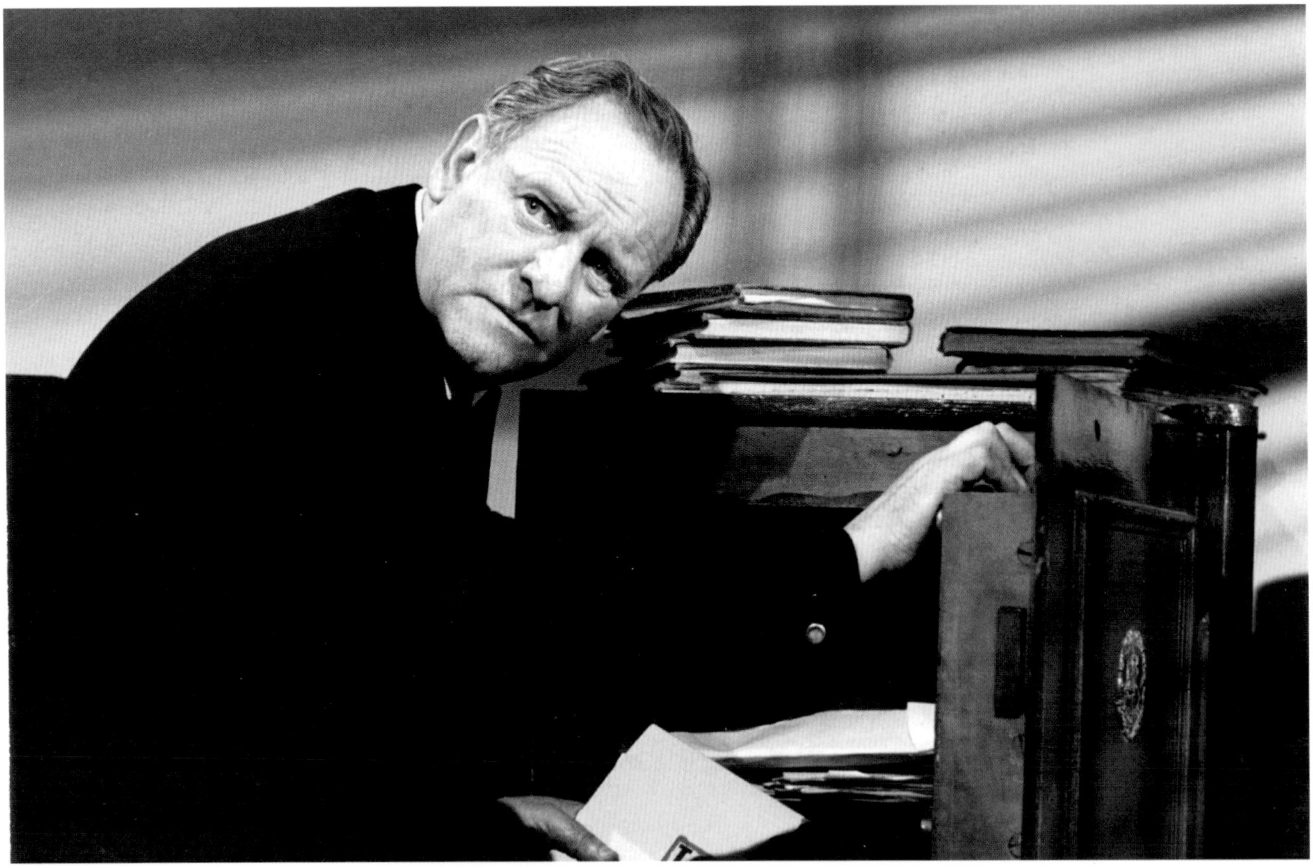

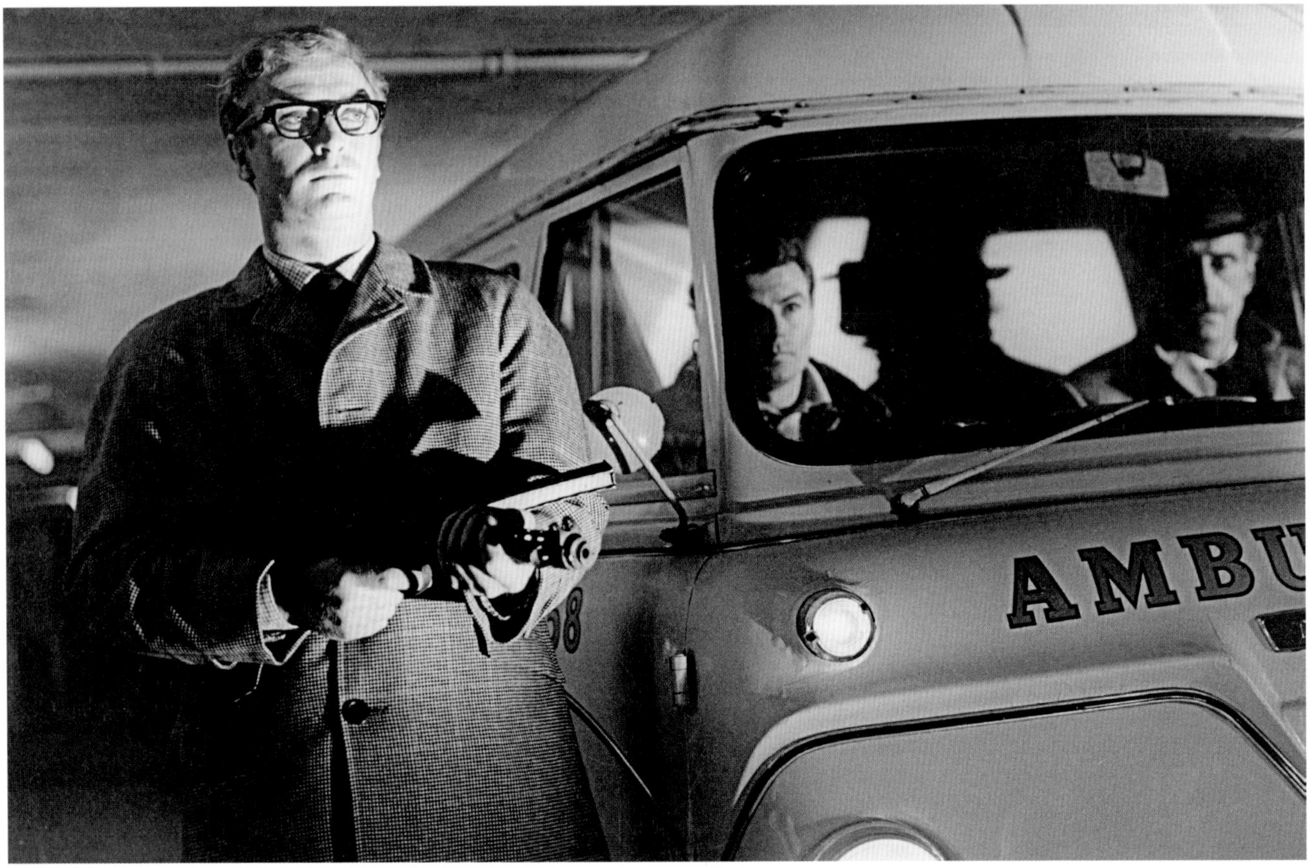
AMBU

anything deepens and enlivens the action. Gregory Peck's decency and rigidity are put to effective use playing Steve Van Dyke, a stubborn, shrewd American officer charged with retrieving a GI who has been kidnapped and whisked to the Soviet zone. His task is complicated by the arrival of the soldier's father, a Trumpish millionaire (played by Broderick Crawford) who thinks his commercial nous can teach the Russians some respect: "I often wonder what would happen if one of our soldier diplomats got tough with these people. Not phony tough, but real tough, the way I've had to be tough in my business on the way up." Van Dyke inducts him into a grey world of utilitarian compromise and deceit, learning along the way that he himself has been more compromised and more deceived than he'd thought possible. After a series of plots, counterplots and con tricks, the film ends with a radio news bulletin explaining that the corporal's prompt return, via regular diplomatic channels, is being interpreted as evidence of the Russians' sincere desire for peaceful relations.

Geopolitical realities weren't the only ones, or even the main ones, that studios responded to: spy films multiplied because they made money. In particular, the success of Bond stimulated a plethora of spoof-Bonds and anti-Bonds, which seemed to offer a more realistic version of espionage. Hence Michael Caine's Harry Palmer in the Len Deighton adaptation *The Ipcress File* (1965) and its sequels – a working-class spy, underpaid and dragged down by dull, repetitive work, oppressive hierarchy and form-filling. *The Ipcress File* is, incidentally, an entry in another Cold War subgenre, the brainwashing film, along with *The Mind Benders* (1963) and, most famously *The Manchurian Candidate* (1962) – though given that the script is by George Axelrod, who also wrote *The Seven Year Itch* (1955) and *How to Murder Your Wife* (1965), I'm inclined to see the Cold War elements as camouflage for its real theme, the war between American men and women.

Harry Palmer comes on as an underdog, but you can see how glamorous he is when you compare the Deighton thrillers with Robert Tronson's *Ring of Spies* (1964), an account of the Portland spy ring, which throughout the 1950s passed information to Soviet spies from the Admiralty Underwater Weapons Establishment. It is, blatantly, a propaganda film, ending with a warning to the audience: "There may be a spy, willing or unwilling, in this very theatre – perhaps in the very row where you are sitting!" and giving the impression that the spies were at it for no more than a few months before they were caught by smart policework (they were actually caught because of a tip-off from a defector, though that wasn't public knowledge at the time). Still, it is in some ways one of the most realistic spy films ever made: Harry Houghton (Bernard Lee, a very long way from M), a naval attaché demoted to clerical work, is a drunken, oafish lech, clearly unfit to be entrusted with secrets, spurred to spy by greed and resentment rather than loyalty or ideals. His mistress and accomplice, Liz Gee, wonderfully played by Margaret Tyzack, is a repressed spinster, desperate for his attention, happily swallowing the obvious lie that they're stealing papers to help our American allies.

Ring of Spies shows up not just the slickness of Bond, but the gritty, doom-laden romanticism that variously enhanced or afflicted later Cold War thrillers – as the 60s wore on, the struggle to find new variations on the themes led to increasing self-consciousness and the almost baroque elaboration of double-crosses, culminating in the

ANATOMY OF A SCENE
DR. STRANGELOVE... (1964)

1. In a classic comic scene, a fleet of B-52s has been sent to Russia without consent, leaving the US President with an awkward call to make.

2. "Dimitri. You know how we've always talked about the possibility of something going wrong with the Bomb. The hydrogen bomb, Dimitri".

3. "Yes of course it's a friendly call, Dimitri!... Well, If we're unable to recall the planes... We're just going to have to help you destroy them!"

4. "Don't say you're more sorry than I am, Dimitri. I'm capable of being just as sorry as you are. So we're both sorry, alright".

(Top)
James Mason as George
Smiley/Charles Dobbs
in Sidney Lumet's John
le Carré adaptation
The Deadly Affair (1966).

(Above)
US agent George Segal
is tortured by resurgent
Nazis in Michael
Anderson's *The Quiller
Memorandum* (1966).

hot mess of John Huston's *The Kremlin Letter* (1970). The cast is fabulous: Nigel Green, George Sanders – in drag! – Niall MacGinnis, Richard Boone; and it is full of odd, memorable incidents; but the characters, with names like the Whore, the Warlock and the Highwayman, are ciphers and the plot (adapted too faithfully from a novel by Noel Behn) is tortuous and obscure. By the end, everyone has been betrayed, and the hero Rone (a charmless Patrick O'Neal) is offered the choice of killing an innocent mother and her children or having his lover die in a Moscow prison: it is not clear how we have got here or why the choice is being offered.

The angst is done so much better by John le Carré. In *The Spy Who Came in from the Cold* (Martin Ritt, 1965), the British spy Leamas – played by Richard Burton – realises too late that his affair with the naive young communist Liz has implicated her in the secret service's plot to discredit an East German functionary, and therefore secure the position of another East German who is working for the British. As Liz, Claire Bloom projects a winning innocence and beauty as a counterpoint to Burton's self-loathing and world-weariness – rather as she had done in *The Man Between* more than a decade earlier, as love-object for James Mason's self-loathing and world-weary German fixer. At the end of that film, Mason sacrificed himself to make sure she could escape over the border into West Berlin; *The Spy Who Came in...* goes a step further – having failed to save her as they flee across the Berlin Wall, Burton allows himself to be killed. No redemption here, only a choice of betrayals; le Carré seems to have taken to heart E.M. Forster's anxious aphorism on loyalty: "If I had to choose between betraying my country and betraying my friend I hope I should have the guts to betray my country." The justification for that position is provided by Cyril Cusack's Control: "Our policies are peaceful but our methods can't afford to be less ruthless than those of the opposition. Can they? I'd say, since the war our methods, our techniques that is, and those of the communists have become very much the same…" If we're really no better than the other side – and since both sides seem prepared to risk the destruction of the world in pursuit of their aims, it's not an entirely opaque position – betraying one's country hardly seems like a problem at all.

The Deadly Affair (1966) was directed by Sidney Lumet from le Carré's 1961 novel *Call for the Dead*. Here, Mason plays George Smiley, though for rights reasons renamed Charles Dobbs: investigating the suicide of a civil servant, Smiley/Dobbs discovers that his old friend Dieter Frey is now spying for the

other side; what's more, Dobbs's nymphomaniac wife Ann (an improbably cast Harriet Andersson) has fallen in love with him. The relationship between sex and spying here is hard to pin down, though. Le Carré didn't quite get Ann figured out until *Tinker Tailor Soldier Spy* (1974 – and filmed twice, by John Irvin for the BBC in 1979 and by Tomas Alfredsson in 2011: critical opinion seems to favour the earlier version; I don't see any necessity to choose between varieties of excellence). Despite their differences in style and pacing, both work as reminders that spying and acting have much in common: disguise, pretended emotion, the confusion of noble motives with greed and ego. That is part of the reason that my favourite Cold War thriller is *The Quiller Memorandum* (Michael Anderson, 1966), in which George Segal's faintly smart-arsed American secret agent (but working for a British agency – the discrepancy is not explained) allows himself to be hunted through Cold War Berlin by resurgent Nazis, in order to find their headquarters. The pleasure of the film lies largely in the way Harold Pinter's script exploits the comic and sinister potential of the conventions of movie espionage – the anxiety about being overheard that means things are never quite named, the elaborate code phrases: "Do you

smoke this brand?" "No, I don't think I know that brand. Is it smoother than other brands?" Quiller's contact Pol (Alec Guinness) smirks his way through the ritual of recognition; Quiller himself is sighing heavily by his third go at the ritual. None of the actors can agree on how to speak this new style of dialogue, with its repetitions and aporia; at times it's almost like a seminar on contrasting approaches to acting Pinter.

The Cold War trailed on for another 20 years, but the thrillers slowed down after the early 1970s, to be replaced in the Reaganite 80s by a new brand of anti-communist action films – *Firefox* (1982), *Red Dawn* (1984), *Rambo: First Blood Part II* (1985) – which abandoned subtlety and moral anxiety (and, to a large extent, acting). But the naivety always feels like a con: you can't get your virginity back, and the pretence that you can be straightforwardly the good guys in a compromised world, a world where fear is here, is the biggest lie of all. The best thrillers of the Cold War remain gripping not just because of the sophistication of the plotting and the subtlety of the acting, but because they feel like attempts to work out the moral choices that face you in a world that has become fundamentally immoral, of staying calm while you're jolting down the road with nitro in the back.

(Above)
Gary Oldman dons George Smiley's glasses in Tomas Alfredsson's adaptation of John le Carré's *Tinker Tailor Soldier Spy* (2011).

CAN YOU TRUST A GANGSTER?
THE JAPANESE THRILLER

BY ALEXANDER JACOBY

In the first English-language history of Japanese cinema, in 1959, Joseph Anderson and Donald Richie wrote dismissively of the Japanese crime film: "In all, this genre, ironically one of the few real influences fostered by the Occupation which still survives, is utterly worthless."

Yet in an answering irony, during the Heisei period (1989-present) the crime thriller became one of the most popular of all Japanese film exports. With the release of his directorial debut, *Violent Cop (Sono otoko kyobo ni tsuki*, 1989), actor and media personality Takeshi Kitano pioneered a new style of crime film, in which violent action was recorded by an often static camera in a slow-paced, meditative style. Kitano's films pushed the boundaries of the genre. In *Sonatine* (1993), much of the film focused not on violence itself, but on the anticipation of violence; while in *Hana-bi* (1997), winner of the Golden Lion at the Venice Film Festival, the generic narrative was almost irrelevant to the portrayal of a tragically doomed marriage and a disabled man's slow recuperation. While diversifying his output, Kitano has continued to work with gangster material, such as the *Outrage* trilogy (2010, 2012, 2017), to the present day.

In the 1990s and early 2000s, directors such as Shinji Aoyama and Rokuro Mochizuki followed Kitano's lead, presenting understated films which often focused less on crime itself than on the personal lives and everyday experience of criminal protagonists: the title of Mochizuki's *A Yakuza in Love* (*Koi gokudo*, 1997) was characteristic. The opposite pole was represented by Takashi Miike, who crafted outrageous, deliberately extreme films such as *Ichi the Killer (Koroshiya Ichi*, 2001), with its baroque ultra-violence.

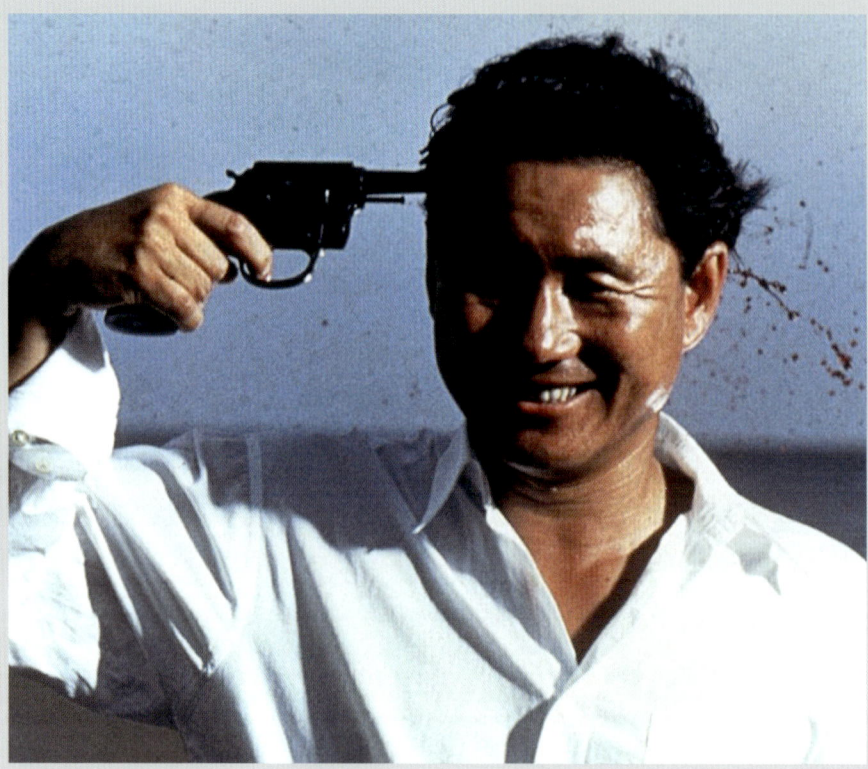

Takeshi Kitano in 'Sonatine' (1993)

Some of the major crime movies of the Heisei period used the conventions of the genre to explore questions concerning Japan's place in a modern and increasingly globalised world. Transnational themes were frequent: Kitano went to Hollywood to film *Brother* (2000), about Japanese yakuza active in Los Angeles, while Miike's *Rainy Dog* (*Gokudo kuroshakai*, 1997) depicts a Japanese criminal in Taiwan. Himself of Korean heritage, Kaizo Hayashi made *The Most Terrible Time in My Life* (*Waga jinsei no saiaku no toki*, 1994), about the ambiguous relationship between a Yokohama private detective rejoicing in the jokily *noirish* name of Maiku Hama and a Taiwanese immigrant involved with a group of ethnically Chinese criminals calling themselves "the New Japs". Here, anxieties about globalisation come clearly to the fore.

In fact, the crime thriller has a long history in Japan. As early as 1933, Tomu Uchida directed the taut, fast-paced *Policeman* (*Keisatsukan*), with obvious influences, both in plot and style, from the then popular cycle of Hollywood gangster films. The effect of pre-war censorship can be detected in the film's focus on lawman rather than lawbreaker, and the film was released with an endorsement from the Tokyo Metropolitan Police!

During the post-war Allied occupation, another form of censorship spurred the emergence of the Japanese thriller: prohibitions on cinematic swordplay and on many of the ideological assumptions that underpinned the *jidai-geki* ('period films') made many of Japan's traditional samurai narratives unfilmable, and opened a niche for a new action-based genre. Thus thrillers with contemporary settings began to emerge. Among the most distinguished was Akira Kurosawa's *Stray Dog* (*Nora inu*, 1949), about a policeman's obsessive pursuit of the criminal who has stolen his gun; perhaps a modern variation on the *bushido* assumption that "the sword is the soul of a samurai". Kurosawa was to return to the thriller genre some years later with *High and Low* (*Tengoku to jigoku*, 1963), in which the kidnapping of a boy for ransom is used to pose a sharp moral dilemma: will a wealthy self-made industrialist ruin himself to rescue, not his own son, but the child of his chauffeur?

Perhaps the most distinguished classical exponent of the Japanese thriller was Shochiku-based director Yoshitaro Nomura. Drawn from the work of popular novelist Seicho Matsumoto, films such as *Stakeout* (*Harikomi*, 1958), *Zero Focus* (*Zero no shoten*, 1962) and *Castle of Sand* (*Suna no utsuwa*, 1974) constitute a remarkable sequence of mysteries and policiers combining the stylistic and narrative economy of Hollywood with a subtle attention to Japanese social realities and the pictorial and symbolic qualities of Japanese landscapes.

In the 1960s and 70s, two studios were to make the thriller a central focus. Nikkatsu had targeted youthful audiences since the mid-50s, and had a roster of young male stars who could suitably be deployed in action contexts; in the 1960s, 'Nikkatsu Action' became a trademark. These films unfolded in a stylised audiovisual world of bright colours or chiaroscuro monochrome. Seijun Suzuki, in films such as *Tokyo Drifter* (*Tokyo nagaremono*, 1966) and *Branded to Kill* (*Koroshi no rakuin*, 1967), is usually held to be the exemplar of what the critic Mark Schilling called an "aestheticised, absurdist worldview, in which the code of the tough guy devolves into choreographed grotesquerie". But in many respects this was shared by colleagues at Nikkatsu such as Toshio Masuda (*Red Handkerchief*/*Akai hankachi*, 1964), Takashi Nomura (*A Colt Is My Passport*/*Koruto wa ore no pasupoto*, 1967) and Yasuharu Hasebe (*Bloody Territories*/*Arakure*, 1969), all of whom gravitated towards action- and suspense-based narratives in recognisable but stylised settings.

Toei, by contrast, was to become famous for the realism of its thrillers. In the 1960s, the studio had specialised in films about the original yakuza, the professional gamblers of the Edo period (1603-1868) and later. In their *ninkyo-eiga* ('chivalry films'), stars such as Ken Takakura were heroic figures, acting according to a chivalrous yakuza code (*jingi*). But director Kinji Fukasaku took the genre into the post-war era and into a deromanticised milieu from which chivalry had been excised. The opening scene of Kinji Fukasaku's *Battles Without Honour and Humanity* (*Jingi naki tatakai*, 1973) depicts the desperate world of Hiroshima under the American occupation, where the existence of a black market fed into the activities of criminal gangs; the opening credits, indeed, play under the shadow of the atomic bomb's mushroom cloud. Drawing his narrative from the memoirs of a real gangster, Fukasaku opted for a hyperrealist style of handheld camera, with onscreen text suggesting newspaper headlines. *Battles Without Honour and Humanity* spawned eight sequels and Fukasaku was the representative face of the Japanese thriller in the 1970s and into the 1980s.

Indeed, when *Violent Cop* was first mooted, it was Fukasaku who was hired to direct. Only scheduling difficulties gave Kitano his first directorial credit, which would again transform the style of the genre.

Toshiro Mifune and Takashi Shimura in Akira Kurosawa's 'Stray Dog' (1949)

CAN YOU TRUST THE STUDIOS?

CHEAP THRILLS: PULP FICTIONS AND B THRILLERS

BY NICK PINKERTON

'Pulp fiction' and 'B movies' aren't genres, but categories of narrative art defined by their downmarket status, their deviation from the middle-class standard, by their very cheapness: cheap overhead, cheap thrills, cheap dames and, for those who toiled away at them, paychecks that kept them living on the cheap. As bargain-basement literature, the American pulp was successor to the Victorian penny dreadful, the black sheep cousin of the high-end slick. The B picture was cut from the same discount cloth, a bit of filler made to follow the A headliner, rounding out the bottom half of the then-ubiquitous double-bill, more respectable than a serial but not by far. It might be produced by a dedicated B unit at one of the major studios, it might be an independent undertaking, or it might be the work of one of the Poverty Row players: Republic, Monogram, PRC. Whatever the case, it was important that the finished product not tie up too much money or take up too much space – it should run about six reels, between approximately 50 and 75 minutes.

Both pulp and B could and did refer to work in several different lines: jungle adventure stuff, sci-fi, Orientalist exoticism, weird tales, detective whodunnits, war stories or, pertinent to our interests, that curious creature called the 'thriller'.

In *Reinventing Hollywood*, his study of developing storytelling modes in the 1940s American cinema, David Bordwell identifies the American thriller as being largely an import, a collision between the indigenous hardboiled detective school and incoming Anglo influences: the stage dramas of Patrick Hamilton as well as the much-ballyhooed arrival of Alfred Hitchcock in the employ of Darryl F. Zanuck. The result of this was a new breed of mystery – most often murder mystery – in literature and film, a form which often sidelined or did away entirely with the figure of the detective to focus instead on the potential victim or even the perpetrator. Years later in some Parisian café some of these movies would be classified as *films noirs*, but this phrase would've been indecipherable to the trade papers or the ticket buyers of the day back stateside, who only knew that they were queuing up to see a good thriller.

In a 1950 essay titled 'The Simple Art of Murder', Raymond Chandler wrote about Dashiell Hammett, the man who more than any other was regarded as having established the school of hardboiled fiction that offered a literary foundation for the *noir* thriller, suggesting that he, as opposed to the Agatha Christie acolytes of the world, "took murder out of the Venetian vase and dropped it into the alley… gave murder back

"Killers are my business . . . and behind every one there's a WOMAN!"

MURDER is my BEAT ·A·

starring
Paul LANGTON · Barbara PAYTON

An Allied Artists Picture · Distributed by Associated British-Pathe Ltd.

CERT. 'A' · LENGTH 6940 ft.

(Above)
Cash-strapped
B-movie maestro
Edgar G. Ulmer's
noir thriller *Murder
Is My Beat* (1955).

to the kind of people that commit it for reasons, not just to provide a corpse; and with the means at hand." In fact the break that Hammett's work signified with the classic detective story was not quite so decisive as all of that. Chandler himself was a would-be toff who was inordinately proud of his private school education at Dulwich College in South London, and many an early thriller in what would come to be known as the *noir* mode still has the rarified air of high society about it: the cavernous nightspots of H. Bruce Humberstone's *I Wake up Screaming* (1941), or the high-gloss sheen that cinematographer Joseph LaShelle lends to Otto Preminger's *Laura* (1944). The A thrillers of the 1940s may have dealt with characters in straitened circumstances and may have traipsed over to the wrong side of the tracks, but they were the products of a boom industry, and studios that were in the pink – you had to go elsewhere to find films in which you could feel the bite of lack.

"Money. You know what that is, the stuff you never have enough of… It's the stuff that has caused more trouble in the world than anything else we ever invented, simply because there's too little of it." This observation comes from Edgar G. Ulmer's *Detour* (1945), a movie in which the absence of the stuff you never have enough of is acutely sensed, and is mouthed in voiceover by Tom Neal, playing Al Roberts, a gifted pianist with concert hall ambitions who's reduced to working nightclubs and thumbing his way from New York to California. En route he's waylaid by Ann Savage, playing perhaps the most hard, shrill, embittered and opportunistic femme fatale in the history of the type – not that Neal was any prize himself. His lunkish screen presence is defined by a combination of squinty dimness and a coiled potential for violence which played out in the actor's own life – in 1951 he brutally concussed the actor Franchot Tone in a fistfight over a woman; in 1965, while working in the landscaping business in Palm Springs, he was convicted of involuntary manslaughter in the death of his wife Gale Bennett.

None of this is mentioned to sensationalise sad and sordid events, but rather to recall that when dealing with the B film, we are very far from the world of rigorous vetting and studio handlers. Money insulates, protects; where its absence is sensed, the possibility of danger is sensed as well. Seeing a flimsy studio set where the walls shake when a door slams, we have a feeling that this isn't quite above board, that bad things might really happen here. David Lynch, though no die-hard cinephile, often seems to be the contemporary filmmaker who has most internalised this lesson of the B quickie, finding analogues in his digital efforts for the sense of ambient threat posed by rough-edged, junky thrillers.

For most of the filmmakers we're concerned with, the aesthetic of want was not a choice. Ulmer, like Al Roberts, fancied himself as an artist whom circumstances had forced to toil in the less dignified sub-basements of pop commerce, though he struggled through his career to keep his panache intact. He was an infamous fabulist, but it can be confirmed that as a youth Ulmer was in some way involved with the production of *People on Sunday* (1929), a slice-of-life film made by a loose collective of artistically ambitious Berlin-based would-be cineastes, including Robert and Curt Siodmak, Fred Zinneman and 22-year-old taxi dancer Billy Wilder. A little more than a quarter-century and a continent away from this youthful lark, Wilder would be adding to a growing collection of awards thanks to his CinemaScope screen adaptation of a hot Broadway property, *The Seven Year Itch*, while all Ulmer had to show for his 1955 was a western *ménage à trois*, *The Naked Dawn*, and *Murder Is My Beat*, a *noir* thriller distinguished by atmospheric train shots and the pouty performance of Barbara Payton, the woman who'd been at the centre of the Neal-Tone brawl.

Ulmer's own career had been derailed by a bit of hanky-panky. While working on his first and last studio feature, Universal's *The Black Cat* (1934), he'd fallen in love with a woman who, unfortunately, was married to studio head Carl Laemmle's favourite nephew – and so, out on to the skids. *Detour* was one of 11 films Ulmer produced over the course of four years under head of production Leon Fromkess at the very-far-from-prestigious PRC, which kept a measly lot on Santa Monica Boulevard that it'd got for a song from the foundering Grand National Pictures, another Poverty Row outfit. The most noteworthy of those films were also thrillers: the 19th-century Paris-set *Bluebeard* (1944), starring John Carradine as a painter and puppeteer who also dabbles in the medium of murder; and *Strange Illusion* (1944), a psychological thriller which exploited the same mania for dime-store Freud that could be found in high-end pictures like Hitchcock's *Spellbound* (1945).

Ulmer's stint at PRC – wags claimed the initialism stood for 'Pretty Rotten Crap' – was but one chapter in a peripatetic, catch-as-catch-can career which found him dabbling in 'race' movies, Yiddish-language films, and anything else he could turn a hand to. PRC was a temporary shelter for many a greying journeyman, like William Beaudine, who cranked out the entertaining *Killer*

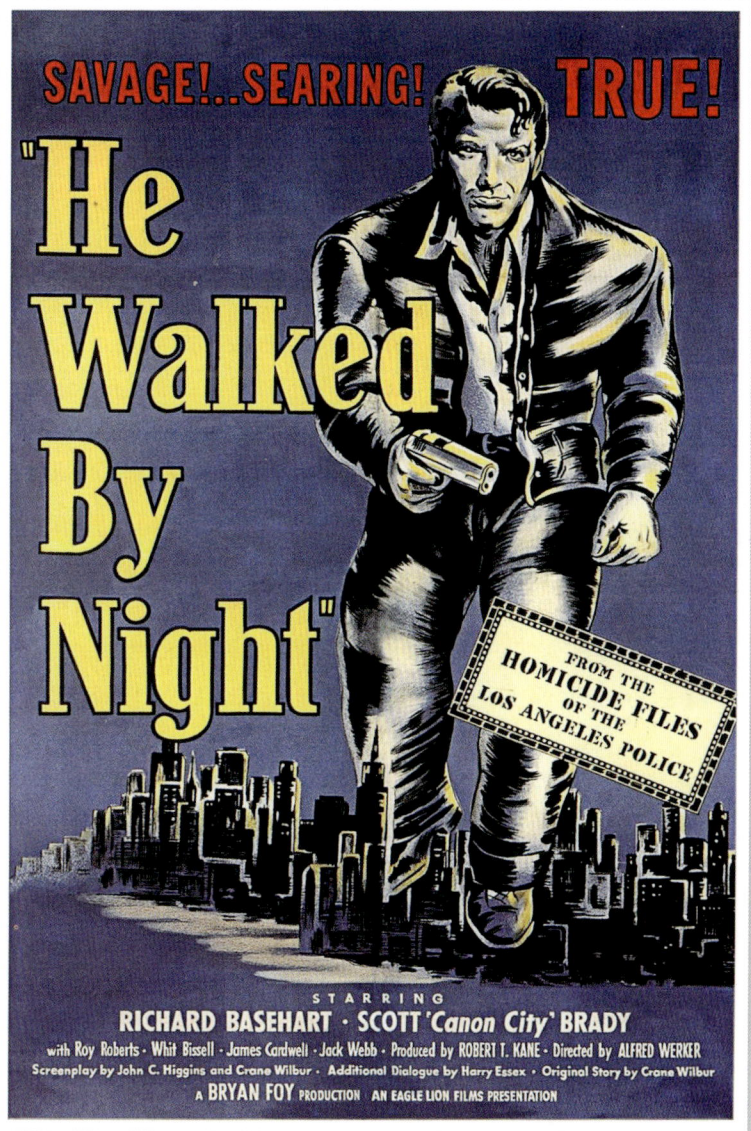

(Above)
An uncredited Anthony Mann co-directed B thriller *He Walked by Night* (1948) for Eagle-Lion Films.

at Large (1947) there, though for others it was a stop-off on the way to better things. Anthony Mann, working with the cinematographer and master *noir* tenebrist John Alton, made *Railroaded!* under the auspices of PRC shortly before the company ceased to operate under that name in 1946, then turned out two highly influential docufiction films, *T-Men* (1947) and *He Walked by Night* (1948), under the imprimatur of Eagle-Lion Films, formed when British producer J. Arthur Rank bought PRC. These docufictions made a virtue of their non-existent production values, using grubby-looking location shooting and stock footage as markers of veracity, and they created a new standard for screen realism in post-war Hollywood – Jack Webb, who played a forensics specialist in *He Walked by Night*, was inspired to create his own show in the docufiction mode, the result being radio and television juggernaut *Dragnet*. At the same time, Poverty Row took its cues from Hollywood in subject matter: the success of Edward Dmytryk's *noir* exposé of American anti-Semitism, *Crossfire* (1947), begets John Reinhardt's *Open Secret* (1948) for Eagle-Lion, in which a small-town cell of bigots is discovered by an investigating John Ireland – soon to star as Bob Ford in *I Shot Jesse James* (1949), the directorial debut of Sam Fuller, another rabble-rousing talent who preferred to work on the margins, at this point in the pay of impresario Robert L. Lippert's Screen Guild Productions.

PRC/Eagle-Lion was but one of the studios that made up Hollywood's so-called 'B-Hive.' The largest was Republic, based in Studio City, founded when processing lab owner Herbert J. Yates lassoed together six small studios who owed him money. Republic was best known for the cheapie westerns it ground out at its Encino ranch, though as the 1940s wore on it ventured occasionally into *noir*-ish territory. Most of these films were ten-day wonders by contract directors like Lesley Selander, the auteur of such titles as *Passkey to Danger* and *Traffic in Crime* (both 1946), or Philip 'Nephew of John' Ford, whose *The Last Crooked Mile* (1946) contains a plum post-*Detour* role for Ann Savage, though Republic also had its brand on Mann's bizarre plastic surgery thriller *Strange Impersonation* (1946), and distributed Fritz Lang's *House by the River* (1950), an underrated tortured-conscience tale in the cheapjack Southern gothic mode. Monogram Pictures had formerly been part of the Republic group, but struck out on its own in 1937, specialising in chintzy crime pictures, with a particular emphasis on series starring Asian sleuths Mr. Wong and Charlie Chan – among the latter were *The Shanghai Cobra* (1945) and *Dark Alibi* (1946), early outings for the great Phil Karlson.

Much B production, however, was undertaken by the studios themselves, who had dedicated B units – the most famous of these was that run by Val Lewton at RKO, and which specialised in horror movies. RKO was also an incubator for a young Richard Fleischer, who'd made a pretty spiffy docufiction job, *Trapped* (1949), for Eagle-Lion, and who broke into the big leagues on the strength of *The Narrow Margin* (1952), a movie whose rib-cracking close-quarters combat set-piece is rightly legendary. It was difficult to pull off the transition managed by Fleischer – some other notable success stories come to us from Columbia Pictures' B unit, which churned out Blondie movies while housed at a safe distance from the prestige stuff at the ancillary Sunset Studios. Joseph H. Lewis made his first *noir* efforts there, including the gothic-inflected *My Name Is Julia Ross* (1945), a film whose 'gaslighting' plot plays on the loss

(Left)
Charles McGraw and Marie Windsor in Richard Fleischer's rib-cracking mob thriller *The Narrow Margin* (1952).

(Right)
Nina Foch played the 'gaslighted' victim in Joseph H. Lewis's psychological thriller *My Name Is Julia Ross* (1945).

of identity commonly experienced by women in marriage, and which is as startlingly candid in its misandry as *Detour* is in its misogyny. Back when Budd Boetticher was credited as 'Oscar' he too got his start at Columbia, on a Boston Blackie picture, though he did his best early thrillers at Eagle-Lion, including 1948 gumshoe-undercover-in-a-booby-hatch picture *Behind Locked Doors*, featuring Ed Wood favourite Tor Johnson.

Considered as cheap, disposable entertainments, the B picture was in direct competition with television far more than was the A spectacle, which offered inducements of production value that you weren't going to get at home, and so the B-Hive, even more than the big studios, felt the pinch that came with the ascendance of the networks. Republic strove to rise to the challenge: would-be mogul Yates had always harboured ambitions of having class, and despite a success like John Ford's *The Quiet Man* (1952), this ambition would go some way towards sinking his company – the studio lingered on for some years after, but never fully recovered from betting the house on a Trucolor gender-swap western dircted by the brilliant Nicholas Ray, *Johnny Guitar* (1954). Eagle-Lion closed shop in 1950; Monogram made it to '53, then pivoted to pricier product under the name Allied Artists Productions, which originally referred to the high-end unit within Monogram. As Allied it produced Karlson's bracing, vituperous *The Phenix City Story* (1955), a docufiction exposé of graft and violence in an Alabama sin city, and it can claim credit for launching the career of Robert Aldrich with *World for Ransom* (1954), an Orientalist *noir* using sets and performers from the short-lived Aldrich-directed TV series *China Smith*.

Where the Bs had once been a training ground for the likes of Mann, Karlton, Boetticher,

and Lewis, up-and-comer directors in the future would frequently follow Aldrich's path from small screen to big. Some did, but not all: the death of Poverty Row corresponded roughly to the rise of the independent operators, outfits like Kubrick-Harris Pictures Corporation, founded by two New Yorkers (Stanley Kubrick and James B. Harris) who'd come out West to make an ingenious low-budget heist movie, *The Killing* (1956, UA), from an adaptation by Jim Thompson, a crime novelist whose hardscrabble southwestern upbringing gave him a firsthand experience of the lower depths that the other guys only wrote about. Where even Edmund Wilson would cop to a fondness for Chandler's prose, Thompson belonged to a much more brutal, blood-and-guts school. His approximate contemporaries included the Philadelphian low-lifer David Goodis, whose work inspired, among other things, Jacques Tourneur's atmospheric Columbia cheapie *Nightfall* (1957), and New Jersey caveman Mickey Spillane, whose private dick hero Mike Hammer was rendered as a rampaging gorilla by Robert Aldrich in his *Kiss Me Deadly* (1955), produced by Parklane Pictures, a company whose sole means for existence was to produce Spillane adaptations.

It was through such independent operations that the spirit of the B thriller lived on. Allan Dwan, a relic from the days of the silents who'd made some enormously charming pictures at Republic, hooked up with Benedict Earl Bogeaus, a Chicagoan who'd made a pile in real-estate and zipper manufactory, and made some of the best films of his life, including the impossibly lurid Technicolor *noir Slightly Scarlet* (1956), shot by Alton, the presiding genius over so many of these films. Boetticher did his best work in the *noir* mould, such as *The Killer Is Loose* (1956) through

GUN CRAZY (1950)

1 In a model of low-budget, ingenious filmmaking, Edgar G. Ulmer films a bank robbery entirely in one shot from the back seat of a car.

2 After we see her partner head into the bank, and with the camera now in a different position, we see Annie step out to stall a passing cop.

3 As her partner exits with the loot, Annie clobbers the cop with her gun, before she and her partner climb back into the car.

4 The camera shifting back to its original position on the back seat, Annie looks over her shoulder as she and her partner make their getaway.

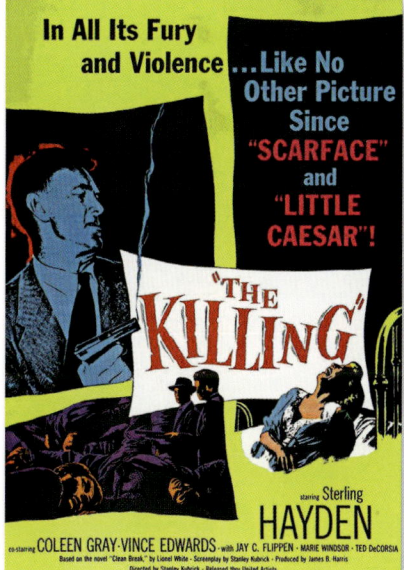
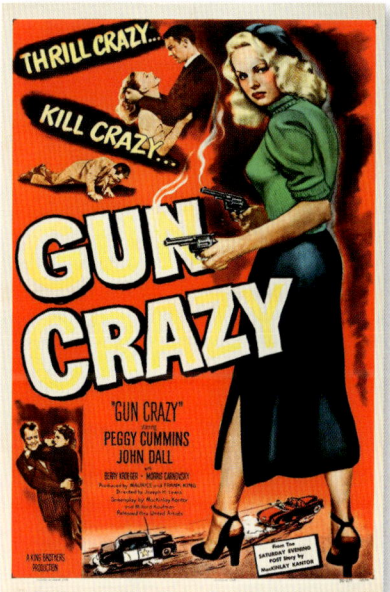

Crown Productions, which also underwrote Gerd Oswald's *A Kiss Before Dying* (1956), a high-gloss production (DeLuxe Color! CinemaScope!) pervaded by a funeral chill, in which working-class striver Robert Wagner angles to marry his way into a copper fortune at any cost. Lewis made his masterpieces by working at the fringes, shooting *Gun Crazy* (1950, UA) with cash from the King (née Kozinsky) Brothers outfit, and *The Big Combo* (1955) through star Cornel Wilde's Theodora Productions, which would handle Wilde's own wild efforts as a director – such operations were becoming more and more common among stars shaking loose of their studio straitjackets, such as Ida Lupino, who directed several first-rate *noirs* under her The Filmmakers Inc. banner.

As the 50s wore on, the low-budget thriller lost market share to science fiction and teen movies at the drive-in, and to television at home – Hitchcock, who'd succeeded in making his name brand synonymous with the murder movie, franchised with anthology series *Alfred Hitchcock Presents*, which ran on CBS and NBC between 1955 and '65. If you are looking for a direct descendant of the B thriller in the 1960s, you would do best to turn to Europe, where television was limited in subject matter by the improving agendas of nationalised broadcast industries, allowing for all manner of local variations on the formula to flourish: the German *Krimi*, the Italian *giallo*, the French *policier*, and the British take on the B, whose own history stretches from Edmond T. Greville's spiv thriller *Noose* (1948) to the likes of Hammer's *Hell Is a City* (1960). In due time a host of American talents would bring the *noir* spirit

back home to roost – names such as John Flynn, Eric Red and Walter Hill spring to mind – and today you can still find traces of the B in direct-to-video movies, the orphan pop films of our time.

Why do these cheap, sometimes rattletrap movies have such a lifespan? In the heyday of the B thriller, even the perspicacious critics who dared to dig through the dross to find the best work could only do so much to combat Pecksniffian prejudices against such low-born material – then as now, importance is usually conferred by how much money's been spent, and the best budget work is discovered by posterity, if at all. And it should be said there was a lot of dross: setting aside the rare exception like Ulmer, who spent the whole of his career on the periphery of polite Hollywood, many of the filmmakers named here are better known for the work they did when they had access to bigger budgets. But if we allow that poverty can be improving to movies – and I think it can – the improvement it offers comes in two forms. The first is ingenuity; think Val Lewton making *Cat People* (1942) without cat people, for example, or the shooting of a bankjob from the backseat of a car in *Gun Crazy* (1950). The other is an intangible we'll call 'edge' – that slight air of potentially dangerous energy that more well-heeled movies don't have. What the Bs lack in pricey crane shots, they make up for in daring – the frank exploration of mutual aggression between the sexes in *Detour* and *My Name Is Julia Ross*; the hot, racially charged violence of *The Phenix City Story*; the cool, calculating nastiness of *A Kiss Before Dying*. There was one advantage shared by pulp fiction and the B movie – they had nothing to lose.

(Above)
The publicity posters for pulp and B thrillers typically promised thrills that were even more lurid than the films themselves.

CAN YOU TRUST THE BUDGET?
THE BRITISH B THRILLER

BY VIC PRATT

Patrick Magee (right) conducting beastly business in 'Never Back Losers' (1961)

Spare a thought, thrill-seekers, for the modestly budgeted marvellousness of the Great British B picture. Though overshadowed by more expensive extravaganzas from across the pond, British B thrillers offered action, adventure, excitement, eccentricity and much more besides. Shining a lamplight on the seamier side of life in Blighty, theirs was an unpretentious reminder of the concerns and aspirations of everyday people in an austere, pre-permissive Britain, in contrast to the distinctly middle-class preoccupations of many 'main feature' attractions.

B pictures began in the 1930s, when US cinema managers, vying for the coins of cash-strapped patrons, spruced up their shows with a 'full supporting programme'. Shorts, cartoons and a low-budget B picture played before the longer, more lavish A picture. In Britain, to stem a tide of transatlantic product flooding picture houses, protective legislation was passed, compelling domestic cinemas to programme a percentage of homegrown product.

Undaunted, American studios swiftly set up British production arms, and a stream of inexpensive UK-made features – 'quota quickies' – were churned out. Many were mysteries and thrillers, based on the works of popular writers of the day, including *Bulldog Drummond* scribe Sapper and *The Four Just Men* creator Edgar Wallace.

Derided by contemporary critics as a blight on British cinema, these were in fact often fast, furious fun and provided an in-at-the-deep-end training ground for famous filmmakers of years to come. The great Bernard Vorhaus made an excellent early effort of crime novelist J. Jefferson Farjeon's breathless *The Ghost Camera* (1933) with starchy but stylish Henry Kendall as the well-spoken crime-busting lead, while the then-unknown David Lean did the editing. Two years later, Vorhaus knocked out another fine Farjeon adaptation, *The Last Journey* (1935), in which a tormented train driver went off the rails at the thought of his wife having an affair.

British B thrillers were fewer and farther between through the war years: light-hearted variety and reassuring escapism were thrust to the fore. But once overseas conflict concluded, a proliferation of small British production companies sprang up, beginning a boom that lasted until the 1960s. Among the throng were Hammer, before it got its fangs into horror, Merton Park, Adelphi, Danziger Productions, Butcher's Film Service and New Realm. A multitude of modest crime flicks aped the shadowy *film noir* of US studios, with laconic bourbon-drinking tough guys, deadpan private-eye-style voiceover narrations, and beautiful but frosty femme fatales.

The House Across the Lake (Ken Hughes, 1953) was a splendid early Hammer example. It featured imported US lead Alex Nicol as a whisky-swilling writer – intriguingly, one who pens hardboiled crime novels (all the rage in post-war Britain, available from US-influenced publishers like Boardman Books, and knocked out by such legendary hacks as Hank Janson). Unfortunate enough to become involved with the glamorous Carol Forrest (Hillary Brooke), our antihero gets wrapped up in a plot to do away with Carol's rich husband Bev (Sid James, reminding us he really could act, well before the lewd guffaws of his *Carry On* caricature).

Media-fuelled public panics were played out on screen in such punchy pictures as *Wide Boy* (1952), also by Ken Hughes, which saw fleshy B-picture stalwart Sydney Tafler as an in-too-deep black-market spiv, with the inevitable manipulative moll in tow, trying to flog one pair of knocked-off nylons too many. Meanwhile, contemporary concerns about juvenile delinquency – thought by the popular press to be the result of impressionable British youngsters watching naughty American films or reading evil imported horror comics – were exploitatively mined in future Bond director Lewis Gilbert's *Cosh Boy* (1952), in which snivelling, molly-coddled teen mummy's boy Roy (James Kenney) runs wild, robbing old ladies and getting his girlfriend (Joan Collins) into trouble, until he finally ends up with what he should have been given in the first place: a good taste of the belt.

Post-war petrol rationing was on the way out, and reckless speed freaks were seen taking to the road causing mayhem in the tiny Highbury Studios production *To the Public Danger* (1947). Featuring a formative spot of acting by future *Doctor Who* series producer Barry Letts, this was also an early directorial exercise by Terence Fisher (later to shoot the 1958 *Dracula*), and was based on a play by Patrick Hamilton. Highbury's mystery caper *Penny and the Pownall Case* (1948) riffed shamelessly on Norman Pett's great newspaper comic strip *Jane* (in which the harassed but glam heroine often accidentally lost her clothes in the course of some slightly spicy adventures), and provided early roles for Christopher Lee – already suave, sinister and charismatic – as well as a mousy, pre-blonde Diana Dors, here given a gratuitous chance to grab viewers' attention by tussling teasingly with a roommate in an appealingly unnecessary bedroom jim-jams catfight.

As the British B thriller blossomed, action sometimes combined with an exploration of everyday modern life. *Devil's Bait* (1959), a tense tale about a poisoned loaf of bread sold to an unwitting customer, included a kitchen-sink-style sub-plot about a jaded baker and his wife coming to terms with their monotonous marriage over a nice cup of tea and a biscuit. *The Third Alibi* (1961), meanwhile, was a complex

murder mystery that hinged upon the very latest middle-class consumer luxury: a spanking new reel-to-reel tape recorder, used to establish a crooked composer's alibi at the time of a murder. It was directed by unsung auteur of the improbable Montgomery Tully, a prolific B-picture specialist whose other wonderfully weird works include *The House in Marsh Road* (1960), a ludicrous suspense drama in which a gold-digging husband's fiendish plot to murder his rich wife goes up in smoke thanks to the inflammatory efforts of a pyromaniac poltergeist named Patrick.

In pre-permissive Britain, B-picture thrillers often titillated and tut-tutted simultaneously. *Cover Girl Killer* (Terry Bishop, 1959), from Butcher's, was a splendidly sleazy proto-slasher pic that saw a pre-Steptoe Harry H. Corbett, sporting crumpled raincoat, thick spectacles and grisly toupee, as a myopic murderer of the dirty-mag pin-up girls who disgust him so. Of course, while he went about his puritanical

crusade, virtuous viewers got an eyeful of various young Soho hussies, without needing to don their macs.

Over at Merton Park Studios, Anglo-Amalgamated shot a more respectable series of films based on the works of prolific thriller writer Edgar Wallace, with a series-opening sequence that really made an impression. While spooky guitar instrumental 'Man of Mystery' twanged atmospherically (subsequently providing a hit single for Stratocaster guitar group The Shadows), a bust of Mr Wallace, wreathed in fag-smoky fog, would turn slowly to create an ominous image that remained burned into the retinal subconscious of generations of British cinemagoers. Among many standouts in this sterling series, *Never Back Losers* (1961) remains a choice exhibit. It features the beetle-browed Patrick Magee as a chain-smoking, cackling master criminal, improbably chauffeured around in a huge tail-finned US automobile, conducting beastly business amid the leafy cul-de-sacs and twitching net-curtains of Mitcham, and must be seen to be disbelieved. While some Wallace series entries were better than others, they regularly boasted cracking casts: *Flat Two* (1962), for example, is lifted by a terrific turn from John Le Mesurier as a debonair but slightly shifty barrister.

Despite the production polish of modest but slickly shot thrillers like these, by the mid-60s, monochromatic British B pictures were looking slightly shabby next to flashier full-colour supporting features from the US. What's more, television was replacing the cinema as the cheap entertainment of choice. The game was up for the British B thriller: it would appear, to echo the words of master criminals everywhere, that they had outlived their usefulness.

CAN YOU TRUST THE CINEMA?

THE INVENTION OF ONSCREEN SUSPENSE

BY PAMELA HUTCHINSON

A thriller is a cinematic con, but we all enjoy being taken in. Directors create this delectable tension by manipulating the audience's perspective, and the passage of time, until the images on screen can no longer be trusted. Over the first three decades of cinema, the silent years, filmmakers developed and refined each other's efforts to fool and excite the viewer until they perfected this trick. We can see that the development of a film grammar and style shadows the early history of the thriller genre, as directors gradually learned the science of suspense.

The first films to be made, those 50-second snatches of real-life made by the Lumières and their peers, seem so transparent that they could never be capable of creating the requisite thrill. The seeds were sown, however, in some early examples of dramatic tension and dramatic irony: a nervous viewer might wonder quite how close the train was going to get to the camera (*Arrival of a Train at La Ciotat*, 1896), or how long it would take for the water-soaked gardener to realise that the culprit was the boy with his foot on the hosepipe, hidden to him, but plainly visible to the audience (*The Sprinkler Sprinkled*, 1895).

Soon, filmmakers turned to more exciting scenarios. James Williamson, a British film pioneer based in Hove, made dramatic, multiple-shot films such as *Stop Thief!* (1901) and *Fire!* (1902), which established some of the basics of film continuity and action. While just a few minutes long, these films combine shots to tell a simple narrative comprising both a crisis and resolution. In the 1901 film, the first shot reveals a thief purloining a joint of meat from a butcher, who gives chase. In the second shot, the thief hides in a water barrel, where he is discovered by a pack of dogs and beaten by the butcher. *Fire!* has five scenes: in the first, a police officer discovers a burning building and alerts the fire brigade, who travel to the fire. Later an interior shot shows a man in a burning bedroom and the fireman appearing to rescue him at the window. The film cuts back to the exterior shot of the house as the firemen continue to drench the fire and rescue another resident. Williamson effectively creates tension by sharing privileged information with the audience: showing how much damage the flames have done before the firefighters arrive or allowing the audience to see the thief's hiding place. However, although these films had drama, they lacked tension.

When Edwin S. Porter, working for the Edison company in New York, made a slightly more elaborate version of *Fire!*, adding a superimposition and a close-up, he managed if anything to decrease the tension. But his mistake highlighted

what was missing from the original. *The Life of an American Fireman* (1903) was flawed because when Porter cut from the interior of the house to the exterior, he re-enacted the action he had already shown, but from a different perspective. The fireman arrived twice, entered the building twice, saved a woman and her baby twice. Second time around, there is no suspense at all. Porter's all-action follow-up *The Great Train Robbery* (1903) would not make the same mistake – the film uses cross-cutting to switch between events taking place in different locations, but with no repeats. In the second half, the time pressure is exacerbated, as the film cuts from a group of bandits escaping from a holdup, to scenes showing the formation of a posse. When the film switches back to the bandits on horseback, the posse is just about to catch up with them and start shooting.

D.W. Griffith was one of the filmmakers who took the idea of cross-cutting further, producing a string of early thrillers at the Biograph company, from 1909 to the early teens. In films such as *The Lonely Villa* (1909), *The Lonedale Operator* (1911) and *An Unseen Enemy* (1912), Griffith cross-cuts between three spaces: the locations of a villain, a victim

and a hero. As the villain attempts to enter the middle space, the home or office where the victim is trapped, the hero is seen at a distance, travelling to the same location to save the victim, who has called for his help. In *An Unseen Enemy*, for example, Dorothy and Lillian Gish play orphaned twins trapped in a room at gunpoint by their "slatternly maid", who pokes a gun through a hole in the wall while she and an accomplice rob the safe next door. After the pair telephone their older brother (Elmer Booth) for assistance, the film becomes a true thriller, cutting not just between their distress and the robbers, but also two 'hero spaces': their brother's delayed return from "his office some distance away" and Dorothy's boyfriend (Robert Harron), who decides to visit at the last minute. Griffith excelled at this technique, using it to especially elaborate and memorable effect in his 1916 epic *Intolerance*, in which he cross-cuts between stories set centuries and continents apart.

In Griffith's early thrillers, it is fascinating to see the extent to which guns, that crucial part of thriller iconography, are a bewildering prop, little understood. Dorothy Gish faints when she approaches the weapon in *An Unseen Enemy*.

In *The Lonedale Operator*, a young woman fools her attackers by pretending her wrench is a firearm, and bizarrely, in *The Girl and Her Trust* (1912), the victim-heroine fires a warning shot at some opportunistic thieves by forcing a bullet through a keyhole with a hammer and a pair of scissors. Many of these films have isolated, rural settings, but 'street films' such as Griffith's own *Musketeers of Pig Alley* (1912) or Raoul Walsh's *Regeneration* (1915) would soon make the seedy, violent behaviour of inner-city criminals, and their weapons, more familiar to audiences.

The Lonely Villa was a home-invasion thriller, exploiting those crucial three spaces, based on a French play by André de Lorde, in which a middle-class husband is lured away from his house by tricksters, who then burgle the house when his wife and children are at home. Four years after Griffith, Lois Weber told a different version of this story, in a short, masterful film, pithily titled *Suspense* (1913). While her husband is at work, a woman (played by Weber herself) is alone in her isolated house, and a prowler is circling. As the man tries to enter the building, where she is barricaded in a bedroom with her

(Above)
Lois Weber's masterful home-invasion thriller *Suspense* (1913) used split-screen to show parallel lines of action.

(Opposite, top)
Dorothy and Lillian Gish played twins trapped at gunpoint in D.W. Griffith's *An Unseen Enemy* (1912).

(Opposite, middle)
Griffith's *The Girl and Her Trust* (1912) sees a young woman confront thieves at an isolated telegraph station.

(Opposite, bottom)
Griffith cuts between the three key locations of the villain, the hero, and the victim in *The Lonely Villa* (1909).

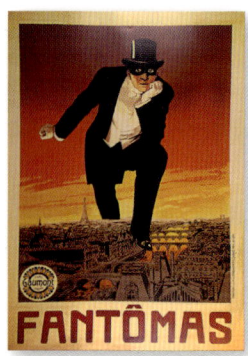

(Above)
Louis Feuillade's crime serial *Fantômas* (1913-14) pioneered the 'cliffhanger' ending between instalments.

(Opposite)
Fritz Lang brought the psychological unease of expressionist cinema to *Dr Mabuse: The Gambler* (1922).

baby, the husband races back home in a hijacked car, pursued by the police. Whereas Griffith used edits, Weber created compositions that contained parallel lines of action. The clearest example is the use of split-screen sequences, where Weber displays all three leads in a three-way formation. Elsewhere, within one frame the husband sees the police reflected in his rear-view mirror; and in another scene the prowler climbs the curved staircase, and a static, high-angled camera captures a mid-shot that transforms into an extreme, unsettling close-up as the actor approaches the lens.

Instead of privileging the audience to see the action laid out as if on a stage, Weber encourages the viewer to shift from one character to another – at other times the action is shot from the overhead perspective of the woman spying the intruder from the bedroom window, or from the criminal's perspective, through a keyhole. *Suspense* is every bit as tense as the examples by Griffith, but its enhanced subjectivity puts the audience at the heart of the action, and makes it an early psychological thriller.

While the greatest American filmmakers of the era were perfecting these matters of thriller technique, global cinema audiences were being further accustomed to the idea of suspense cinema via the spread of adventure serials, from *Fantômas* (1913-14) to *The Perils of Pauline* (1914). Regular doses of crime, espionage, sleuthing and stunts became a reason for the audience to return to the cinema week after week, with the narrative trick of a carefully planned 'cliffhanger' moment at the end of each episode prolonging the thrill until the next visit.

Sergei Eisenstein, in a famous essay called 'Dickens, Griffith, and the Film Today'

describes how the director's technique was inspired by the novelist's: praising their close-ups, and their "parallel montage sequences both". Soviet directors would make an artform out of exaggerating American montage in the 1920s, working their films into a frenzy of rapid cutting, but Eisenstein's manipulation of time in the Odessa Steps massacre in *Battleship Potemkin* (1925) demonstrated a new way to edit suspense into a film. By interspersing images of a pram teetering on the steps with other shots and angles, Eisenstein elongates a moment in time and the audience is held in suspense. Will the baby survive? Eisenstein proved that speed is exciting, but slowness is agonising.

Over in Germany, after World War I, the rise of expressionist cinema added a new dimension to the portrayal of psychology on film, with distorted sets and drunken angles revealing the characters' moral anguish. Fritz Lang channelled this sense of unease into two memorable thrillers, each in two parts: *The Spiders* (1919 and 1920), about an international crime syndicate; and *Dr. Mabuse: the Gambler* (1922), starring Rudolf Klein-Rogge as a maniacal master-criminal. Adapted from a series of novels by Norbert Jacques, Lang's Mabuse films move at an accelerated, ultra-modern pace, with trains, guns and speeding cars as well as handbrake plot turns and a magnificent, monstrous villain in the doctor himself. By 1928, demoralised after the box-office failure of *Metropolis* (1927), and under pressure from UFA to return to his former commercially successful mode, Lang directed *Spione* (1928), which he called "a small film with a lot of action". This international espionage adventure recalls the plot twists of his early 1920s thrillers but there's a clearer dramatic line: an enigmatic

ANATOMY OF A SCENE
BATTLESHIP POTEMKIN (1925)

1. Within the maelstrom of the film's 'Odessa Steps' sequence, Eisenstein shows a baby in a pram, teetering at the top of the steps.

2. Using montage editing to create suspense, Eisenstein cuts to the horrified face of a woman who watches the pram roll down the steps.

3. Cutting to a side-angle view, we see the pram as it continues to move faster and faster, passing falling bodies and marching soldiers.

4. The editing quickens as the pram continues to roll, all the way to the bottom of the steps, where soldiers wait with bayoneted guns.

villain (played once again by Klein-Rogge) is being tailed by a secret agent, who falls in love with a blonde who can't be trusted. Lang uses both cross-cutting and special effects, including superimpositions, to ramp up the tension. Most effective of all are the fetishistic close-ups of guns, cigarettes, diamond bracelets; and low-angled shots of speeding motorcycles. From the outset Lang used speed to create excitement, but in *Spione* he's openly trying to seduce the viewer with the glamour of the underworld. Watching this ultra-sexy thriller, the audience might find themselves cheering for the wrong side.

Hollywood largely neglected the thriller in the 1920s, although Lang and his fellow European émigrés would make it their own in the 1940s, by infusing the gangster films of the 1930s with

expressionist techniques and creating the *film noir*. Instead, stunt films such as Harold Lloyd's *Safety Last!* (1923) or Buster Keaton's *The General* (1926) provided edge-of-the-seat thrills in the cosier realm of comedy. In Britain, however, one director in particular had absorbed the work of Griffith, Lang and Eisenstein, as well as relishing the detective dramas of the London stage. This man, who learned his tricks in the experimental silent era, would go on to execute some of the most audacious cons of 20th-century cinema.

Alfred Hitchcock, who understood that there is "no terror in the bang, only in the anticipation of it" revealed a precocious mastery of suspense with *The Lodger* (1927), his third feature film – combining cross-cutting, shifting perspectives, hints of expressionism and the grisly crimes of a serial killer to expert effect. Not only that, but he employs the simplest suspense trick of them all, which would become one of his favourites, when he dangles his leading man (Ivor Novello) from a set of railings. Hitchcock's final silent film remains one of his finest thrillers, a masterpiece of psychological manipulation. In *Blackmail* (1929), the audience are encouraged to side with a young woman who has killed a man in a clear case of self-defence, but that's only the beginning of the film. Complicit in her guilt, the audience share her anxiety as she attempts to evade a blackmailer. In one famous sequence, lead actor Anny Ondra sits paralysed by guilt at the breakfast table when she is asked to use a breadknife – her murder weapon on the preceding night. The film climaxes with an elaborate spectacle, the chase over the roof of the British Museum, but *Blackmail*'s greatest trick is getting the audience to inhabit the mind of a murderer. As we leave the cinema, we may well trust ourselves a little less than we did before.

CAN YOU TRUST THE SILENTS?
THE EARLY BRITISH THRILLER

BY BRYONY DIXON

On a down-at-heel city street a man is tackled to the ground by a policeman. He struggles frantically and, slipping free of his jacket, makes a run for it. Will he make it? No. A passing sailor intervenes and the thief is thrown to the ground and handcuffed. It's a fast-paced, all-action thriller. One minute long and the first commercial film ever made in Britain, this is Birt Acres's *The Arrest of a Pickpocket,* filmed for the Kinetoscope (a single person film viewer) in April 1895.

Thrilling chases gripped the new audience for moving pictures in Britain, with films such as *The Life of Charles Peace* (1905), with its longer running time allowing for a more nuanced attitude to the villain of the piece; Peace's story is told in episodes, well-known from other media, involving thrilling roof-top chases and a daring escape from a moving train. A master of disguise, Peace repeatedly fools the police till finally he is run to ground – and hanged.

That same year, one of the best-known early British thriller novels, *The Four Just Men*, was penned by a man who would come to be known as the 'King of Thrillers': Edgar Wallace, whose works spawned some 200 films and television programmes. A Londoner of humble origins, Wallace overcame a modest education to become a journalist and an astonishingly prolific writer of thrillers, plays and screenplays, including the first script for *King Kong* (1933). His debut *The Four Just Men* was an instant hit, in large part due to its fast pace, clarity of style and satisfying construction. The story concerns a group of vigilantes who try to prevent a piece of extradition legislation from going through parliament by threatening to kill its principal champion, the foreign secretary.

Wallace dictated his novels, which were sometimes produced in days,

The Four Just Men (1921)

without rewrites. His lowbrow – his word – easily readable thrillers, were hugely popular and eminently adaptable for the screen, and he became involved in the film business as early as 1915, penning a script for *Nurse and Martyr*, about the execution of Edith Cavell. In the 1920s he was a founder chairman of British Lion and directed several films. Alongside better-known titles such as *The Ringer*, *The Crimson Circle* and *The Squeaker* – which were adapted first as early sound films and then as popular German *Krimi* films in the 1950s – he was responsible for ingenious works such as *Melody of Death*, filmed by Stoll in 1922, about a man who thinks he is dying of cancer and turns to crime to provide for his wife after his death (the *Breaking Bad* of its day?); and *The Green Rust,* about an attempt by bio-terrorists to starve the world, filmed as *The Green Terror* in 1920.

As a thriller writer, Wallace was part of a wider tradition of popular product that built on – among other sources – Conan Doyle's Sherlock Holmes stories, largely set in London, involving villains

of superior intelligence, dogged Scotland Yard detectives and clever plot twists; and others that dealt with conspiracy stories, such as Erskine Childers's 1903 espionage tale *The Riddle of the Sands* and John Buchan's 1915 *The Thirty-Nine Steps.*

In the 1920s, the right-wing zealot Noel Pemberton-Billing wrote a play, *High Treason*, which featured classic thriller fare such as international terrorists blowing up the Channel tunnel and flying planes into New York skyscrapers. Marie Belloc Lowndes, whose psychological thriller *The Lodger* was published in 1913 and later adapted by Alfred Hitchcock, was another writer who was often labelled 'prolific' – for which read 'slapdash'. But for the nascent film industry this was not a problem – in fact, it almost seems to be a prerequisite for the success of cinematic thrillers that the books on which they were based were not great works of literature; they needed to be bold, pacy, popular and above all affordable. These murder-strewn dramas had an appealing range for filmmakers, spanning romance, mystery and detection, as well as the psychological suspense narratives seen in *The Four Just Men* and *The Lodger.*

Fast-paced action, which we now regard as an essential component of the thriller, was reserved for big-budget epics, and what British filmmakers lacked in finances, they made up for in ambition, often creating highly condensed montage sequences to stand in for more extended chase scenes. The opening sequence of Hitchcock's *Blackmail* (1929), one of the last British silents *and* one of the first sound films, is a good example: the film opens with a police car screeching through the mean streets of London, on its way to make an arrest.

CAN
YOU
TRUST
OTHERS?

CAN YOU TRUST YOUR LOVED ONES?

TILL DEATH US DO PART: DOMESTIC SUSPENSE

BY SARAH WEINMAN

(Opposite)
Gloria Grahame and Humphrey Bogart in the 1955 adaptation of Dorothy B. Hughes's novel *In a Lonely Place*.

For the first half of the 20th century, crime fiction seemed to fall into two distinct camps: the cosy, exemplified by British 'Golden Age' writers like Agatha Christie, Margery Allingham, Ngaio Marsh and Dorothy L. Sayers; and the hardboiled, by the likes of American writers such as Dashiell Hammett, James M. Cain, Raymond Chandler and Ross Macdonald. These were the novels that sold well, stayed in circulation, and garnered serious critical acclaim.

When I looked at my own bookshelves, though, I found my favourite contemporary crime novels didn't seem to fit either designation. No locked rooms, no mean streets. No country houses, no tough talk. No great detectives, no femmes fatales. These books were, however, full of suspense and psychology and above all, a heightened sense of fear. They were also, by and large, written by women. Writers such as Gillian Flynn, Megan Abbott, Laura Lippman, Alex Marwood, to cherry-pick among dozens of worthy writers.

Who preceded them? Who were the women writing suspense fiction from the dawn of World War II to the beginnings of second-wave feminism? It turned out there were quite a number. Their novels and stories were innovative, exciting, suspenseful. They weren't romanticised fantasies of heroism but pragmatic explorations of day-to-

day life. Most of all, they explored what terror does when it strikes close to home. When it's someone you love – your partner, your parent, your child – whom you cannot trust. Domestic suspense is a mirror image of romance. While romance is about conflict resolving into a happy ending, domestic suspense is about a happy beginning (of marriage, children, or independence) splintering into chaos.

The elevated sense of fear translated perfectly to film, too. Where detective fiction emphasised the intellectual, the puzzles needing to be worked out to a surprising but reasonable-in-hindsight solution, suspense stories feed upon all five senses – as well as the ineffable, intangible intuition that allows some people to fight and others to flee. By emphasising psychology, domestic suspense was perfectly situated to reveal things about character, about emotion, about trauma, and about fear that cinema was well placed to capture. No wonder so many filmmakers found fertile adaptive inspiration from these writers. No wonder, too, that these books caught the eye, over and over again, of Alfred Hitchcock.

We must start with Hitchcock because the vocabulary of suspense in film owes so much to him. He understood, better and earlier than nearly every other filmmaker, that terror increases based on what you know is going to happen, and

suspense lies in how long you must wait until the event you fear happens – or is prevented from happening at the last possible moment.

While the silent film version of *The Lodger* (1927), based on Marie Belloc Lowndes's 1913 novel, did much to establish Hitchcock's filmmaking credentials, another early film – which has the distinction of being the first successful dramatic 'talkie' out of Europe – fits more squarely into the domestic suspense realm. (A silent version also exists.) In *Blackmail* (1929), a woman kills the man who attempts to rape her, and another man – only knowing part of the story – attempts to blackmail her. The tension results as much from whether the blackmailer will succeed as it does from whether Alice, the victim and killer in question, will speak the truth to her detective lover. She is unwilling to trust him because her shame overwhelms, and it is this shame that carries the narrative.

Issues of trust and conflict became ever more prevalent as Hitchcock grew more confident with sound and moved from the UK to the US. He also grew more fixated on stories of murderous husbands and uncertain relationships – such as his adaptation of Daphne du Maurier's *Rebecca* (1940), starring Joan Fontaine and Laurence Olivier; *Suspicion* (1941, adapted from Anthony Berkeley's novel), in which Joan Fontaine's shy heiress marries Cary Grant's outwardly charming gentleman, only to become convinced he is plotting to kill her; and *Notorious* (1946), with Ingrid Bergman and Cary Grant – each of which were defining, influential examples of the form.

Hitchcock's mastery of the domestic thriller also led him to tales of suspense within familial as well as romantic relationships, as in *Shadow of a Doubt* (1943), the director's own favourite. Here, the loved one who young Charlie (Teresa Wright) cannot trust is her namesake uncle (Joseph Cotten). The seed of doubt is planted by a visiting detective, Jack Graham (Macdonald Carey), who informs Charlie that her uncle is one of two suspects in a spate of recent killings. Hitchcock expertly maps Charlie's growing suspicion, and her confusion over whether to trust family (her uncle) or her love interest (the detective), over the course of the film, building up to a thrilling conclusion on a moving train.

Women in the window

As the film professor David Bordwell noted in his 2013 essay 'Murder Culture: Adventures in 1940s Suspense', 1944 was a watershed year for the domestic suspense film. Hitchcock had become a hitmaker, and other directors and film studios lined up to emulate the master, to spin their own versions of *Rebecca*, *Suspicion* and *Shadow of a Doubt*. Thus 1944 saw new film adaptations of *The Lodger* and *Jane Eyre* – which brought out their more gothic elements – as well as treatments of more recent work and of originals like *Gaslight, Experiment Perilous, Phantom Lady* and *The Woman in the Window*.

An article in *Variety* took note of the new suspense trend in original scripts: "The typical tale in the new genre crawls with living horror, is eerie with something impending, and socks its suspense thrill well along toward the middle of the story, instead of doing the crime victim in at the beginning and then building a whodunnit and a detective quiz as the element of suspense." The deeper psychology explored in domestic suspense novels opened the door for similar explorations in film.

Take George Cukor's 1944 version of Patrick Hamilton's play *Gaslight*, a work so influential that its title is now a bona fide psychological term. (British director Thorold Dickinson had already adapted the play in 1940, for a film starring Anton Walbrook and Diana Wynyard.) Cukor's film shows the cunning with which Charles Boyer's character drives his wife, played by Ingrid Bergman, to the brink of madness, simply by the dimming of house lights. Of course it didn't happen, he tells her. Of course it's all in her mind, which displays a deepening fissure. These types of psychological games feel personal, outrageous, because they are played not only to win, but to destroy.

The success of domestic suspense on film fed into further explorations of the subgenre in books. The growth also owed much to WWII and its aftermath, when women went off to work while men enlisted, or were drafted, into military service, dying or being injured in their millions. When the war ended and soldiers came home, they expected to slip naturally into their earlier roles of provider and breadwinner, while their wives were supposed to be happy homemakers and mothers. Sometimes it worked; often it did not. The tension was explored brilliantly in novels by Elisabeth Sanxay Holding, Charlotte Armstrong, Dorothy B. Hughes and (though, puzzlingly, not as source material for film) Margaret Millar.

Holding's *The Blank Wall*, in which a middle-class mother finds herself drawn into a criminal world of blackmail and violence, was filmed by Max Ophuls as *The Reckless Moment* in 1949, and could be summed up as, "Can you trust your daughter and protect her even when you suspect she's a killer?" *Strangers on a Train*, both Patricia Highsmith's novel and Hitchcock's 1951

(Top)
A husband tries to
convince his wife she
is going mad in George
Cukor's *Gaslight* (1944).

(Above)
A middle-class mother
is drawn into a criminal
world in Max Ophuls's
The Reckless Moment (1949).

film adaptation, take the mistrust of spouses far
beyond acceptable norms with the now-legendary
conceit of a pact by two men to kill each other's
wives, and how they must trust one another
to carry it out, or be betrayed in the process.

Mischief, the 1951 novel by Armstrong filmed
by Roy Ward Baker as *Don't Bother to Knock* in
1952, starring a young Marilyn Monroe, is likely
the first treatment of the psychotic babysitter
motif – going outside the trust circle of family to
find someone to care for a child. And *In a Lonely
Place,* Hughes's masterwork, was adapted into
an equally terrific film by Nicholas Ray in 1950,
starring Humphrey Bogart and Gloria Grahame,
albeit one that could not carry over the novel's
audacious conceit – being told from a multiple
murderer's point of view, where the reader is
privy to so much more than the narrator.

But both the book and the film of *In A Lonely
Place* examine the post-war feeling head-on, when
supposed heroes mask lingering demons and
where trauma is inadequately treated. No wonder
the women – Laurel Gray (Grahame) and Sylvia
Nicolai (Jeff Donnell), chiefly – turn out to be the
heroes, transforming their deeply held suspicions
into action as other women are being murdered.

Ray's film brilliantly depicts the seeds
of mistrust building within Laurel over Dix's
behaviour. What ought to be a romantic reckoning
devolves into something more disturbing when Dix
cannot control his temper, assaulting a stranger in
what we'd now call 'road rage'. Laurel is appalled,
but feels she has no choice but to get back into
the car – only for Dix to put his arm around her
neck, mimicking the gesture he imagines the serial
strangler employs. His immediate recitation of a
line from the script he's working on – "I was born
when she kissed me. I died when she left me. I
lived a few weeks while she loved me" – takes on
a disquieting pallor. As Imogen Sara Smith writes
in her essay for the Criterion Collection release, "It
is clear that this love is the last chance for both of
them, the failure from which they won't recover."

Crimes passionels

While domestic suspense in fiction went into
decline in the 1960s and 70s, there was more of a
delay in cinema – and French cinema, in particular,
remained a hotbed of domestic intrigue. Much
of it owed to adaptations of Patricia Highsmith
and Charlotte Armstrong novels, whose works
proved ideal for movie treatments. The success
of *Strangers on a Train* naturally prompted others
to seek out Highsmith's work, though nine years
elapsed before Rene Clément adapted *The Talented*

Mr. Ripley as *Plein soleil* (1960), starring Alain Delon, and another three until Claude Autant-Lara turned *The Blunderer* into *Le meurtrier* (1963).

Other French filmmakers mined Highsmith stories for their own explorations of marital discord and bourgeois malaise, most notably Claude Miller with *Dites-lui que je t'aime* (1977), based on *This Sweet Sickness*; and Michel Deville's *Eaux profondes* (1981), an adaptation of *Deep Water*.

But it was Claude Chabrol in particular who saw the merits of adapting domestic suspense works into eerie, quirky movies. *La rupture* (1970) distances itself from the tight rhythm of Armstrong's *The Balloon Man*, published two years previously, instead opting for a more languid, non-linear approach to the encroaching madness felt by Hélène (Chabrol's then-wife Stéphane Audran) after a series of psychological games perpetrated by her in-laws.

La rupture arrived at the height of Chabrol's most fertile moviemaking period, when he was most consumed with themes of domestic obsession, conflict and murder – lack of trust and changing loyalties figured prominently in Chabrol's other films featuring Audran, such as *Les Biches* (1968), *La femme infidèle* (1969), *Le Boucher* (1970) and *Wedding in Blood* (1973).

Chabrol returned to Armstrong as adaptive muse three decades later with *Merci pour le chocolat* (2000), a reworking of her early novel *The Chocolate Cobweb*. And he also found inspiration from Highsmith with *Le cri d'hibou* (1988), based on *The Cry of the Owl*, as well as from the British novelist Ruth Rendell, when he adapted her celebrated

novel *A Judgement in Stone* – about a housemaid who conspires with another woman against the family who employ her – as *La Cérémonie* (1995), starring Isabelle Huppert and Sandrine Bonnaire.

Trouble at home

Domestic suspense films began to cluster anew in the early 1990s. The pendulum seemed to swing back at a time when the culture was recovering from the dog-eat-dog conservatism of Thatcher and Reagan, and there was a newfound appetite for movies in which people who professed to love each other saw that love curdle into something more sinister.

Fresh retreads on earlier types of peril emerged, too. The underlying horror of Armstrong's *Mischief* or Evelyn Piper's *Bunny Lake Is Missing!* – babies in peril from psychotic babysitters or kidnappers – returned in *The Hand That Rocks the Cradle* (1992), featuring Rebecca De Mornay's chilling depiction of a woman who will stop at nothing to insinuate herself into a family, supplanting the mother played by Annabella Sciorra.

Husbands and wives were at particular loggerheads in films during this era. One of the creepiest examples was *Sleeping with the Enemy* (1991), based on the novel by Nancy Price. While domestic violence was not a taboo subject on screen, the powerful images of Patrick Bergin beating Julia Roberts, and the ways in which she tried to fight back, struck a chord at a time when there was more awareness of the problem – and a given disorder, 'battered woman syndrome',

(Left)
Stéphane Audran fears her boyfriend (Jean Yanne) may be a killer in Claude Chabrol's *Le Boucher* (1970).

(Above)
Julia Roberts fights back
against her violent
husband (Patrick Bergin) in
the marital thriller *Sleeping
with the Enemy* (1991).

(Above)
Nick Dunne (Ben Affleck)
is implicated in the
disappearance of his
wife Amy (Rosamund
Pike) in *Gone Girl* (2014).

(Below)
Vengeful nanny Rebecca
De Mornay (left) supplants
mother Annabella
Sciorra in *The Hand That
Rocks the Cradle* (1992).

for abused wives who killed their spouses.

Other examples of the marital thriller during this juncture include *A Kiss Before Dying* (1991), a decades-delayed adaptation of Ira Levin's clever, groundbreaking novel (even if the film was more conventional); *Deceived* (1991); *Shattered* (1991); *Mortal Thoughts* (1991); *Consenting Adults* (1992); *Unlawful Entry* (1992); *Guilty as Sin* (1993); *Malice* (1993); and *Dream Lover* (1993), which flipped gender expectations to make James Spader the gaslighted husband of Mädchen Amick's outwardly perfect wife.

The cyclical nature of domestic suspense asserted itself again in the 2010s. In books, this was a direct response to the economic crash of 2008, when the idea of seemingly safe financial nets proved to be a fiction, and when the so-called middle-class lifestyle proved to have a shorter generational shelf life. Trust within a marriage or between parents and children or other loved ones could not hold because the very things that glued people together – money, status, power – were no longer there, leaving avarice and destruction as replacements.

More of these psychological underpinnings are on display in Gillian Flynn's 2012 novel *Gone Girl* than in David Fincher's film adaptation two years later. The disappearance of Amy Dunne, and the suspicion laid upon her husband, Nick, gets twisted in spectacular fashion with a mid-narrative reveal that recasts their relationship as a more brutal battle-of-wits, each getting revenge against the other wherever possible.

The changes in plot for the film were by design: the complicated tone shifts between Amy and Nick Dunne show them to be equally loathsome and complicit, and their gamesmanship ends up condemning one another to an eternity of hell.

But in the film, someone had to be the hero and someone had to be the villain – hence the decision to make Nick the more outwardly sympathetic character, even if Ben Affleck's portrayal was more consistent with the character in the novel.

Gone Girl's astonishing success spawned many imitators, to the point where it became a running theme, then a joke, that a hit suspense novel had to have the word 'girl' in it. The best known and most commercially viable remains Paula Hawkins's *The Girl on the Train*, and if the 2016 film adaptation could not come close to replicating the main character's drunken disorientation and unreliable narration, it certainly did show why one cannot trust one's own memory.

Other recent examples merge domestic suspense with other genres. *The Invitation*, Karyn Kusama's 2015 thriller, just as easily belongs in the horror genre, as a dinner party among current and former spouses descends into cult-conceived madness and murder. It perhaps also isn't too much of a stretch to characterise Jordan Peele's 2017 hit horror film *Get Out* as in part a domestic suspense, seeing as it involves a couple stretched to their psychological limits as a result of spending time with family.

Domestic suspense will endure for a simple reason: people need to channel their fears into something cathartic. We can look forward, hopefully, to more women writing and directing such films, for the female gaze offers fresh potential for the subject of terror and mistrust. We can also look ahead, in books and in film, to more ways in which the power wielded by those we most trust can be perverted, betrayed, and circumvented. For the shakiest fault lines run between those we profess to love, and the worst danger lurks closest to home.

ANATOMY OF A SCENE
SUSPICION (1941)

1 Lina Aysgarth fears her husband Johnnie plans to kill her – he had been quizzing a friend about untraceable poisons.

2 The suspense mounts as Hitchcock shows Johnnie carrying a glass of milk up the stairs for her. Is it laced with poison?

3 The simple glass of milk looms with a sinister menace. Hitchcock placed a light in the glass to enhance the effect.

4 Johnnie places the milk at Lina's bedside. He seems tender and affectionate, but the look on Lina's face betrays her doubts.

CAN YOU TRUST WHITE PEOPLE?

RACE AND BLACK ANXIETY IN THE THRILLER

BY KELLI WESTON

A chilling warning frames Jordan Peele's directorial debut *Get Out*. Even before the audience understands it explicitly (in the wake of the film's massive success, few of its many threads have been left unexplored), they surely feel it intuitively. A young man – Andre Hayworth (Lakeith Stanfield), we find out later – has just been abducted in the middle of the night, in a suburb of all places. An ominous melody follows this abrupt and mysterious assault, hinting at the danger ahead. The chorus whispers, *"Sikiliza… Kwa Wahenga"* – Swahili for 'listen to [your] ancestors'.

The film unfolds through the eyes of black photographer Chris Washington (Daniel Kaluuya), an orphan, seemingly unmoored; for convincing as it is, the British actor's American accent betrays no specific regional graces. As Chris and his white girlfriend Rose Armitage (Allison Williams) head to the countryside to meet her parents, it appears he leaves only his best friend Rod (Lil Ren Howery) behind to feel his absence. Once they arrive, much of the humour and horror that occurs during that weekend at the Armitages' arises from Chris's isolation. Perhaps without knowing it, he desperately seeks community, someone he can understand and who understands him in return, someone who can raise his numbers, for historically black people

do not fare well in thrillers, and even worse when surrounded by white people in the woods.

What begins as a present-day *Guess Who's Coming to Dinner* (1967) soon descends into something far more insidious, more in line with *Rosemary's Baby* (1968). Rose and her parents Dean (Bradley Whitford), a neurosurgeon, and Missy (Catherine Keener), a psychiatrist and skilled hypnotherapist, seem well-meaning enough – her aggressive brother Jeremy (Caleb Landry Jones) less so – yet Chris finds himself subject to a barrage of microaggressions. Jeremy comments on his physique and likens him to a "beast". Dean insists that he would have voted for Barack Obama a third time. At the Armitages' annual garden get-together, white guests fondle him and ask invasive questions about his body and sexual prowess. It's no wonder Chris longs for allies. But each time he encounters another black person – the groundskeeper, the maid, and finally Andre, who now goes by the name Logan and arrives at the Armitages' as the partner of a much older white woman – there is something disturbing about the encounter. They all behave strangely – not unfriendly, but also not quite genuine. Things take an even more bizarre turn when Chris tries to take a photo of Logan with his phone. The camera flash sends Logan into a

panic; his nose bleeds and he grabs Chris, shaking him and frantically screaming, "Get out!"

As it turns out, the Armitages have been dealing in black bodies. That is, they have been lobotomising black people and transplanting the brains of ageing white people into them. Only a sliver of the host's consciousness remains, immobilised in a dark, endless void that Missy calls "the sunken place". It is from this sunken place that Andre, or what is left of him, briefly emerges, roused by the camera flash.

Already, 'the sunken place' has effectively replaced the colloquial expression 'Uncle Tom' as a way of describing those black people perceived to have betrayed their community, either in ideals or actions. It is the more generous term, for it suggests not duplicity, but brainwashing or conditioning beyond the perpetrator's control. Such is the impact of *Get Out*, a film that has provided new language for thinking about race simply by considering the essence of black anxiety. Few thrillers before it have been concerned with such a question.

On the rare occasions black characters actually make it into horrors or thrillers, they are often the first to perish. This, too, is part and parcel of black fear, the dispensability of a 'raced' body, rarely the hero's body or a body worth saving. There are, of course, notable exceptions. Those black actors who have managed to become heroes in thrillers generally tend to be established stars – examples include Sidney Poitier in Norman Jewison's *In the Heat of the Night* (1967), Laurence Fishburne in Bill Duke's *Deep Cover* (1992), Will Smith in *Enemy of the State* (1998), and Denzel Washington, who has established himself as a mainstay of the thriller, from Carl Franklin's *Devil in a Blue Dress* (1995) to several Tony Scott films, as well as Jonathan Demme's version of *The Manchurian Candidate* (2004). Furthermore, those films either presume a black audience, thanks to those black directors and black stars, or purposefully evade race altogether.

Before the arrival of *Get Out*, it was George A. Romero's *Night of the Living Dead* (1968) – one of Peele's many stated influences alongside *Rosemary's Baby* and *The Stepford Wives* (1975) – that came as close as any film to representing the ever-present danger of existing in a black body, when its hero Ben (Duane Jones) survives a zombie onslaught only to be killed by white vigilantes. If Romero, at least publicly, often shied away from the film's political connotations, Peele wholeheartedly embraces the implications of his. *Get Out* blatantly engages with black suspicion of white people, or perhaps more accurately with black fear of white cannibalism, a fear that has, naturally, plagued the former ever since her introduction to America. Because for all its contemporary trappings, *Get Out* may well be the most penetrating cinematic depiction of slavery, from the nature of the institution to its far-reaching psychic consequences.

Peele himself has said as much of the film: "The real thing at hand here is slavery… it's some

dark shit." Kaluuya has called the film "12 Years a Slave: The Horror Movie" and journalist Steven Thrasher wrote an online piece for *Esquire* titled, 'Why *Get Out* is the Best Movie Ever Made About American Slavery'. Earning its distinction as a social thriller (Peele's own favoured categorisation), the film deftly connects the theft and exploitation of black bodies past to present, from slavery to sports, showing how the American tradition of profiting from disposable black bodies continues to this day. Chris does not know it at the time, but the Armitages' annual get-together is not really a party at all, it is a slave auction. The invasive questions, the preoccupation with his body, the groping – all these resemble the business of slave markets. Much has been made, too, of the central role cotton plays in his grand escape. After Chris has been 'bought', the Armitages confine him to a downstairs chamber, where he is strapped to an old chair and forced to watch a television programmed with Missy's hypnosis. He stuffs the cotton spilling from the chair into his ears, blocking out the television's audio cues, so when Jeremy comes to collect him for the operation, he can break free. 'King Cotton', the staple crop of the South – a crop so vital it fuelled the expansion and continued horror of slavery – ironically becomes his saviour, enabling him to exact his revenge.

It should be noted that *Get Out* was shot in Alabama, a state whose own bitter racial history in many ways mirrors the themes Peele sought to emphasise. But he sets his film in a New England-like milieu, thereby directly implicating those northern, presumably liberal, white Americans for their complicity in racist structures, if not their own outright racism, which is far less publicised than their Southern brethren.

There is a vicarious excitement to watching a thriller, done well, in which the protagonist is flung from their safe, everyday life into a world of peril, and perhaps white audiences experience *Get Out* much the same as any other thriller in that regard. But for black audiences, the experience must be nothing short of validation. So much of the film's tension mirrors real life in all its hostility and violent carelessness toward the raced body. At the very least, black audiences recognise all too well the unfortunate position Chris finds himself in, forced to navigate a predominantly white space where his blackness quickly becomes a spectacle. When he meets blind art dealer Jim Hudson (Stephen Root), for a moment Chris is relieved; his blindness comes as a welcome reprieve. If this man cannot see his race, he cannot possibly judge him for it. Hudson clearly becomes a symbol of

(Top)
Denzel Washington has starred in innumerable thrillers, among them Jonathan Demme's take on *The Manchurian Candidate* (2004).

(Middle)
The essential thriller themes of mistrust and survival in a hostile world find analogues in such slave narratives as *12 Years a Slave* (2012).

(Bottom)
Jordan Peele has admitted that George A. Romero's *Night of the Living Dead* (1968) was a key influence on *Get Out*.

a 'colour-blind' or post-racial society, the kind of false liberal fantasy that inspired Peele to make the film in the first place. But later Hudson will cast the winning bid to inhabit Chris's body; he is impressed by Chris's 'eye', his gift for photography, a talent he himself never possessed even when he could see. When Chris asks him why they choose black people, Hudson laughs and tells him that his race makes no difference. "I want your eye, man!"

In this way Peele reveals the emptiness of the post-racial promise. Slavery, in the beginning, was not about race either. Ta-Nehisi Coates, author of *Between the World and Me*, has written, "Race is the child of racism, not the father." Racism was born out of the necessity to justify the assault and abuse of bodies that were black. Hudson cannot see how his intent to violate and destroy the man to exploit the fruits of his body is itself evidence of his faith in his own preeminence, his own supremacy. Ultimately, only he benefits from his colour-blindness. Chris does not. And what of that gaze Jim covets so much? Chris has used it, as the early scenes of the film reveal, to capture black people living: a pregnant black belly, a black man clinging to bags of balloons. Surely his perspective cannot be divorced from the man himself, but Hudson does not appear to consider that the talent and the man are one and the same. For him, for all the bodysnatchers who the Armitages supply, the skill exists purely in the muscles and bone, and they need only bend it to their will.

Outside of the film, modern debate over the white gaze and appropriation has argued that the success of white supremacy has resulted in history being forgotten and ownership – or rather, authorship – misplaced. *Get Out* expressly addresses the fears of a people from whom much has been taken and follows their fear to its logical end: a people afraid of being snatched themselves. Womanist scholar bell hooks explains, "The overriding fear is that cultural, ethnic, and racial differences will be continually commodified and offered up as new dishes to enhance the white palate – that the Other will be eaten, consumed, and forgotten." Their ancestors could not know what the future held for them, but the descendants of these people carry the knowledge of a not so distant past in which bodies like theirs fed an insatiable appetite, and therefore dread what form such an appetite might take next.

Even though Chris eventually escapes, *Get Out* turns out to a be a film far more cynical than its equally grim predecessor, Steve McQueen's *12 Years a Slave* (2012), a somewhat more straightforward look at the evils of slavery. Solomon Northup (Chiwetel Ejiofor) is kidnapped from his home in New York and sold into slavery in 1841, where he endures and is forced to bear witness to unspeakable horrors until one stranger's kindness secures his freedom. Solomon spends those 12 years trusting different white people, almost all of whom betray him, until his hopes are eventually rewarded. Samuel Bass (Brad Pitt) succeeds in getting a letter from Solomon to friends back home. In *Get Out*, every white person Chris trusts, from Rose to Jim Hudson, deceives him. Even so, Chris cannot bring himself to kill Rose (and interestingly, Missy's death is also not shown, which may say something about the power of white femininity in the framework of such a black male-driven text). Ultimately Chris is saved by Rod, his best friend, whose concerned investigations into his whereabouts bear fruit at just the right moment.

At the end the two black men ride away together and the chorus returns. Listen to your ancestors.

ANATOMY OF A SCENE
GET OUT (2017)

1. Late one night, Chris finds his girlfriend's mother Missy awake in the sitting room. She tells him to sit, and then begins to hypnotise him.

2. She asks Chris about his late mother. He cries as he recalls finding her body as a child, and then realises he is unable to move in his chair.

3. The mood has suddenly turned sinister. "Now, sink into the floor" says Missy. Chris suddenly finds himself falling through darkness.

4. The sitting room is now an unreachable window in the distance. Missy leans in and tells Chris: "Now you are in the sunken place".

CAN YOU TRUST THE STORYTELLER?

BY LEE CHILD

Last year I saw the new Broadway musical *Hamilton*, and it was every bit as good as the hype said it would be. For a writer it had extra appeal. Its rap-style lyrical structure imposed a strict scheme for beats and rhymes. I found myself constantly thinking ahead, in repeated split-second micro-bursts of speculation: how will he rhyme that? What word will he use? I found myself guessing and predicting. Sometimes I was right. It was an extra dimension of fun. It added to the show's many other extraordinary virtues.

I had a similar experience the first time I saw the movie *Se7en* (1995). Not in split-second bursts, but a long slow burn. From the first frame the story is exactly what all writers wish would come to them fully formed in a dream: a rock-solid self-defining structure, and a tight and perfectly symmetrical vertical axis. The clock is always ticking – how long does it take to count to seven? – and against that relentless timeline, the characters fight it out. On our side, two detectives, one old, one young, both no doubt troubled in different ways, but to be understood as two halves of a whole, as a realist compromise, standing in for a single mythic superman, both wise and vigorous.

Against which, therefore, in true David-versus-Goliath fashion, must be pitched a formidable opponent. In the old days, the KGB or the Mafia were good in that role. Infinitely powerful and completely uninhibited. However lantern-jawed you made your David, he was always going to be the underdog. But the old days are gone, and this is a dim, claustrophobic movie, so the antagonist has to be a lone individual, and therefore a psychopath, which we're learning can be just as scary. Uninhibited, certainly. Powerful

Brad Pitt in the finale of 'Se7en' (1995)

in a certain unpredictable way.

At this point in the movie the writer in the audience sinks down in his seat and whispers to himself, "Damn, I wish I had thought of this." Seriously. There is no higher compliment. No bigger disappointment. But you get over it fast. Your storytelling instincts start buzzing with the simple joy of ranging ahead, of figuring out how this story really should be told, which is obviously the way you would do it yourself, which is… and all of a sudden you know how you would do it. You've been keeping score. It's five down, and you know which two are left. You know how you would do it. It would be stunningly elegant, and it would ask a big question.

They won't do it.

Too ballsy.

They do it.

Unbelievable. For a second you feel irrationally proud to be part of the storytelling community. The elegance is in the question: can the good guy be made to complete the bad guy's

work? He knows what he's doing. He's figured it out too. He knows he should back off. But can he trust himself? The provocation is immense. It's what you thought they wouldn't have the balls to do. But they did. The guy gets asked the question. We all do. Every audience member must answer. We all know what we're doing. We all figured it out at the same time. It's a brand new David-versus-Goliath contest all by itself. It's what we should do, versus what we want to do. In the teeth of terrible provocation. Could we trust ourselves? Probably not. Which is a tough conclusion. Most things in life are built on the belief we can trust at least ourselves.

Is that the message of the movie? Probably not. Can we trust ourselves to judge? Maybe. The movie certainly looks like it has a message. It is wonderfully stylised, in a movie-magic kind of way. It's always raining, on soaking-wet low-rise brick buildings. It looks like Manchester. Really it's Los Angeles. But the universe is tight, and people rush from place to place, hunched into raincoats, like a Lowry painting. The palette is dark, the floors are dirty, the mood is sombre, and the era is resolutely analogue. The bad guy's props are wonderfully gothic. The film stock itself has been forced by a special process, so that it pulses and glitters. The movie is meticulously visual, and almost every frame has a kind of terrible beauty. It's exactly the kind of cared-about production we expect to carry a message. It's hard to believe it wouldn't.

Do we trust ourselves to judge? Suppose we thought it's just a beautifully solid story, beautifully told, a Swiss-watch piece of entertainment, and suppose we thought, "You know what? That's all we need."

CAN YOU TRUST WOMEN?

FEMMES FATALES AND WICKED LADIES

BY IMOGEN SARA SMITH

Vamps, vixens, Jezebels or femmes fatales: built into the archetypes of the dangerous woman is the assumption that sex is her chief weapon. But it is not, by itself, what makes her most interesting, or even most dangerous. When Brigid O'Shaughnessy (Mary Astor) walks into the office of private eye Sam Spade (Humphrey Bogart) in *The Maltese Falcon* (1941), she looks like a lady stopping by on her way to lunch at The Ritz, with her furs and a smart little hat tilted over her cameo profile. Her manners are demure, her voice as sophisticated as dry vermouth. Spade sees through Brigid's "schoolgirl manner" and through the phony story she tells him; yet each time one of her falsehoods is exposed she has another ready. Her layers of deception are like the black enamel covering on the jewelled falcon that Brigid, and everyone else in the movie, is chasing after: there may or may not be anything real underneath.

Even her rueful confession – "I've always been a liar" – is another gambit, like her offer of her body, and her appeal to male chivalry and vanity ("I'm so alone and afraid… you're brave. You're strong…") He sees through this too, always appreciating her performance with that amused, sceptical appraisal that was Bogart's specialty. But just because she uses her fear as a ploy doesn't mean she's not really afraid. Astor deliberately

hyperventilated before shooting her scenes to capture Brigid's breathless, panicky desperation to be believed. Beneath her darting eyes and nervous energy is a continually recalculating intelligence and a willingness to do, say or be whatever the occasion requires. Brigid – aka Miss Wonderly, aka Miss LeBlanc – turns out to be even worse than Spade suspected, not just a cheat but a cold-blooded killer. Under it all is tiredness and a sort of blur; she looks drowned in the bottomless pool of her own lies.

Duplicity, even more than greed or selfishness, is the defining characteristic of the femme fatale; even more potent than her sex appeal is her ability to manipulate men with lies and play-acting. The figure is spawned by male anxiety – not about women's emancipation during World War II, as many have argued, but an age-old fear of being deceived by women. Unlike the 'new woman' of the interwar years, the classic *noir* femme fatale is never an independent working girl. She always uses men to get what she wants, exploiting the most traditional feminine wiles. Conniving temptresses multiplied in movies during the post-war years, in a society that discouraged women from pursuing careers and at the same time typecast them as gold-diggers, punishing them for using the only form of power they had.

(Above)
Barbara Stanwyck's
Phyllis Dietrichson reels
in prime sap Walter Neff
(Fred MacMurray) in
Double Indemnity (1944).

(Opposite)
Mary Astor as the coldly
calculating killer Brigid
O'Shaughnessy in *The
Maltese Falcon* (1941),
with Humphrey Bogart.

Phyllis Dietrichson (Barbara Stanwyck) in
Billy Wilder's *Double Indemnity* (1944) married for
a home and security, just as women of the time
were expected to. The only difference is that she
eliminated her husband's first wife to get him, and
now wants to cash him in for his life insurance
policy. Has the idea occurred to her before
insurance salesman Walter Neff (Fred MacMurray)
shows up at her door? We never know, but you see
it form in her narrowed, glinting eyes as he leers up
at her in her towel and makes a tacky joke about
her sunbath ("No pigeons around, I hope,") and
she looks down, seeing a pigeon. She reels him in
with a mixture of lady-like coyness and blatant
sexuality, playing dumb and deftly trapping him
in a web spun by his own cleverness. Stanwyck,
known for the lacerating honesty with which she
faced down hypocrites, crafts an act that's as false
as her character's platinum wig, as transparent
as her tight white sweater, yet convincingly
deadly. She uses surface fakery to distract from
her deeper game, all while letting us glimpse the
cold pit of corruption beneath her glossy allure.

The deadliest of all the classic-era femmes
fatales may be Kathie Moffat (Jane Greer) in
Jacques Tourneur's *Out of the Past* (1947): not
because of her body count (three), but because
she is the most enchanting. When she first

appears, dazzling the detective Jeff Bailey (Robert
Mitchum), who has been sent to find her by the
gangster boyfriend she tried to kill, she's less a
bombshell than a bewitching moonbeam. Greer
was 22, and her huge, fathomless dark eyes
and sultry contralto are set off by baby-faced
freshness and a smile bursting with sweetness.
Kathie effortlessly beguiles Jeff with her mixture
of cool, enigmatic reserve and dry humour,
holding back yet offering the subtlest of come-
ons. They are a perfect match and their romance
is genuinely rhapsodic, nothing like the usual
mating of a black widow and her sucker-prey. *Out
of the Past* is one long jazzy, lyrical improvisation
of the theme of disillusionment, so it's important
that the illusion itself be so irresistible.

Everyone loves the moment when Jeff replies
to Kathie's protestations of innocence with, "Baby,
I don't care." But as it turns out, he cares very
much. When he finds out she lied to him, that
she is willing to kill anyone who gets in her way,
he conceives a loathing for her as ardent as his
former love; when his new girlfriend says that
no one is all bad, he retorts, "She comes closest."
We always see Kathie through his eyes – half her
scenes are part of a long flashback narrated by
Mitchum in a mesmerising voiceover – and she
changes like the weather, from the radiant, girlish

charmer in Mexico, dressed all in white; to the gangster's mistress, glamorous in black gowns and furs but furtive and shifty; to the gloating killer, in a severe, nun-like head covering, who deludes herself she can still get Jeff to love her again. Kathie is not really a schemer like Phyllis, just an utterly selfish, cowardly and opportunistic woman. As Jeff puts it, disgustedly, "You're like a leaf that the wind blows from one gutter to another."

This suggests that what's fatal is not so much the *femme* herself as a man's blind infatuation with her. ("All women are wonders, because they reduce all men to the obvious," says the ill-fated Leonard Eels in *Out of the Past*.) John Brahm's *The Locket* (1946) builds a particularly potent case that the femme fatale springs from men's impulse to idealise the women they love, and to punish them when they fall short. Nancy (Laraine Day), *The Locket*'s disturbed and disturbing anti-heroine, is described by each of her three suitors as "perfect", the girl of their dreams. They are undone when they discover that beneath her impeccable facade she is a lying, homicidal kleptomaniac. The film is constructed as a series of nested flashbacks, as Nancy's past victims (one played by Robert Mitchum) try to warn their successors – only to be dismissed as crazy or spiteful rivals. Nancy herself is a victim as much as a villain, her psyche warped by a traumatic childhood experience of being falsely accused of theft and forced to lie, and she is driven to chronic fabrications by her need to remain desirable to men. "I want you to want me, very much," she tells the last of her fiancés. The pathos of this declaration suggests the way Judy (Kim Novak), in *Vertigo* (1958), after shattering Scottie (James Stewart) with her impersonation of the imaginary dream girl Madeleine, is so desperate

(Above)
Margaret Lockwood as a serial husband-killer in British director Lance Comfort's *Bedelia* (1946), with Ian Hunter.

OUT OF THE PAST (1947)

1 Jeff Bailey passes slow days in an Acapulco café, hoping to meet Kathie Moffatt, whom he has been paid $40,000 to find.

2 All of a sudden, in Kathie walks, and Jeff says: "Then I saw her, coming in out of the sun. And I knew then I didn't care about that 40 grand".

3 The camera, taking Jeff's viewpoint from across the bar, lingers admiringly to watch as Kathie lights a cigarette and orders a drink.

4 Jeff lets a coin drop and roll across to Kathie's table. As he picks it up, a local guide asks him to sit. "With pleasure señor". Jeff is fatally smitten.

to regain his love she allows him to transform her into the dead woman he wants her to be.

"I loved a woman who doesn't exist," complains a disillusioned husband in British director Lance Comfort's *Bedelia* (1946), starring Margaret Lockwood, a line echoed in David Fincher's *Gone Girl* (2014), when the anti-heroine says of her husband, "Nick loved a girl I was pretending to be." Adapted by Gillian Flynn from her own novel, *Gone Girl* tries to have its cake and eat it too, giving us the persuasive self-justifications of Amy (Rosamund Pike), who elaborately fakes her own murder in order to frame her cheating husband, Nick (Ben Affleck), and his own baffled viewpoint. The film opens with Amy turning an indecipherable gaze to the camera as Nick wonders in voiceover, "Who are you? What are you thinking?" The heart-shaped gold locket in Brahm's film, which never reveals its secret, is an apt symbol of the way women are perceived by men as mysterious, inscrutable creatures. Amy, like Nancy, is consumed by the need to maintain a facade of perfection and have it affirmed by a man – when her husband neglects and belittles her, she feels death is an appropriate punishment – even as she complains about having to play the role of "cool girl", the eternally game and fun fantasy girlfriend. At first the movie encourages us to sympathise

with Amy and enjoy her diabolical cleverness, but in the end the number of misogynist stereotypes she embodies is overwhelming: the judgemental princess obsessed with controlling her lovers; the temptress who tricks men into sex and then cries rape; the biological blackmailer who gets pregnant in order to hold a man hostage.

As a femme fatale who is motivated not by greed but by a twisted form of love, Amy belongs in the interesting company of Gene Tierney's Ellen in *Leave Her to Heaven* (1945) and Jean Simmons's Diane in *Angel Face* (1953). Both these women transfer an obsession with their fathers on to a husband or lover, and fear abandonment so much that they will kill others, and even themselves, to hold on to the men they love. In *Leave Her to Heaven*, Leon Shamroy's luscious Technicolor photography makes Tierney inhumanly beautiful; she dons a frilly baby-blue negligée to throw herself downstairs in order to abort her pregnancy, and watches stonily from behind cat's-eye sunglasses and glowing scarlet lips as her husband's paraplegic younger brother drowns. Her single-minded devotion to her husband and home make her a monstrous caricature of the ideal post-war woman, revealing a terrifying void behind the burnished fantasy of domestic bliss.

These films, with their trendy Hollywood

(Above)
Gene Tierney's scarlet-lipped Ellen looks on as her paraplegic brother-in-law drowns in *Leave Her to Heaven* (1945).

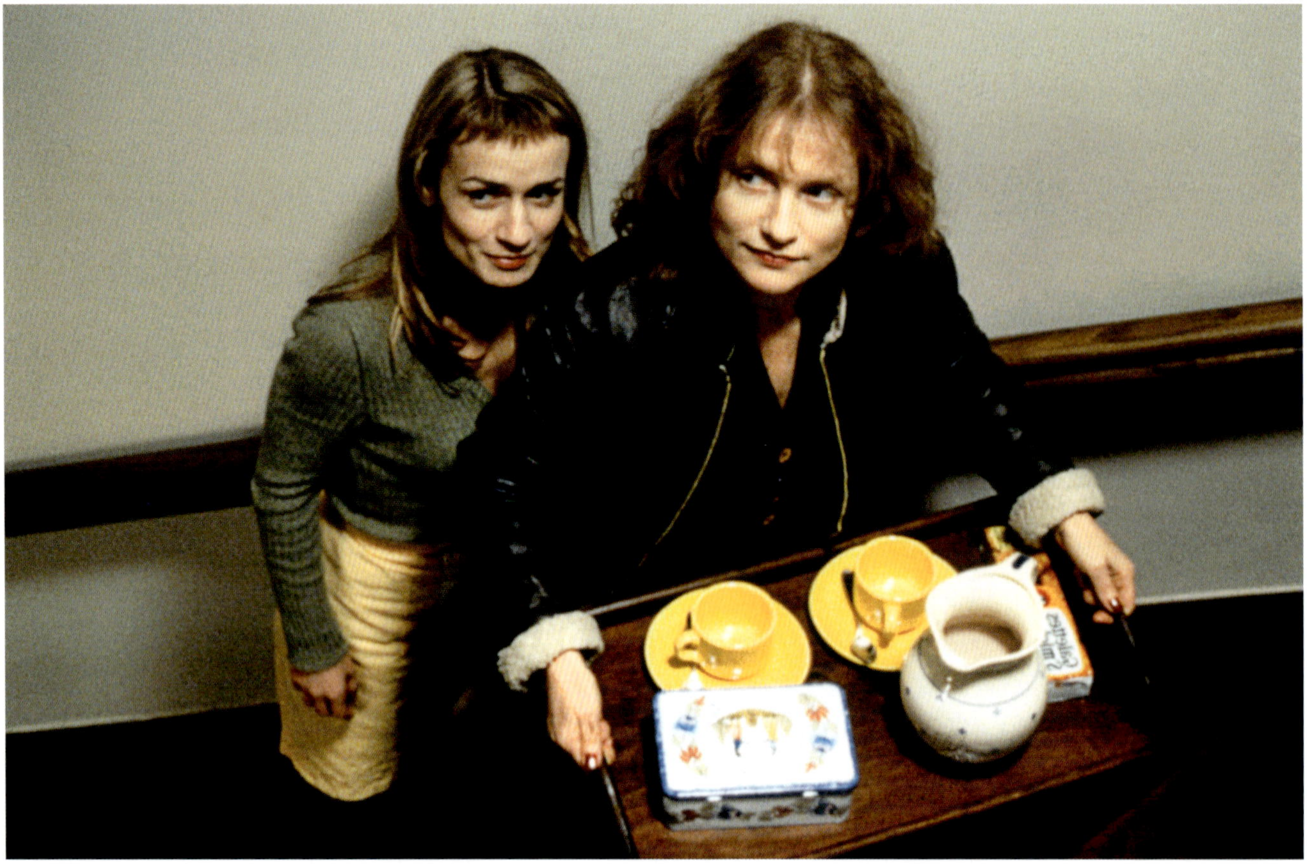

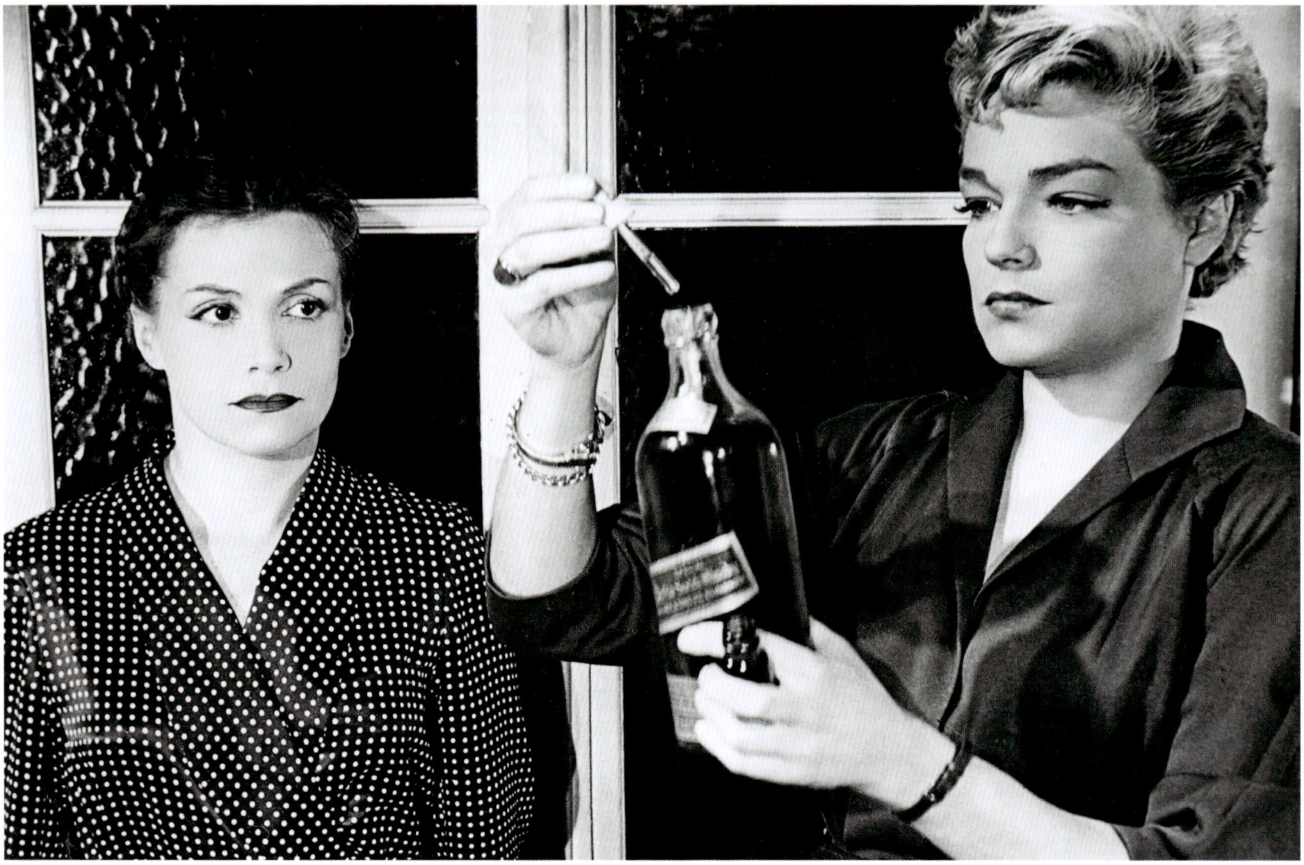

Freudianism, trace the psychological roots of the women's destructive drives – and play on fears of female neurosis and insanity – while films such as *Double Indemnity, Fallen Angel* (1945), *Beyond the Forest* (1949) and, most overtly, *Crime of Passion* (1957) imply the limited options and stifling confinement that could push ambitious women to plot escapes through crime.

Then there are films that present – and seem, often, to perversely celebrate – women who are just plain bad: sociopaths without a shred of empathy or conscience. Such characters turn up in classic-era *noir* – Lizabeth Scott in *Too Late for Tears* (1949), beaming as she motors to Mexico with a suitcase full of stolen money and a few corpses behind her; the icily impassive schemer played by Rita Hayworth in *The Lady from Shanghai* (1947) – but reach their full toxic bloom in gleefully amoral post-Production Code films such as John Dahl's *The Last Seduction* (1994). Linda Fiorentino's character is named Bridget (only one of the film's allusions to classic *noir*; at one point she floats a scheme to murder abusive husbands for their life insurance, smirking that one will bring double indemnity) but she could hardly be less like Mary Astor's *soignée* Brigid O'Shaughnessy. Though she flaunts miniskirts and peek-a-boo hair, and is happy to exploit the role of the victim (gaining leverage at various points by posing as a battered wife and a rape victim), the keynote of her character is her assumption of masculine prerogatives. She is not merely tough and callous, but vulgar and aggressive; she mocks a lover for wanting more than just sex, and later – when she wants him to commit a murder – for being burdened by morals. Though she lies and manipulates, she never hides her real nature; she does not so much seduce as browbeat her weak and dim patsy into obeying her.

With explicit scenes unthinkable during the classic *noir* era, neo-*noir* thrillers suggest a cynical argument for the prevalence of femmes fatales: that they provide a big, steaming helping of sex to movies while at the same time demonising female sexuality as either a calculating tool or a voracious, destructive force. The basic paradox of the femme fatale is that she is undeniably an embodiment of misogyny and male anxieties about being duped or devoured by women – yet her enduring popularity springs from the way people enjoy rooting for these heartless women, and revel in watching them trick, exploit and even kill men. It is presumably the man-bites-dog novelty that gives these stories their kick, the fun of seeing women shed their expected virtues of compassion and selflessness.

Real cases of female killers are comparatively rare, but they are amplified by an echo chamber of fictional versions. Ruth Snyder, the Queens housewife who convinced her lover Judd Gray to help murder her husband after insuring his life, inspired James M. Cain to write both *Double Indemnity* and *The Postman Always Rings Twice*, which in turn inspired a string of direct and indirect adaptations. The grisly case of Christine and Léa Papin, French sisters who were convicted of brutally murdering the wife and daughter in the family they worked for as maids, inspired Jean Genet's play *The Maids* and numerous other works, including Claude Chabrol's *La Cérémonie* (1995). Here, as with all the stories of sirens luring men, fascination springs from the way one of the women (Isabelle Huppert in Chabrol's film) psychologically dominates the other, and how their intimacy, whether sexual or not, propels them to unthinkable violence.

Films in which women prey on other women paint a black picture of female rivalry: for instance, jealousy and resentment between sisters that escalates to violence. This subgenre ranges from Roberto Gavaldón's elegant, melancholy *The Other One* (*La otra*, 1946), starring Dolores del Río as identical twins, to the gothic horror of *What Ever Happened to Baby Jane?* (1962). Is there a crueller deception than the final twist of Henri-Georges Clouzot's *Les Diaboliques* (1955), in which the pretence of female solidarity – an insufferable man's wife and mistress conspire to kill him – proves to be a sham? Simone Signoret gives a fascinating twist to the femme fatale: not a dame who seduces men with beauty or sex, but one who seduces a weaker woman with her strength and guise of sympathy.

The ultimate taboo, of course, is the mother who plots against her own child, who is a death-giver rather than a life-giver. Angela Lansbury, in John Frankenheimer's *The Manchurian Candidate* (1962), might be the ultimate female villain, with her liquid-nitrogen-fuelled portrayal of a woman who turns her son into a robotic pawn in the service of her cause. The typical dangerous woman – whether she is a mother or lover – is an influencer who does not act herself but inspires or goads or manipulates a man into acting, demonstrating both women's power and its limitations. Lansbury's Eleanor is deliciously frightening because even as she plots an assassination and government takeover, her awfulness is so recognisable and ordinary – her embarrassing pushiness, her relentless hectoring, her soul-sucking kisses. The femmes fatales of *film noir* are nightmares wrapped in fantasies, while Lansbury's matronly monster is a nightmare wrapped in a plain old bad dream.

(Opposite, top)
Sandrine Bonnaire (left) and Isabelle Huppert as friends-turned-killers in Claude Chabrol's *La Cérémonie* (1995).

(Opposite, bottom)
Simone Signoret (right) and Véra Clouzot as the co-conspirators in Henri-Georges Clouzot's *Les Diaboliques* (1955).

CAN YOU TRUST A LADY?
THE BRITISH FEMME FATALE

BY JOSEPHINE BOTTING

The jury's out on whether there truly is such a thing as British *film noir*, but there is no doubt that after World War II British cinema reflected the distinctly darker mood of the times. Victory had brought neither spoils of war nor peace of mind, communities were fractured and people displaced, food was scarce and times still hard. The Blitz spirit was gone and it was every man for himself.

And every woman. British cinema began to offer a greater number of edgy female roles, beyond the 'tart with a heart' type often portrayed by Jean Kent, or the wicked lady personified by Margaret Lockwood. These British femme fatales were as ruthless and single-minded as their American counterparts and equally skilled at using their sexuality to manipulate the men around them, in films that tapped into a desire to recapture the tension and uncertainty of the war years.

With a typically British failure of confidence, actors were often imported to lend exotic allure and generic authenticity to thrillers: note Simone Simon in Lance Comfort's *Temptation Harbour* (1947) and Gloria Grahame in Lewis Gilbert's *The Good Die Young* (1954). But Britain had no shortage of wily women – although the films often restricted them to a more domestic sphere, craving warmth and security rather than affluence and power.

The illicit liaison is the transgression of choice for the British femme fatale and few carried it off with more conviction than sleek, green-eyed Christine Norden. In Anthony Kimmins's *Mine Own Executioner* (1948) she takes the upper hand in seducing Burgess Meredith's troubled psychiatrist, having already honed her skills as a "loose… dance-hall minx" in Harold Huth's demob drama *Night Beat* (1948) and

Linden Travers in the controversial 'No Orchids for Miss Blandish' (1948)

later completing her credentials as the murderous wife in Vernon Sewell's 1951 Hammer B picture *The Black Widow*. Norden was unusual in 1940s British cinema for her voluptuousness and sexual confidence, and the scandals of her private life rivalled her onscreen exploits. Dubbed 'Britain's number one oomph girl', she was married five times and had a long and scandalous affair with Alexander Korda, 31 years her senior. Yet she was no dumb blonde and her talent shone through, earning her praise as a "siren who can act".

Also blonde but lissom, haughty and brittle, Sally Gray qualifies as a femme fatale in several films, notably Edward Dmytryk's *Obsession* (1948), in which she plays a serial philanderer who drives husband Robert Newton to plot the murder – and subsequent dissolving in acid – of his love rival. Gray helps the police rescue her beau but shows her true colours by rejecting him at the end, leaving him to seek solace with her decidedly more faithful pet dog.

The gruesome nature of the murder plot caused the release of *Obsession* to be held up by the BBFC, yet even more controversial was St John Legh Clowes's *No Orchids for Miss Blandish* (1948). This notorious film was panned by critics as much for the brash stateside accents and American slang as for its unsavoury plot. Linden Travers is scintillating in the complex title role; dark-haired and high-cheekboned, curvaceous and sensual, her refined exterior hinted at a seething passion beneath. Graham Greene had described the image of her "buttocks over the billiard table" in Edmond T. Gréville's *Brief Ecstasy* (1937) as one of the most erotic ever seen in British cinema. In *No Orchids for Miss Blandish*, she plays a wealthy heiress engaged to a socialite whose physical advances leave her cold. Only when she winds up in the clutches of gang leader Slim Grissom are her passions awakened by the thrill of his immorality and she relinquishes her fortune for the chance of happiness with him. But their love can't overcome his destiny and after he is shot dead by the police, she jumps off a balcony. Sadly, Travers left the film business after *No Orchids*, depriving audiences of her rare combination of sweetness and passion.

Trailed by Rank as the 'British Jean Harlow', Norwegian-born Greta Gynt was another versatile star who with a sly smile and raised eyebrow could communicate everything from triumph to disdain. Compelling as a sultry nightclub singer in Bernard Knowles's *Easy Money* (1948) and a treacherous girlfriend in Francis Searle's *Whispering Smith Hits London* (1952), Arthur Crabtree's *Dear Murderer* (1947) provided her ultimate femme fatale role as a faithless wife seeking excitement in a string of lovers. Critics praised her ability to combine "beauty with Borgia-like

The 'British Jean Harlow' Greta Gynt in 'Dear Murderer' (1947)

habits" as she drove a cuckolded Eric Portman to murder her lover, only to find she already has another one on the go.

Petite and deceptively demure, Elizabeth Sellars enlivened many British thrillers of the period, the best being Robert Hamer's *The Long Memory* (1952), a kind of North Kent version of French director Marcel Carné's classic *Le Quai des brumes* (1938). Lying to protect her drunken, crooked father, she condemns her boyfriend Philip (John Mills) to prison for a murder he didn't

commit. On his release, she realises her deception has put her marriage and home at risk, so she blackmails a gang leader and tries to flee the country.

For over a decade, the British femme fatale adorned many downbeat thrillers but, as befits that time of austerity, she was less interested in diamonds and furs than more modest comforts. As Christine Norden's barroom floozy in *Night Beat* says: "What does anybody want? Bread, kisses, a chance to get out of the rain…"

CAN YOU TRUST MEN?

MAN TROUBLE: MISOGYNY AND THE THRILLER

BY HANNAH MCGILL

(Opposite)
Jane Fonda as stalked prostitute Bree Daniels, and Donald Sutherland as private detective John Klute, in Alan J. Pakula's *Klute* (1971).

"Women have very little idea," Germaine Greer wrote in *The Female Eunuch* in 1970, "of how much men hate them." The idea of misogyny as not a rare or even a common pathology, but a bone-deep component of every male's make-up, has been a contested one among feminists – Greer's feminist contemporary Betty Friedan regarded men as "fellow victims" of archaic gender models; more recently, *Times* columnist Caitlin Moran declared, "One of the first rules of any useful kind of feminism is to politely but firmly say 'Not today, dear' to any woman quacking on about how men are the enemy." Still, the notion of all women being menaced by all men has regained currency in recent years, with the rise of a fourth wave feminism that emphasises the inevitable complicity of males in patriarchal dominance and 'rape culture'. (Even the tempting defence "Not all men!" has been reclaimed as weary feminist parody of male denial and complicity.)

In the reliably gender-troubled realm of cinema, the idea of maleness in general – rather than an individual man or men – as a threatening entity is to some extent a matter of perspective. The mass of thrillers from all eras that position women solely or largely as victims or eye candy might strike some viewers as exposing misogynistic conditions. However, such a reading might well be incidental or contrary to the filmmaker's intentions. The fact that *Taxi Driver* (1976) places its female characters in a misogynistic context is signalled in the scene in which a passenger informs his driver Travis Bickle of his plans to kill his wife, and asks him whether he knows "what a .44 Magnum's gonna do to a woman's pussy". That the character is played by the director, Martin Scorsese, lends the scene a knowing jokiness, however; and like the nameless subject of his speech, the film's other female characters are of interest not for their own experiences or predicaments but for what they trigger in the psychology of a man.

It's not difficult, meanwhile, to list examples of the thriller genre in which a woman ostensibly in need of male help turns out to be playing the system to her own advantage – from the countless double-crossing dames of 30s and 40s *film noir*, to Hitchcock's far-from-dumb blondes, to the post-feminist femmes fatales of *Basic Instinct* (1992) and *Gone Girl* (2014). Such narratives are interestingly double-edged, playing as they do to both misogynistic characterisations of women as manipulative fake victims, and the feminist hankering for resourceful and empowered female leads. But what about those thrillers that acknowledge a

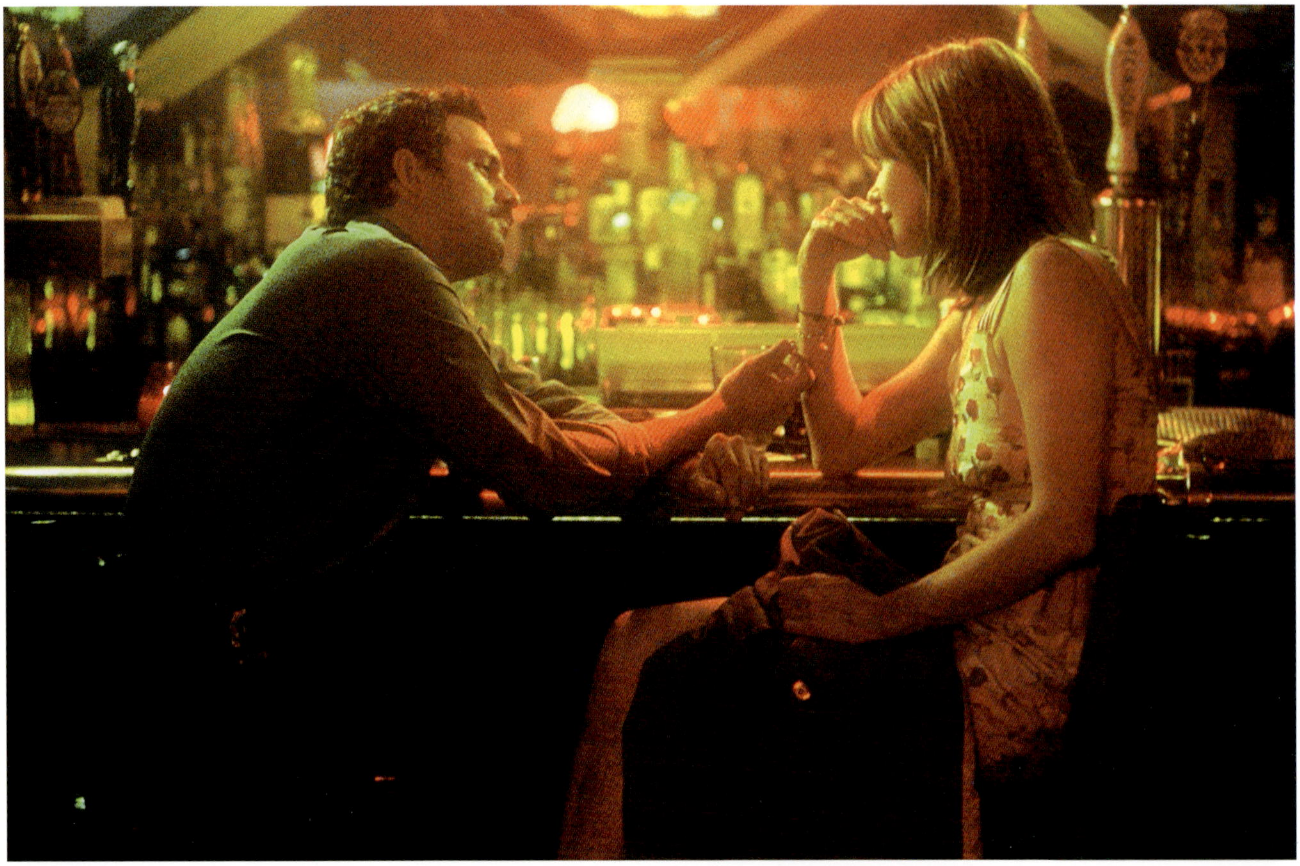

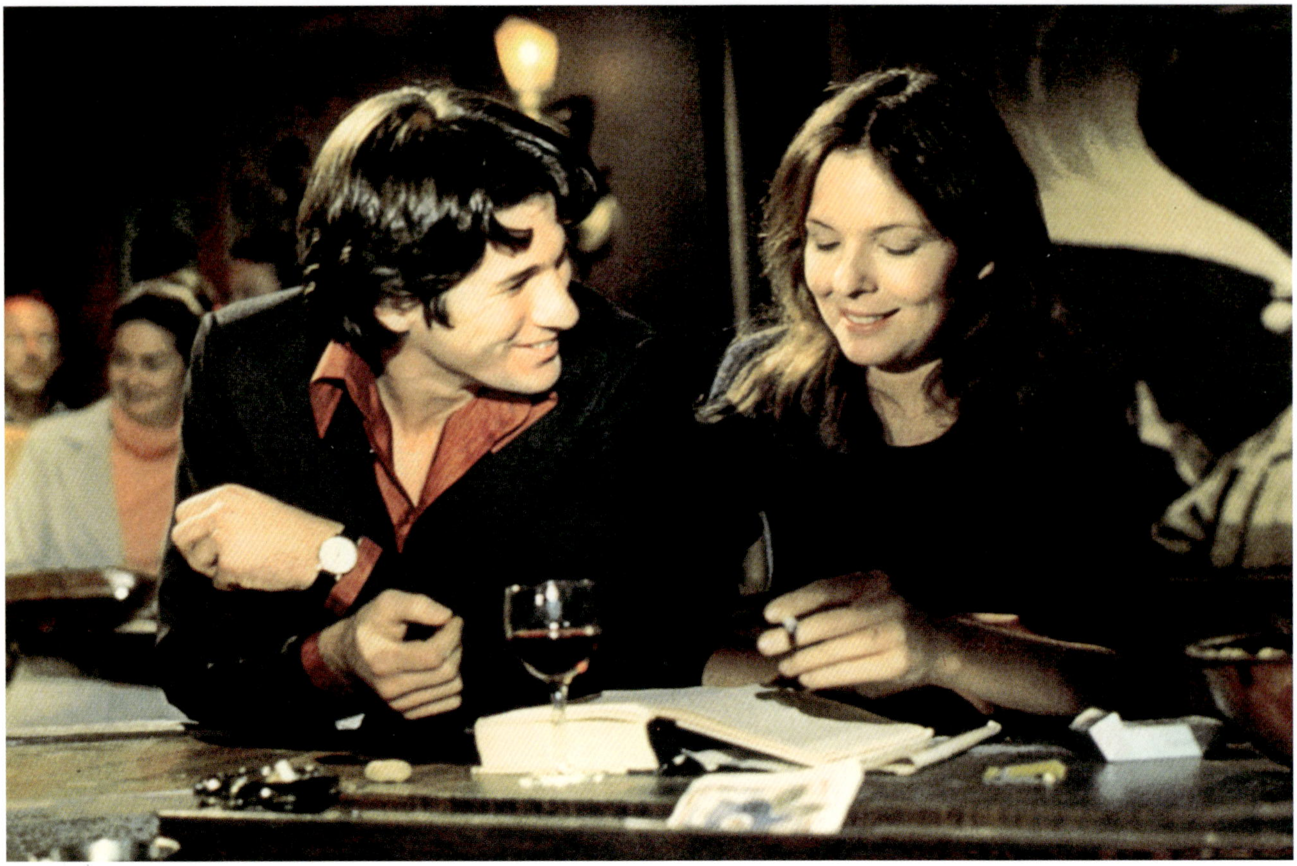

misogynistic context without either colluding with it or gifting a woman the power to flip it?

Klute (1971) might be named after its male protagonist, upstanding private detective John Klute (Donald Sutherland), but it's Jane Fonda's stalked prostitute Bree Daniels who provides its jaded, jittery heart. Once Klute has identified and seen off the man who has been threatening her and murdering other women, and the two have become drawn to one another, the stage is set for Bree to be 'saved' by love. But one of the edgy pleasures of Alan J. Pakula's film is its refusal of this narrative. Bree is not grateful to have won the attention of a respectable man. She's resentful, instead, at her feelings being stirred; she longs, her therapist hears, to be "faceless and bodiless and left alone". When she attacks Klute with scissors, it expresses the fact that he is not the antidote to the patriarchy she subconsciously wishes to disempower, but a part thereof. Even the alternatives to hooking that Bree entertains – modelling, acting – depend upon her being judged as an object, and the idea of permanent domesticity with Klute is also ambiguous in its appeal. "I may be back in a couple of weeks," Bree tells her (female) therapist at the film's close.

Of course, Bree's dissatisfaction can be read as a sexist trope – an illustration of female inscrutability, neurosis and duplicity. But it also conveys with startling clarity the paucity of fulfilling outcomes for a woman in a thriller. We might even choose to read Bree's post-coital taunt to Klute – "Are you upset you didn't make me come?" – as a comment on this lack of satisfying options.

The idea that a woman might be at risk even from those to whom she turns for help reaches a nightmarish pitch in *In the Cut* (2003). Jane Campion's dreamy, scary, blackly comic meta-thriller constantly blurs what excites Frannie (Meg Ryan) with what endangers her. The film introduces to the erotic thriller genre the grim truth that to women, sexual violence is no anomalous, startling plot point, but a universal shared experience, commonplace enough to be the source of black humour rather than shock. Here, the roll-call of suspects commonly required by the murder mystery genre is replayed as a bleak feminist joke: of course the perverted thrill-killer could be any of the guys Frannie knows, because the perverted thrill-killer could *always* be any one of the guys a woman knows. Campion's film avoids the punishing negativity of *Looking for Mr. Goodbar* (1977), in which a woman's risky sex life is seen to lead directly to her murder, but a similar shade

of mordant pessimism can be detected in both films. Go ahead and be smart or dumb, pretty or plain, brazen or modest: however you define or present yourself, there'll still be a good number of guys out there whose fondest wish is to kill you.

As an English professor, Frannie has long intellectualised the drama of gender by analysing it on the level of language. She researches slang, which she finds to be "either sexual or violent"; her verbal sparring with students, suitors and cops abounds with similarly carnal double meanings. As a professional, Frannie is confident with language. As a woman, however, she is permanently stuck outside of it – excluded from its shortcuts and assumptions; always the object and never the subject of hateful jokes and erotic reveries alike. The idea of a language designed to be used *about* women, not *by* them, was replicated by the numerous critical responses to *In the Cut* that upbraided Campion for daring to play with the apparently sacrosanct conventions of the erotic thriller, and Ryan for straying too far from her familiar romcom poppet persona.

That Frannie favours poetry, the form identified by feminist theorists such as Julia Kristeva as best-placed to disrupt patriarchal language and lead to an *écriture feminine*, hints at her desire to break out of oppressive structures. That she finds much of her poetic stimulus via glib mass-produced posters on the New York underground is characteristic of the film's promiscuous mingling of the high with the low, the grubby with the sublime.

One of Frannie's subway encounters is with a tanka by the Japanese feminist and social reformer Akiko Yosano, which runs, "Now, thinking back on the course of my passion / I was like one blind, unafraid of the dark." The simile encompasses both the terror of a redoubled unknown, and the power inherent in being in one's element. If a blind person is frequently at odds with a world constructed with sightedness in mind, he or she sheds any disadvantage, and indeed might gain the upper hand, in darkness. It's not hard to discern a parallel with the female protagonists of thrillers, who in the absence of physical advantage over men must often find ways of weaponising traits customarily associated with female vulnerability: sexual allure, emotional intuition, physical slightness, social unassertiveness. In *Wait Until Dark* (1967), both the blindness of the lead character, Susy, and the passivity that is expected of her are doubled in the blank-eyed china doll that serves as the film's MacGuffin. The symbolism may have appealed to star Audrey Hepburn, who was herself accustomed to being defined by delicate looks and a demure

manner. Susy's literal struggle is against the three
thugs who enter her home in search of the doll
and the drugs it contains; but implicitly she is also
battling the infantilisation and underestimation
of women and of people considered 'impaired'.
Because Susy already lives in darkness, she can be
unafraid of the dark. This idea – of women using
the ingenuity of the underdog, and exploiting
their attackers' low expectations of them –
recurs in two films that bear the clear influence
of *Wait Until Dark*: *Mute Witness* (1995), in which
the female witness to a grisly murder is literally
voiceless, and *Panic Room* (2002), which sees the
anger generated by an ugly marital separation
fuel a mother's resistance to a home invasion. In
both films, women save themselves not only with
guile and graft, but by transcending or subverting
language. Billy (Marina Zudina), lacking the ability
to communicate conventionally, is particularly
well versed in the use and interpretation of body
language; she is also, as a special effects artist,
adept at manipulating visual information, and not
easily duped herself. Female survival in *Panic Room*
also hinges on non-verbal communication. Meg
(Jodie Foster) may be ill-suited to verbal aggression
("Say 'fuck'!" her daughter urges when she first
engages with the intruders), but she is empowered
in the ensuing standoff by her 'feminine' facility
for sending out subtle and misleading messages, as
well as by her maternal devotion to her daughter.

Where a film depicts a woman who is in
possession of social power, in the unambiguous
form of a badge and a gun, her professional trials
are liable to be accompanied by slighting attitudes
from male colleagues, and/or an unsupportive
home life. Kathryn Bigelow's *Blue Steel* (1989) sees
female cop Megan, played by Jamie Lee Curtis,
take pride in following all of the rules of her
profession – including the judicious deployment of
physical violence – only to have her professional
credibility and personal safety jeopardised by
the impulsiveness and emotionality of men. The
very sight of a woman wielding a gun triggers an
erotic obsession in onlooker Eugene (Ron Silver),
a Wall Street banker loaded with signifiers of
material success but deeply insecure about his
sexual authority. Eugene gets plenty of help –

(Right)
Audrey Hepburn as a
blind woman whose
New York home is
invaded by thieves in
Wait Until Dark (1967).

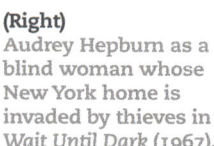

(Above)
FBI agent Clarice
Starling (Jodie Foster)
faces sexism from all
sides in *The Silence
of the Lambs* (1991).

though sadly not the kind he desperately needs – from a sexist law enforcement establishment too mired in its own prejudices to see the truth of Megan's situation. *Blue Steel* is full of men whose obsession with being 'real men' ironically destroys their 'masculine' effectiveness.

In *The Silence of the Lambs* (1991), similar bureaucratic sexism affects FBI agent Clarice Starling (again played by Jodie Foster, an actress frequently positioned in opposition to condescending or hostile men). Clarice is harassed and patronised by men on all sides of the case on which she's working, from her superiors and colleagues, to the killer himself, and the veteran prisoner to whom she turns for advice. Try as she might to keep sex or gender out of her workplace, the men around her keep letting it right back in. (Indeed, the efforts of Hannibal Lecter to embarrass Clarice with lascivious and personal remarks now seem to eerily anticipate the tactics used by the recent rash of self-styled 'pick-up artists', whose favoured tips for eliciting a response from a woman include insulting her appearance and making direct references to sex acts.) The effect is to render Clarice increasingly solitary, until the film's climactic showdown seems to occur not between one criminal and all the forces of law enforcement, but between one woman

and all the forces of misogyny. The peculiar bond that Clarice develops with Lecter, meanwhile, may be said to have something in common with the romantic fervour certain women harbour for imprisoned murderers. Sheila Isenberg, in her 1991 book *Women Who Love Men Who Kill*, found that a motivating factor for such 'death row brides' was a deeply repressed envy of the murderer's defiance of social and moral rules. "It is his ability to murder that attracts her. He acted on his rage, however unsuitably. She could never act on her rage."

Not having committed a crime may not, however, prevent a woman being deemed culpable by association. For a woman, after all, *innocence* denotes not only non-culpability, but also sexual purity. Volker Schlöndorff and Margarethe von Trotta's *The Lost Honour of Katharina Blum* (1975) asks us to consider what is meant by 'honour'. The eponymous Katharina (Angela Winkler) does nothing other than what poets, songwriters and pick-up artists through the ages have wheedled women to do more willingly and less discriminatingly: she acts on an instant attraction, and makes love to a man she likes. When her lover turns out to be a wanted robber and terrorist, Katharina becomes a target for a tabloid media that cares far more about fomenting sensation than it does about whether she actually bears

any responsibility. Implicitly, Katharina's lack of sexual purity has made her fair game: journalists and police alike interrogate her sex life as if it holds the key to her moral character, and eschew treating her decently on the basis that she's already proven herself to be a 'whore'. The general public, meanwhile, bombards her with obscene messages and photographs, in a dispiritingly direct foreshadowing of the sexualised online abuse that greets any woman who finds herself the subject of news coverage for any reason whatsoever today.

Katharina kills her chief tormentor out of an ambiguous mix of self-defence and revenge. The two concepts might be said to merge to some extent when a woman acts against an aggressor who embodies harm to her entire gender. The 'rape-revenge' subgenre takes this idea and runs with it – in heels. To what extent the likes of *I Spit on Your Grave* (aka *Day of the Woman*, 1978) and *Ms. 45* (1981) can be considered critiques of misogyny is debatable: the former revels in its rape scenes, and arguably dehumanises perpetrators and victim alike; the latter emphasises its female protagonist's encroaching derangement and near-sexual enjoyment of killing at least as much as the male violence that surrounds her. A rather more subversive and startling post-feminist idea drives the grinding, gritty *Baise-moi* (2000):

that rape is only considered the outrage that it is because of outmoded ideas about the importance of female chastity. "I leave nothing precious in my cunt for those jerks," declares Manu (Rafaëlla Anderson) after being gang-raped. The violent rampage upon which she then embarks with her friend Nadine (Karen Bach) is not so much an attack on the patriarchy as it is a rejection of any and all structure. Catherine Breillat's *Á ma soeur!* (2001) is another raw, wilfully messy take on female resistance – and gives us another rape survivor who declines the status of victim.

It's possible to read the challenging technical and narrative choices made in *Baise-moi* and *À ma soeur* as an artistic expression of their protagonists' nihilistic brand of feminism. Who, these films demand, made your rules of what constitutes a 'good movie'? For the other films discussed here a clear tension exists: that produced by critiquing sexist systems via the conventions of a genre expressly tailored to the male gaze. We neither have to hate all women nor blame all men to see that thrillers are no less mired in their sexist language than Frannie Avery is in hers. And the fact that these movies continue to stir impassioned debate about just how feminist they truly are indicates how disputed the territory is on which their protagonists tread.

CAN YOU TRUST QUEER CHARACTERS?

GENDER OUTLAWS AND HOMICIDAL HOMOSEXUALS

BY SIMON MCCALLUM

A French lake, all but deserted on a balmy summer's evening. A young gay man, Franck, who spends his days sunbathing and cruising for casual sex in the dense woodland surrounding the lake, spots the dangerously handsome Michel – latest object of his desire – drowning another man.

This scenario and the ensuing dilemma at the heart of French director Alain Guiraudie's mischievous *Stranger by the Lake* (2013) offer a knowing wink to one of the thriller genre's most well-worn tropes: the disturbed homosexual villain. *Stranger by the Lake* is open to multiple readings; the knee-jerk one being that sexy/menacing Michel is a one-dimensional psychopath and poor Franck a reincarnation of a certain pernicious old stereotype: the lonely, desperate, morally bankrupt gay man, in this case willing to overlook a spot of murder in his craven pursuit of love. Franck might well end up as Michel's next victim and he knows it, but for him it's worth the risk – and gay men are addicted to risk, right? Forever loitering in public lavatories and rooting around in the bushes with strangers…

These connections tap into a tangled web of cinematic representation spun by decades of institutionalised homophobia. In their search for the ultimate villain, filmmakers around the world have reflected and often amplified prevailing prejudices that equate homosexuality – and more broadly any deviation from societal norms of sexuality and gender identity – with moral weakness and depravity. Novelists and playwrights must shoulder some of the responsibility for this since many of the thrillers open to a queer reading here derive from a literary source.

Let's rewind to the 1930s and reacquaint ourselves with the Master of Suspense himself. Beloved of queer theorists, Alfred Hitchcock was drawn to deviants of all stripes, and in Hitch's day to be queer most certainly was to be classified as a deviant. The birth of cinema came just a few years after the publication of Krafft-Ebing's *Psychopathia Sexualis* in 1886, with debates around the pathology of homosexuality intensifying in both Europe and the US. Homosexuality was not removed from the American Psychiatric Association's list of mental disorders until 1973, and in the UK sex between men was only partially decriminalised in 1967. Sporadic witch-hunts against gay men persisted on both sides of the Atlantic throughout the 20th century.

One of Hitchcock's most fascinating queer villains appears in what was only his third 'talking picture', *Murder!* (1930). The mixed-race actor and circus trapeze artist Handel Fane, played by Esme Percy, is a loner among a touring theatre troupe.

(Above)
Stranger by the Lake
(2013) plays with the
well-worn cinematic
trope of the disturbed
homosexual villain.

Often required to cross-dress, he becomes prime suspect in the murder of actress Edna Druce, found battered to death with a fire poker; another actress in the troupe, Diana Baring (Norah Baring) has been wrongly convicted and awaits hanging. Fane's otherness is signified by his violation of gender norms and the secret of his 'half-caste' heritage; this otherness can be read as a metaphor for homosexuality at a time when censorship proscribed any explicit mention of the subject. Knowing the game is up, and haunted by images of the innocent, 'ordinary' Diana, Fane commits spectacular suicide, making ingenious use of his trapeze. Queer villains like to go out with a flourish.

A taste for murder

While crimes of passion dominate the thriller genre, queer characters have long been carving out a special niche for themselves by killing for kicks. Following his move to Hollywood, Hitchcock made *Rope* (1948), one of his most formally and thematically experimental works. Based on a 1929 play by Patrick Hamilton inspired by the 1924 Leopold and Loeb case – in which two men abducted and murdered a Chicago schoolboy – the film sees two wealthy Harvard graduates strangle a former classmate as a demonstration of their

perceived superiority, and proceed to host a dinner party with the body concealed in a chest. The killers, played by John Dall and Farley Granger (himself openly bisexual), commit this "perfect crime" in the Manhattan penthouse they share. Homosexuality was taboo in the Production Code, but it's clear the pair are to be read as a couple.

Like Leopold and Loeb, they are fascinated by Nietzsche's concept of *Übermenschen*, 'supermen' who transcend the codes of conduct mere mortals have to live by. Already outsiders by dint of their sexuality, queer villains are often depicted as aesthetes who intellectualise and rationalise their actions, with an ability to compartmentalise necessitated by living life in the closet. Leopold and Loeb's real-life 'crime of the century' inspired several other works, including Richard Fleischer's *Compulsion* (1959) and Tom Kalin's icon of the New Queer Cinema *Swoon* (1992), which zeroed in on the killers' likely homosexuality.

Deadly duos crop up frequently in thrillers; the intimacy of a criminal bond sometimes coupled with implicit or overt lesbianism. Claude Chabrol's *La Cérémonie* (1995), loosely based on Ruth Rendell's novel *A Judgement in Stone*, stars Sandrine Bonnaire and Isabelle Huppert as an unstable maid and postmistress who wreak violent revenge on the

happy family they can never be part of. Rendell's novel, like Jean Genet's 1947 play *The Maids* before it, was inspired by the scandalous case of Christine and Léa Papin, who in 1933 murdered their employer's wife and daughter. The Lancashire motorways offer a bleaker backdrop for bisexual serial killer Eunice (Amanda Plummer) and naive acolyte Miriam (Saskia Reeves) in Michael Winterbottom's *Butterfly Kiss* (1995); while the Wachowskis injected a dose of black comedy and S&M kink into their debut *Bound* (1996), in which a butch ex-con (Gina Gershon) and a gangster's moll (Jennifer Tilly) turn the tables on the male crooks.

Rope's Farley Granger returned to the Hitchcock fold for the celebrated *Strangers on a Train* (1951), a classic example of the thriller's implicit correlation between queerness and amorality. Based on Patricia Highsmith's debut novel, the film hurls the psychopathic Bruno Anthony (Robert Walker) into the life of Granger's tennis star Guy Haines like a hand grenade. Guy's life is about to get extremely difficult when he inadvertently agrees to "swap murders" with Bruno to help cover their tracks. Bruno will deal with Guy's brash and unfaithful wife, who has refused him a divorce, leaving him free to marry his true love, in return for dispatching Bruno's hated father.

(Above)
Guy (Farley Granger) and Bruno (Robert Walker) 'swap murders' in Alfred Hitchcock's *Strangers on a Train* (1951).

(Below)
Jennifer Tilly (left) and Gina Gershon as a couple who turn the tables on the male crooks in *Bound* (1996).

(Top)
Bitchy, effete Waldo Lydecker (Clifton Webb) moulds Laura (Gene Tierney) into his perfect woman in *Laura* (1944).

(Above)
Cruising (1980), starring Al Pacino as an undercover cop, drew protests from the gay community.

(Below)
The controversial *Basic Instinct* (1992), starring Leilani Sarelle (left) and Sharon Stone, was picketed during filming.

Whereas Guy is naive but not fundamentally evil, since he doesn't take Bruno's suggestion seriously, Bruno is the genuine article, a true psychopath. There is some sexual ambiguity to the character of Guy, but charming mother's boy Bruno is more clearly signalled as homosexual, paying obsessive attention to the handsome tennis player and willing to stop at nothing to get his wife out of the picture.

Hitchcock's post-war output coincided with (and in the case of films like *Strangers on a Train* fed into) that distinct subgenre of the thriller that came to be known as *film noir*. *Noir* had an important and largely malign role in screen representations of homosexuality. A new model of villain was born: the 'sissy'; sly, dry and fastidiously dressed. Trappings of femininity signal danger and deviance, an apparent lack of physical prowess compared to the scruffy-macho heroes – something to be suspicious of, even feared. Peter Lorre's slippery, perfumed crook Joel Cairo in John Huston's *The Maltese Falcon* (1941) is a touchstone here. Rendered by his accent, mannerisms, hair and make-up as an exotic, foreign 'other', Cairo is backed up by Wilmer (Elisha Cook Jr); the censors prohibited any explicit reference to their sexuality but if the film had been made later Cairo and Wilmer would likely be an item.

The association of femininity with homosexuality is mined further in Otto Preminger's *Laura* (1944). Bitchy, effete newspaper columnist Waldo Lydecker (Clifton Webb) lives in a fussy apartment bursting with art. Waldo sets about moulding the mousy Laura (Gene Tierney) into his idea of the perfect woman – a woman as another work of art, not a sexual partner. He's a villain in the most insidious sense, totally selfish and concealing a haywire moral compass beneath a veneer of respectability, wit (he's actually quite vicious) and 'good taste'. Obsession with surface reflects the emptiness beneath, ie, childlessness, the absence of a heteronormative family unit. Stereotypes persist about gay men having good taste as if this fills some perceived void; Waldo is just one of many incarnations in popular culture.

After *Strangers on a Train,* Patricia Highsmith, a lesbian who at times struggled with her sexuality, wrote under a pseudonym *The Price of Salt*, eventually filmed by Todd Haynes as *Carol* (2015). But it was in 1955 that she introduced her most famous creation to the world: Tom Ripley. The amoral yet sympathetic conman appeared in a series of five novels, starting with *The Talented Mr Ripley*, filmed by René Clément as *Plein soleil* (1960) with Alain Delon

as Ripley; and by Anthony Minghella in 1999, with Matt Damon in the role. Ripley's repressed homosexuality – a trait Highsmith was reluctant to be drawn on – is intimated in Minghella's film, as his obsession with playboy Dickie Greenleaf (Jude Law) and resentment of Dickie's wife Marge (Gwyneth Paltrow) tips over into murder. Ripley's elaborate scheme to assume the identity of his 'perfect man' sets the tone for the devilish series of adventures to come.

The killer inside me

Queer villains often lash out at the straight world that's rejected them, but other queers have to watch out too. The self-hating homosexual is armed and dangerous in *Cruising* (1980); William Friedkin's serial-killer thriller prompted widespread protests from the gay community with its portrayal of a cop (Al Pacino) tracking a creepy gay killer through New York City's leather bars. Pacino's character is so drawn into this S&M underworld he might have been 'turned', as if homosexuality is something you catch by snorting a bottle of poppers. Echoing the *Cruising* controversy, Joe Eszterhas's leaked script for *Basic Instinct* (1992) provoked an outcry before Paul Verhoeven's 'neo-*noir*' erotic thriller even opened, with filming locations and later screenings picketed by the Gay & Lesbian Alliance Against

Defamation (GLAAD). In a star-making turn, Sharon Stone plays Catherine Tramell, a rich and beautiful crime novelist whose dalliance with posturing San Francisco detective Nick Curran (Michael Douglas) is complicated by the presence of her lover Roxy (Leilani Sarelle). Roxy is a man-hating butch of lesbian stereotypes past, while Catherine's bisexuality is an immediate red flag for danger (bisexuals can't be trusted). The ice pick used by the film's blonde killer during acrobatic sex represents the man's ultimate fear of penetration – and his rejection by the female of the species.

The 'mad dyke' trope isn't quite dead and buried, even in the 21st century. Richard Eyre's *Notes on a Scandal* (2006), based on the bestselling novel by Zoë Heller, saw Judi Dench play lonely spinster Barbara, a secondary school teacher who latches on to flighty colleague Sheba (Cate Blanchett) with passionate zeal. Sheba's having an affair with an underage male pupil and Barbara uses this secret to inveigle herself into her life. Barbara is bitter and unbalanced and riled many queer viewers, yet Sheba is arguably the real villain of the piece. A parallel reading suggests that societal homophobia is to blame for Barbara's repressed sexuality and consequent 'acting out'; progress of sorts.

Transgender representation – what little there is of it – has proved especially problematic

(Above)
Peter Lorre (centre) as slippery, perfumed crook Joel Cairo in John Huston's *noir The Maltese Falcon* (1941).

(Opposite, top)
Razor-wielding killer
'Bobbi' in Brian De
Palma's fetishistic
homage to Hitchcock,
Dressed to Kill (1980).

(Opposite, bottom)
Ted Levine as serial
killer 'Buffalo Bill' in
The Silence of the Lambs
(1991). The character
met with criticism.

in mainstream cinema. Reflecting prejudice and misunderstanding in wider society, many thrillers have muddled questions of sexuality and gender identity, equating transvestitism with transgender, while cross-dressing becomes a plot device to denote deviant sexuality or a split personality. Brian De Palma's *Dressed to Kill* (1980) paid fetishistic homage to Hitchcock's *Psycho* (1960), the latter film's schizophrenic motel-keeper Norman Bates (Anthony Perkins), still living at home with 'mum', given a flashy 1980s update in the form of razor-wielding killer 'Bobbi'. Ostensibly a trans patient of psychiatrist Dr Robert Elliott (Michael Caine), awaiting gender reassignment surgery, Bobbi is in fact Dr Elliott in a blonde wig, a murderous manifestation of his thwarted desire to be a woman. To be trans is a harbinger of mental illness; to be resisted at any cost.

While De Palma's film was enjoyed (or dismissed) by many in the LGBT community as campy exploitation, deeper unease greeted the portrayal of serial killer Jame 'Buffalo Bill' Gumb (Ted Levine) in Jonathan Demme's *The Silence of the Lambs* (1991). Gumb, who FBI Agent Clarice Starling (Jodie Foster) discovers had been turned down for gender reassignment, skins his female victims with the aim of making a suit out of them. Demme was perplexed by the fierce criticism the character provoked, seeing Gumb simply as a man who hated himself and for whom becoming a woman was an escape route. Well-intentioned though that defence may be, and masterful though Demme's film undoubtedly is, this fails to situate the character within the Hollywood thriller's historically transphobic narrative. In this world to be cisgender (where a person's gender identity matches the gender assigned to them at birth) represents innocence and transgender the polar opposite.

An earlier, exceptionally crude example of the 'corrupt cross-dresser' featured in Alan Gibson's banned shocker *Goodbye Gemini* (1970). Disturbed twin Julian (Martin Potter) is drugged and raped by two drag queens, members of a 'circus' of transvestite prostitutes. Once the ultimate taboo (the death penalty for it was only repealed in Britain in 1861) sodomy lingers in the cinematic shadows as a transgressive threat to heteronormative patriarchy. Unable to depict it in the context of consensual love, filmmakers have more often alluded to anal sex as a violent perversion of the status quo. In John Boorman's *Deliverance* (1972) it is an act borne of genetic deficiency and primordial savagery, with city boy Bobby (Ned Beatty) urged to "squeal like a pig" as he's held down and raped by inbred locals in the Georgia backwoods.

Whether violent, immoral, unbalanced or just plain criminal, do these characters have any redeeming features? And though times are slowly changing, what can we salvage from a century of LGBT representation filtered largely through a heterosexual, cisgender lens? First and foremost there is pleasure to be had for many queer viewers in the high-camp showboating of the more outrageous bad guys/girls, and in the darker psychological thrillers a certain catharsis in seeing revenge wrought on a straight world that has been, and for many still is, unwelcoming and oppressive. The more depraved among them may be beyond 'reclamation', but rooting for the queer baddie is a subversive act in itself, especially when consuming films produced under government-approved homophobic and transphobic censorship. As any actor will tell you, it's always more fun playing the villain.

ANATOMY OF A SCENE
ROPE (1948)

1 The film opens with a man being strangled to death, his contorted face and cries suggesting a moment of sexual climax.

2 Physically spent and panting heavily, the two killers Philip (left) and Brandon heave the limp body into a wooden chest.

3 Brandon turns on a lamp, but Philip implores him to turn it off: "Not just yet, let's stay this way for just a minute."

4 As though in a classic Hollywood post-coital scene, Brandon lights a cigarette, exhales, tips his head back and sighs in relief.

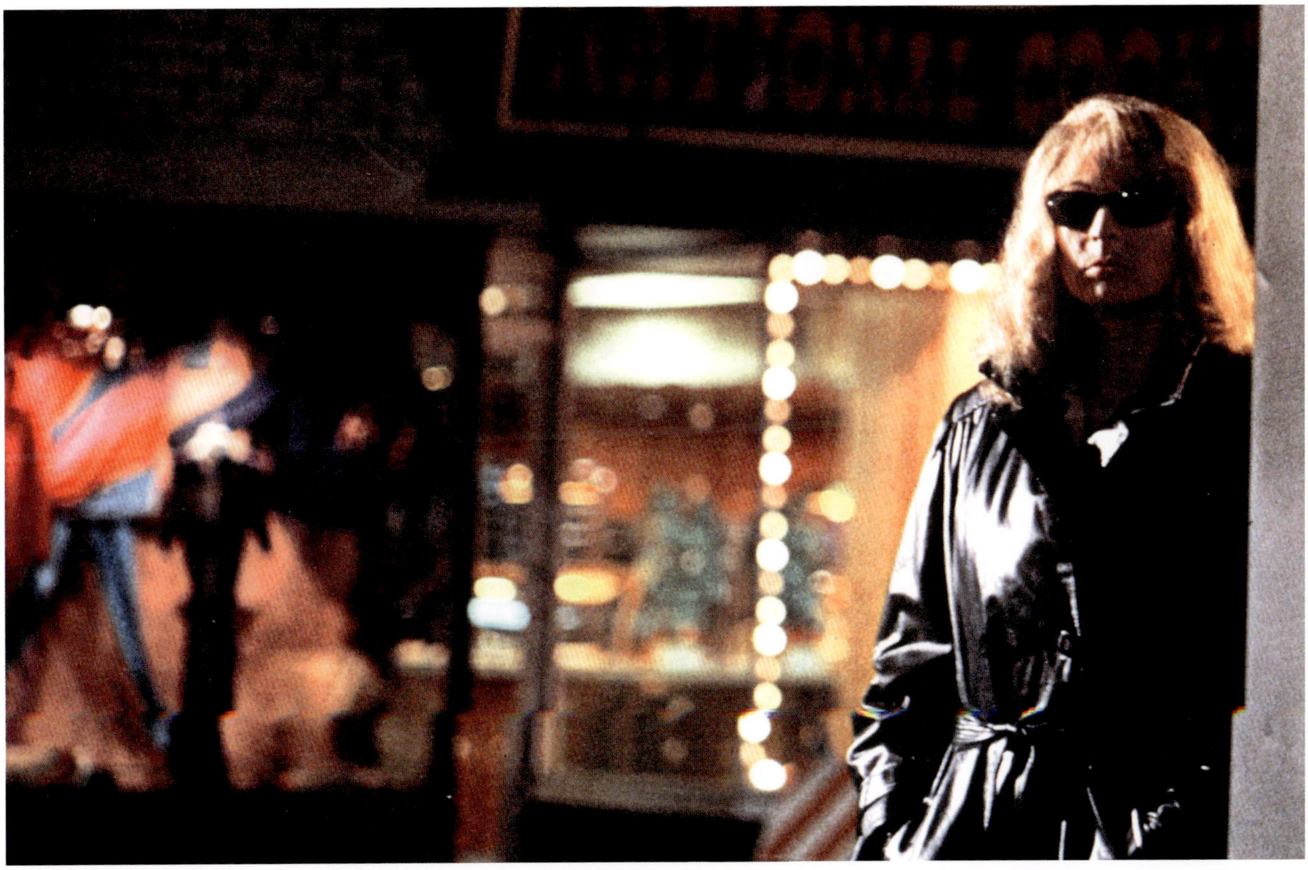

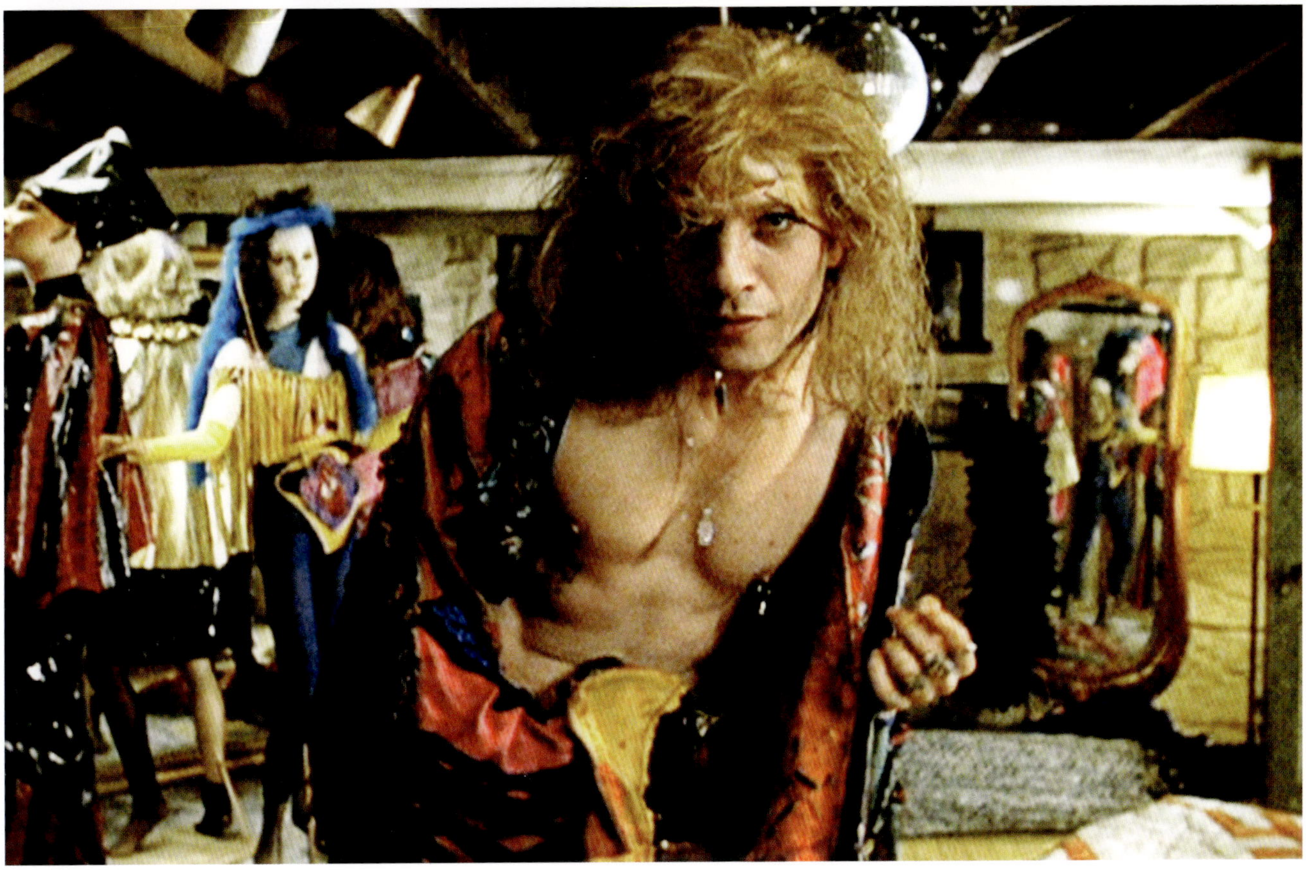

CAN YOU TRUST A STRANGER?

PSYCHOS, SERIAL KILLERS & STRANGER DANGER

BY KIM NEWMAN

(Opposite)
Marion Crane (Janet Leigh) wonders if she can trust motel owner Norman Bates (Anthony Perkins) in *Psycho* (1960).

Perhaps the purest form of thriller is the public information film. The likes of Sarah Erulkar's *Never Go with Strangers* (1971) set out to imprint on their audiences a terror of eccentrics offering children sweeties, lifts home, a trip to see some puppies, or just unwelcome company. Though necessarily vague about the specific fate awaiting foolish children ("He can be rude and nasty," purrs the narrator as the shadow of a "big, frightening" man looms over young Lucy, "and she can't do anything about it"), the short – made in a Britain which remembered the Moors Murders all too well – is all the more persuasive because of its hints of the literally unspeakable. It even risks a special effect, as a playground loiterer morphs into a literal monster – indicating that the Big Bad Wolf of the fairytale and the werewolf of Hammer Films were only masks worn by predators you were much more likely to meet in your 1970s suburb.

Never Go with Strangers is a short, sharp 20-minute condensation, suitable for screening in a classroom (albeit supervised), of the contemporary nightmare scenarios found in *Assault* and *Revenge*, Sidney Hayers's remarkably obsessive 1971 diptych of British schoolgirls raped and killed by 'strange men' and the horrific ripple effects through the affected communities in the aftermath of the crimes.

The intersection of information and exploitation later yielded Kenneth Rowles's 40-minute *Take an Easy Ride* (1976), which begins as a sober, narrated account of the perils of hitchhiking – targeting young girls who could be the children from *Never Go with Strangers* five years on – before turning into a salacious sex-and-violence programmer. Here the drivers who pick up hikers are as likely to be robbed at knifepoint by psycho nymphets as unwary girls thumbing their way to a pop festival are to be raped and killed or wind up pregnant and dumped after a booze-fuelled threesome with the chic couple cruising for easy prey in their Rolls-Royce.

So many suspense/menace thrillers boil down to awful warnings after the manner of a public information film – even down to the titles. In Pat Jackson's *Don't Talk to Strange Men* (1962), naive teen Jean (Christina Gregg) answers a telephone ringing in a box by a rural bus stop she uses after her regular babysitting shift and, calling herself 'Samantha', begins a fantasy relationship with a smooth-talker who grooms her – not an expression in use in 1962 – in exactly the way today's internet lurkers seduce their victims. It's obvious that screenwriter Gwen Cherrell has researched the habits of these strange men – the touch of petulance and controlling behaviour he

(Right)
Public information films such as Sarah Erulkar's *Never Go with Strangers* (1971) warned children of dangerous strangers.

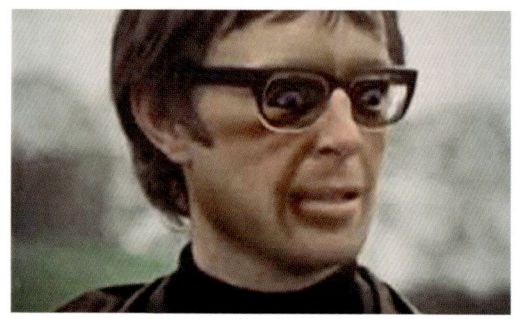

shows when he threatens never to call again to punish 'Samantha' for not immediately answering is chillingly believable. That there was a lot of this sort of thing going on (at least in the movies) is evidenced by the fact that Jean's younger sister, who eventually keeps Samantha's date with the stranger, is played by Janina Faye, who had already been traumatised by an encounter with a drooling old lech (Felix Aylmer) shaking a bag of candy in Cyril Frankel's equally bluntly titled *Never Take Sweets from a Stranger* (1960). The lesson has to be reinforced over and over, so that even the titles run together: *When a Stranger Calls* (1979), *Don't Answer the Phone!* (1980), *Never Talk to Strangers* (1995), *Don't Hang Up* (2016), *Don't Breathe* (2017).

The killing kind

The myth of the wandering murderer is deeply ingrained, appearing in Jack the Ripper pictures from Alfred Hitchcock's *The Lodger* (1927) and G.W. Pabst's *Pandora's Box* (1928) onwards. Hitchcock's film, unlike the Marie Belloc Lowndes novel it and most subsequent adaptations are based on, complicates the situation by making its stranger (Ivor Novello) an innocent man unjustly suspected of being the Ripper-type murderer – as opposed to the culpable Mr Slade (Laird Cregar) in John Brahm's 1944 remake, which stays closer to Lowndes's vision. Even as early in his career as *The Lodger*, Hitchcock was turning familiar stories inside-out. His serial killers – Uncle Charlie (Joseph Cotten) in *Shadow of a Doubt* (1943) and Norman Bates (Anthony Perkins) in *Psycho* (1960) – are isolated, lonely and eccentric but accepted as part of the family or a community.

Before the term 'serial killing' came into common parlance, the FBI termed such crimes 'stranger murders', referring to the fact that motive was harder to discern in cases where killer and victim didn't know each other. "That's the trouble with sex crimes," says the policeman (Alfred Marks) in Gordon Hessler's *Scream and Scream Again* (1970), "there's no motive… except the sex." Raymond Lemorne (Bernard-Pierre Donnadieu) in George Sluizer's *The Vanishing* (*Spoorloos*, 1988) isn't even interested in the sex, though he targets a pretty young girl. He abducts and kills as an experiment, selecting a random stranger (Johanna ter Steege) but then getting to know his next victim, the bereaved boyfriend (Gene Bervoets) who will literally give anything to know what happened. We see Raymond as a family man, even practising his abduction techniques on his young daughter, but realise that in order to be who he is, he must hold back a submerged portion of his personality even with those close to him. A trace of public information film lingers – like Buffalo Bill in *The Silence of the Lambs* (1991), Raymond copies a trick of the serial killer Ted Bundy by wearing a cast on his arm as a stratagem to ensnare kindly passers-by. Victims trust a man who seems to need help. Similar vanishings – the result of chance encounters in

(Opposite)
The stranger (Ivor Novello) arrives to take his room in Hitchcock's Jack the Ripper-inspired silent *The Lodger* (1927).

(Left)
Laird Cregar in John Brahm's 1944 version of *The Lodger*, which stayed closer to Marie Belloc Lowndes's novel.

roadside diners or service stations while partners are distracted – recur, from *Dying Room Only* (1973) through *Breakdown* (1997) to *Death Proof* (2007), emphasising the randomness of running into the wrong person or situation on the road.

Lost highways

"My mother told me never to do this," Jim (C. Thomas Howell) says as he lets John Ryder (Rutger Hauer) into his car in Robert Harmon's *The Hitcher* (1986) – and, like so many other young protagonists, he should have paid more attention to the various 'stranger-danger' public service announcement films that were the US equivalents of *Never Go with Strangers*. But long before Ryder stuck out his thumb or those young hitchers took their easy ride, the highways were haunted by sinister strangers – in the *noir* era, few villains are as chilling as the psychopathic hitchers Steve Morgan (Lawrence Tierney) in Felix E. Feist's *The Devil Thumbs a Ride* (1947) or Emmett Myers (William Talman) in Ida Lupino's *The Hitch-Hiker* (1953). Like Ryder, these villains are barely human – Myers has the unnerving habit of sleeping with his eyes open, so that his hostages (Edmond O'Brien, Frank Lovejoy) never know whether he's alert and deadly or not. It's a signature move of the creepy hitcher to settle comfortably into the car with the unwary motorist and come up with an ominous line that unmistakably marks him out as a maniac – Myers admires a driver's wrist-watch and says, "I had a watch like this once when I was 17 – nobody gave it to me, I just took it," and Ryder flicks a switchblade and muses, "You want to know what happens to an eyeball when it gets punctured?"

It's in the nature of stories to delve behind the mask and try to come up with a backstory or even ask for sympathy for the menacing stranger – but then he ceases to be a stranger and becomes a part-tragic figure, like Mark Lewis (Carl Boehm) in Michael Powell's *Peeping Tom* (1960). The purest stranger menaces in film are raspy voices at the end of the phone – with that 'the calls are coming from inside the house' urban legend punchline never far off – who torment invalid Barbara Stanwyck in *Sorry, Wrong Number* (1948), coeds Olivia Hussey and Margot Kidder in Bob Clark's *Black Christmas* (1974), babysitter Carol Kane in Fred Walton's *When a Stranger Calls* ("Have you checked the children?") or everyman Colin Farrell in Joel Schumacher's *Phone Booth* (2002).

Even creepier, perhaps, is trucker Rusty Nail (voiced by Ted Levine) in John Dahl's *Joy Ride* (aka *Road Kill*, 2001), who does his menacing over CB radio, though the never-fully-seen, never-says-a-word truck-driving road hog (stunt driver Carey Loftin, seen only as a pair of cowboy boots) in Steven Spielberg's *Duel* (1971) – based on a Richard Matheson short story – is an ultimate in unknowable, unreachable malice. It's possible that the driver in *Duel* isn't even a person, just a component in the filthy petrol tanker he's driving – an engine of sentient destructiveness which roars like a dinosaur as it crashes over a cliff.

Demonising the stranger extends even to those who ought to be familiar – Michael Myers, in John Carpenter's *Halloween* (1978), has a family, a home and a face, but erases his own identity long before he puts on that William Shatner mask and returns to terrorise his old neighbourhood. The long first act of Rob Zombie's 2007 *Halloween* remake entirely misses the point by showing us Michael's typical-for-a-serial-killer early years – abusive parents, white trash squalor, torturing small animals, withdrawing from other kids, giving up speech and making his first masks – before

---

ANATOMY OF A SCENE
THE VANISHING (1988)

1. Attempting to craft the perfect kidnap, Raymond Lemorne tries to convince a woman to drive with him to another part of a car park.

2. His ruse is that he needs help hitching a trailer to his car. Suspicious, but accepting, the woman tells him she will meet him over at the trailer.

3. However it is the woman's husband who comes over, and he angrily recognises the fraud when he easily lifts the trailer using only one hand.

4. Raymond realises that he needs to appear vulnerable – a strategy that succeeds later when he manages to kidnap the film's heroine, Saskia.

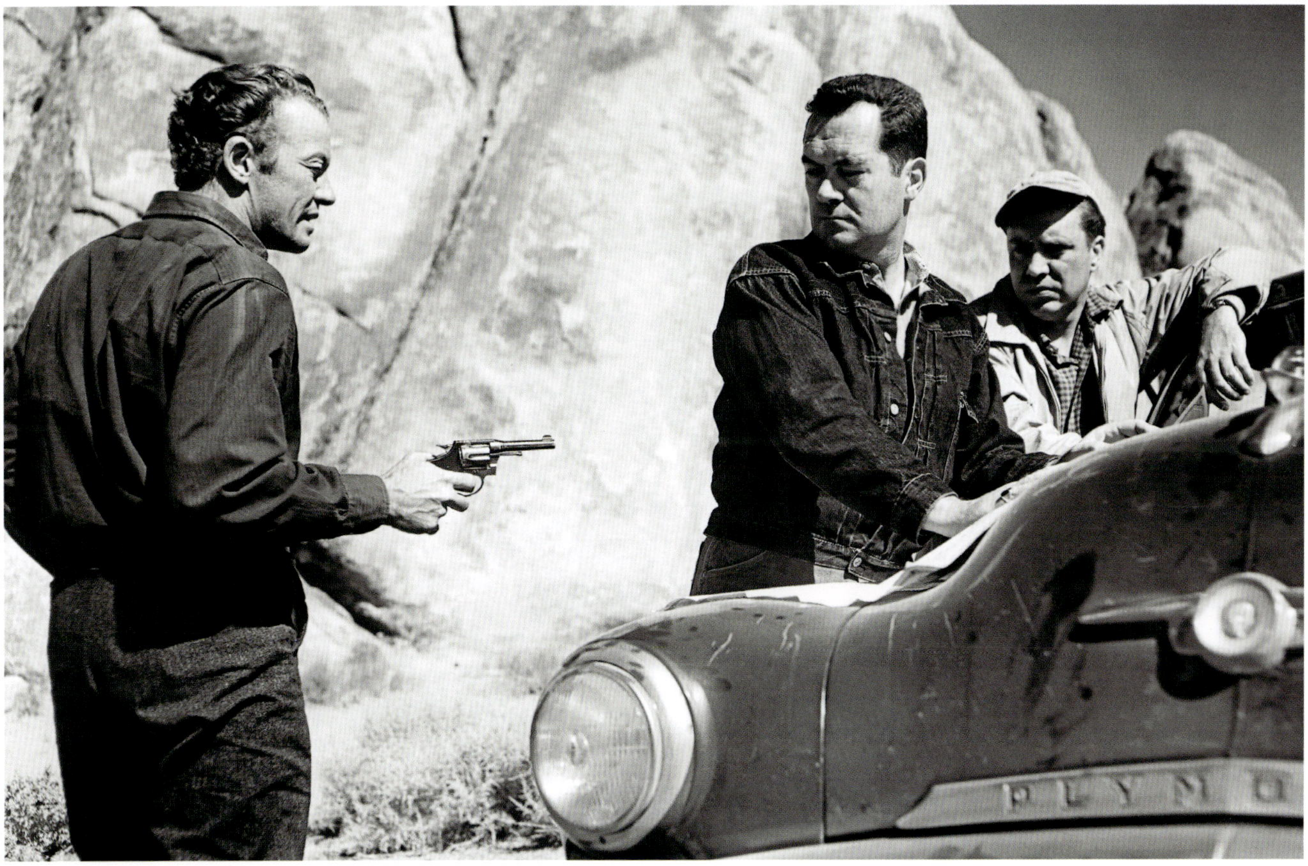

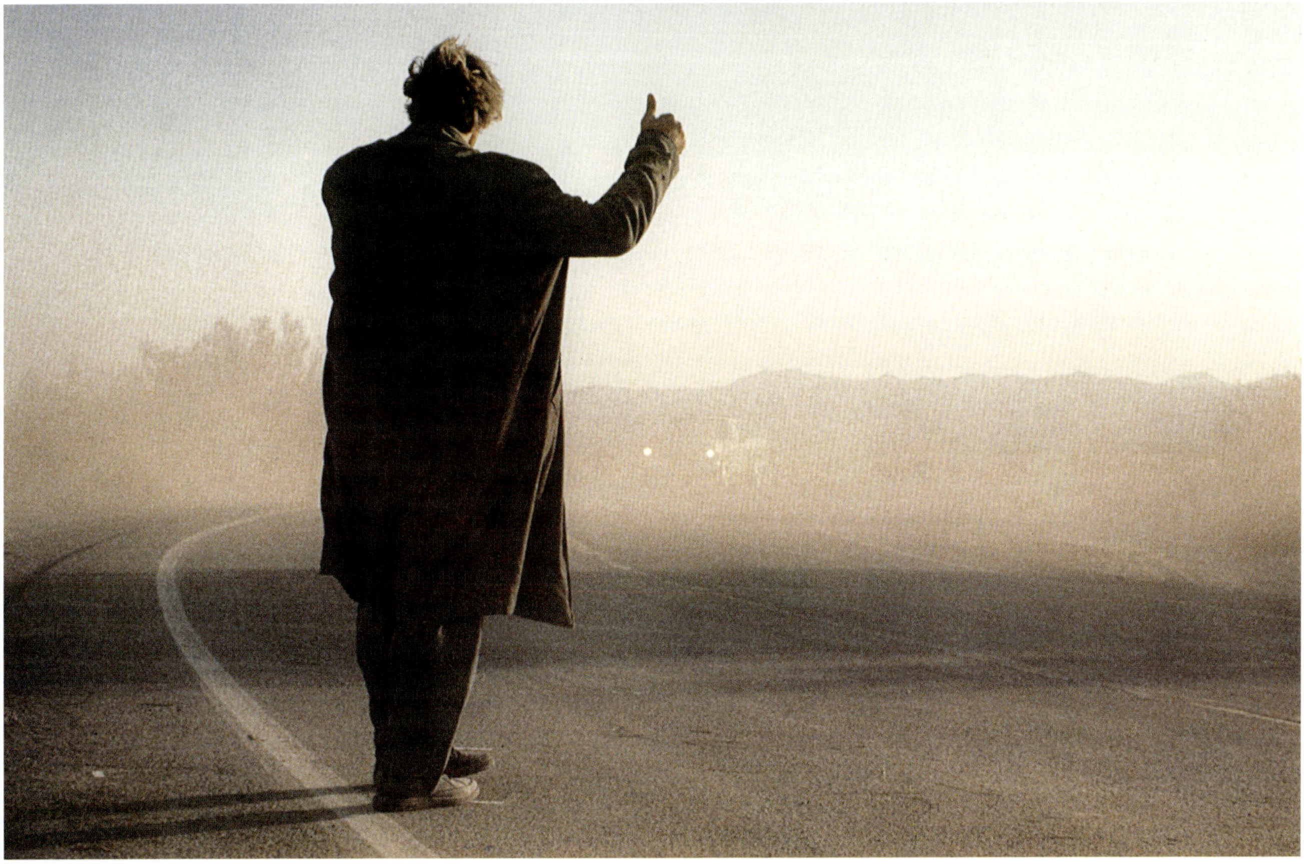

he takes up the knife. Carpenter's Michael isn't even a serial killer, but a shark born in a human skin – the single, shocked "Michael?" from his non-abusive, entirely ordinary mother as he is found after his first killing, revealed as a child in a clown suit, is all we need to understand that horror. By the time Michael escapes from the asylum, he's not even a case study for his doctor (played by Donald Pleasence) – who bleats about empty eyes and pure evil as if he were a middle-class Damien Thorn – and he's become the ultimate stranger, 'the boogeyman'. Again, we're in fairytale territory, close to the Big Bad Wolf who'll eat up little girls and their grannies – or the plausible, fast-talking Devil (John Huston) who talks a farmer out of his soul in William Dieterle's *All That Money Can Buy* (1941). A contemporary incarnation of this folk figure, whose intentions are as vague and unspeakable as those of the public information film strangers, is Arnold Friend (Treat Williams) – either 'a friend' or 'arch-fiend' – in Joyce Chopra's *Smooth Talk* (1985), from a Joyce Carol Oates story, who lounges in his bright gold sports car flexing in a muscle T-shirt and unleashes a torrent of serpentine chatter at teenager Connie (Laura Dern).

Home safety

If going off with strangers is a certain path to doom, then worse still comes of letting them into your home – a paranoid strain of thriller, popular since the mid-80s, deals with the perils of not doing a background check before letting supposedly trustworthy, reliable people over the threshold. Warnings have been issued about one-night stands (*Fatal Attraction*, 1987), tenants (*Pacific Heights*, 1990), nannies (*The Hand That Rocks the Cradle*, 1992), flatmates (*Single White Female*, 1992), cops (*Unlawful Entry*, 1992), foster parents (*The Glass House*, 2001), neighbours (*Lakeview Terrace*, 2008) and adopted children (*Orphan*, 2009). They arrive with smiles, offers of help and a glint of envy or resentment – and, inevitably, the film ends up with a body count (heroine's best friends are especially endangered) and, worse, the trashing of cosy domestic spaces.

These are slow-burn thrillers, as opposed to the more shocking variety of 'home invasion' drama – a theme that was treated with high seriousness in William Wyler's *The Desperate Hours* (1955), a modern-dress version of Joseph Conrad's *Victory*, in which escaped cons (led by Humphrey Bogart) barge into a suburban home and terrorise everydad (Fredric March) until the homesteader is driven to fight back with the tenaciousness of a settler seeing off an Indian attack. The pressure-cooker of weighty themes in this taut, influential movie explodes at the end, prefiguring the horror films of the 1970s – though home invasion stories have often taken an absurd, almost whimsical angle as power shifts balance sadism with barbed social comment in the likes of Roman Polanski's *Cul-de-Sac* (1966), Peter Collinson's *The Penthouse* (1967), Stanley Kubrick's *A Clockwork Orange* (1971), Richard Loncraine's *Brimstone & Treacle* (1982), Nicolas Roeg's *Track 29* (1988) and Michael Haneke's *Funny Games* (1997).

Without exception, these films suggest that the houseproud home-owners who get raped, tortured and killed deserve everything they get for being complacent consumers – often with nasty secrets or warped relationships of their own, which come to light as their whole lives are trashed in front of them. These scenarios have been echoed in a recent run of horror films – *Them* (*Ils*, 2006), *The Strangers* (2008), *White Settlers* (2014) – in which new homeowners are persecuted by mostly unseen murderous pranksters, again usually as a punishment for their relationship shortcomings or their temerity in buying a property to which locals feel they have a prior claim. The point is that the home-owners are the strangers, and the masked killers the ones protecting their turf.

A great gap in the classic public information film litany of horrors – dark and lonely water, abandoned fridges, playing on railway lines, overloading plug sockets – is that their sponsors could not bear to admit one significant danger: that children were more at risk from people who *weren't* strangers. Going back to *Revenge* and *Assault*, we find a significant difference in the actual culprits – one features a stereotypical sweetie-proffering dirty old man (Kenneth Griffith), and much debate about vigilante justice, but the other eventually reveals that the rapist (a trick of the light makes his eyes glow red like the devil) is a trusted authority figure, the local headmaster (Anthony Ainley). Now, there are campaigns to raise awareness of abuse perpetrated in the home and the worst instances of historical child abuse turn out to be the responsibility of people who were not strangers to their victims – teachers, priests, nuns, celebrities. The funny man in the playground was mostly a phantom, while the real threat came from Hitchcock's Uncle Charlie – as revealed by the shadow of a doubt (not a certainty of guilt) – who was always the 'stranger within the home'. If a typical title for a stranger-danger film was once *Never Take Sweets from a Stranger* or *Don't Talk to Strange Men*, now horror films have titles like *Mum & Dad* (2008).

CAN YOU TRUST YOUR COUNTRYMEN?

BERLIN, 1931. M: MURDER IN THE CITY

BY IAIN SINCLAIR

The striking of a soft distorted gong: our alarm. A wake-up call running backwards through the nightmare of the electrified city. Velvet-black frame held a beat or two more than is comfortable: *has something gone wrong with the system, Fritz Lang's first sound film?* Then a child's voice, in the dark, chanting a timeless refrain: "Just you wait, it won't be long. The man in black will soon be here with his cleaver's blade so true." A characteristic high-angle Lang composition, eye of fate, down on the circle of children; the human clock with pointing girl at its centre, arm outstretched. A stoic mandala seeking protection by calling up the bad thing: the stalking shadow, giver of sweets, patron of peddlers. May 1931: dial M for murder. Chalk the letter on the killer's back. The Germans of that period, we know from hindsight, had a taste for nominating scapegoats, separating racial categories by badges that had to be worn.

Flick-knife in trouser pocket, blade dripping with the juice of oranges, the monster with the moon face and unanchored eyes has been turned loose by the asylum, psychosis doctored and perfected. Lang, the dream-architect, with his gift for form, the interplay of warm flesh and cold stone, moves the camera across the enclosed courtyard and up to the lip of the angular balcony where a laundress with an unwieldy Moses basket challenges the children, protesting against the imposition of noise, chorus to a ceremony of inevitable sacrifice. Without Dr Death there is no story. The children of the poor are bred to vanish, intimations of coming horror, eugenic programmes in state hospitals and refuges; ambulances testing poison gas for the great industrial conglomerates.

Madhouses mark the edge of the city and they house terrifyingly damaged patients and worse doctors: Mabuse and Caligari, avatars of endless night. Phantoms cooked up by crazed directors in studio-laboratories break free of the limits of the frame, to confirm the city, this unidentified Berlin, as a labyrinth of signs and symbols, tunnels and cellars beneath nightclubs and ghettoes. Blind troglodytes in caves are printing banknotes. Microphones hidden behind curtains preach apocalypse: exploding planes, torched oil refineries, biological warfare. Plague and the stock market.

M is approved by the new politicians, by Dr Goebbels – "Fantastic! Against humanitarian soppiness." But Lang's last German film before his mythologised escape to Paris – *Das Testament des Dr. Mabuse* (1933) – falls foul of the censor and is not released in Germany until after the war. Mabuse, criminal genius incarcerated in an asylum, remote-controls the city, controls the psychiatrist, feeds on electricity, newsprint, automobiles, mass hypnosis.

A madman playing a madman. It was too close to the truth. This fashionable gimmick, psychoanalysis, is a distorting mirror. The possessed suffer from the delusion that they are actors. In M, Peter Lorre tries out a repertoire of funhouse faces, grimacing at the glass. Dr Mabuse launches his fabulous career by testing a selection of wigs and false noses, shuffling a set of theatrical cards to celebrate his manifold transformations. He shapeshifts, he splits. Invisible, he is omnipresent. Trapped in his bunker, he exploits new technologies of communication. He gambles without risk and fixes share prices. He decorates apartments with fashionable savagery: primitive masks, drapes, cod-expressionist paintings.

Rudolf Klein-Rogge, former husband of Lang's wife and screenwriting collaborator Thea von Harbou, impersonates Mabuse with unblinking Mephisthophelean conviction; a marmoreal presence waiting for his time, when the clocks will go backwards into barbarism. Klein-Rogge joins the NSDAP (National Socialists) and von Harbou follows him. Lang's relations with the party are more feline. He polishes retrospective anecdotes. He fires a fresh cigarette and screws in the fearsome monocle. He decides to shoot the murderer's trial by an underworld court, the climax of M, inside a decommissioned Zeppelin

hangar. The manager of the property is reluctant to sanction the deal. The problem, it appears, lies in the original title, *Mörder unter uns* ('Murderers Among Us'). In a piece of typical Lang business, the director talks of grabbing the man by the lapels – and discovering the hidden Nazi Party badge. The script for *M* is no Brechtian exercise in subversion, alerting the masses to the lethal intentions of the men in long leather coats, but an everyday tale of the serial slaughter of children, inspired by accounts of Peter Kürten, the Düsseldorf stalker.

Shoot approved. How much Lang actually drew from reports of the Kürten case is difficult to establish, since the trial followed the film's premiere. Lang speaks of the ugliest crime he could imagine, the writing of poison-pen letters. And then, scanning the newspapers, he realises in an instant of blinding clarity that he has found his twist: the way the criminal classes, exposed to troublesome police raids, hunt down this alien other, the unprofessional assassin. The harmless man driven to bestiality by his demons. The city is restless. Killing innocents early protects them from a worse future.

Lang and von Harbou do not merely customise the sensational narrative of the Kürten case, they anticipate it. The police inspector summoned from Berlin to Düsseldorf to offer assistance in the

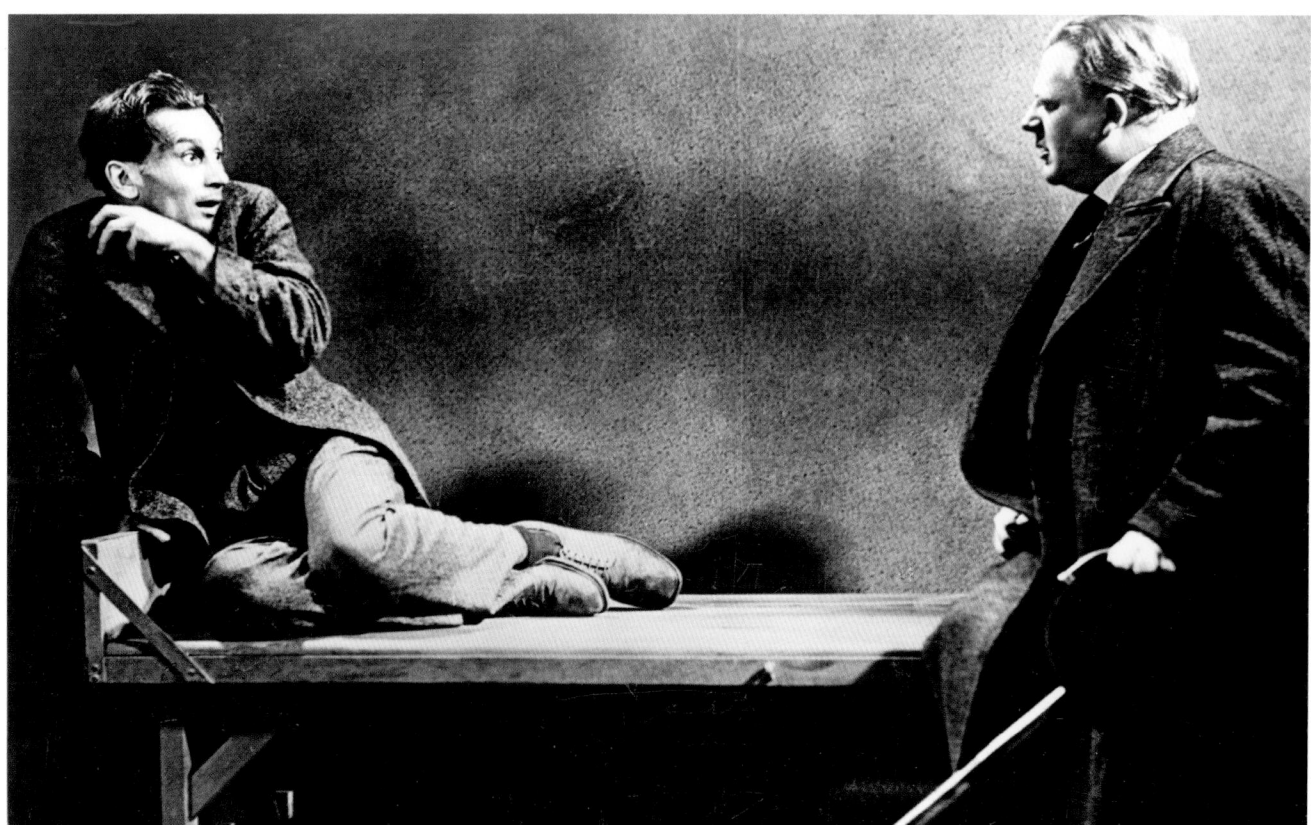

investigation was a Lang informant, the model for his charismatic detective, Inspector Lohmann. The actor who plays Lohmann in *M*, and again in *Das Testament des Dr. Mabuse*, is Otto Wernicke. With his thick mantle of flesh, backswept hair, set of jaw, Wernicke is the doppelganger of Hermann Göring. A dangerous clown with tapeworm appetites and the compulsion to chew and chomp: meat, bread, cigars. And telephones. Lohmann is always barking orders after the killing has taken place somewhere unexpected and they are shooting another page of the script: a growling fugue of self-satisfied amusement as he acknowledges that he has been duped once more. Gaunt underlings tremble and winch him into his Wagnerian overcoat.

The serial nature of the Mabuse films (Lang made an earlier, two-part silent, *Dr. Mabuse the Gambler*, in 1922) parallels the newspaper frenzy surrounding the serial killer in *M*. Crime is the maggot, articulated by wolfish solitaries and emerging demagogues. Lang was notorious for his treatment of actresses who did not meet his impossible standards: mechanical gestures repeated to the point of psychic breakdown, staged slaps, sanctioned abuse. The dictatorship of the celebrated director revelled in the exposure of fellow monsters. The mute Nietzschean super-criminal Dr Mabuse, scribbling in his cell, produces

the *Mein Kampf* of the underworld, a primer for theft, panic, murder as a fine art. Draft pages of this insane document are scattered across the floor of the cell like an abandoned screenplay.

It was a period of leakage and confusion, many of the Berlin filmmakers were poised for flight. Others made their treaties with the dark side. Lang's yarns were shaped around close-ups of clocks: Goebbels across the desk, closing time at the bank, Paris train waiting at the station. *M* is an exercise in relativity, marginal sounds from outside the frame expand the sense of space. Empty corridors, abstracted stairwells, deserted offices: without a human presence to act as a temporal marker, time is endless and unpunctuated. The cuckoo clock oversees a table set for a meal that will never be eaten. Stolen watches are laid out by thieves waiting for instruction. Germany, Lang said, was suffering from a wave of "unconnected sex crimes and mass murders".

M is a film made from echoes, overheard confessions. The name of the child who disappears is called out over series of minatory compositions: *Elsie! Elsie!* Lang favours silence over the emotional syrup of mood music. Plunging stairs. Laundry arranged in a sunlit attic like a spectral art installation. *Elsie! Elsie!*

(Above)
Sign of the times: *Das Testament des Dr. Mabuse* (1933) sees a criminal mastermind unleash a wave of fear and violence.

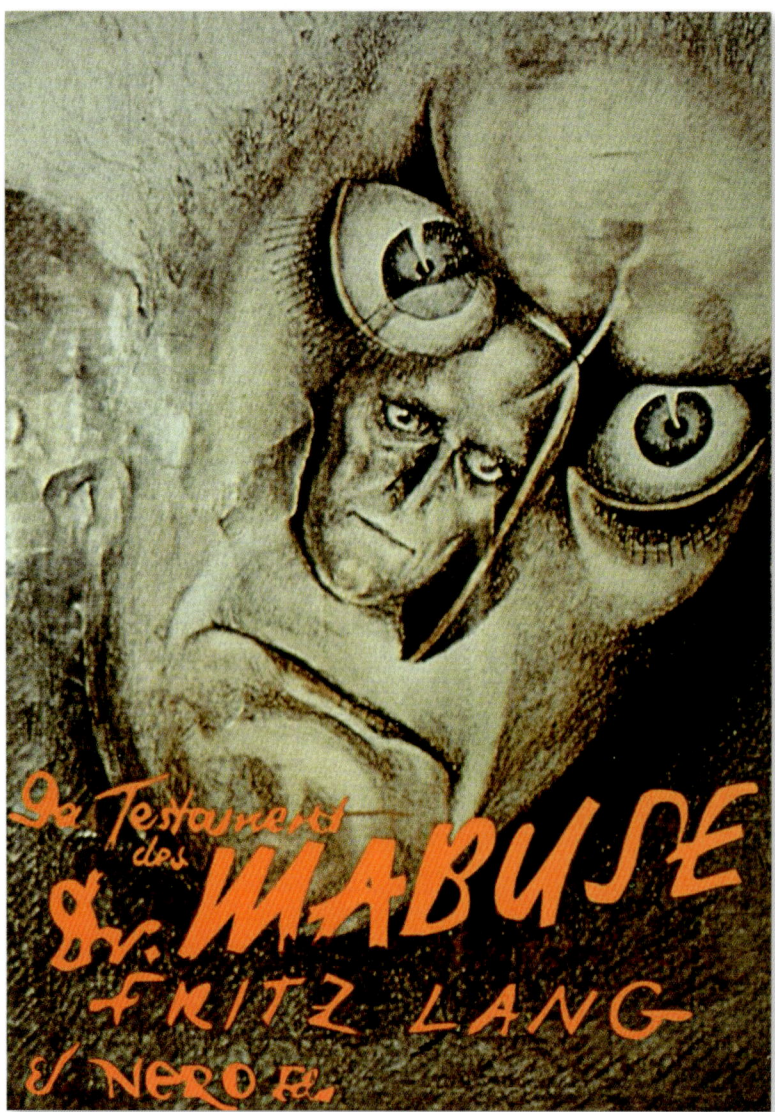

(Above)
The German poster for
*Das Testament des Dr.
Mabuse,* like the film,
conveyed the fear and
paranoia of its times.

Soup-plate with single spoon on bare table. Ball rolling across a patch of studio garden. Writhing balloon-puppet caught on telegraph wires. *Extra! Extra!* Death in the city. Little Elsie. Elsie Beckmann. Chinese whispers, reverberations. In 1938, Max Beckmann paints *Death:* Lang's dark-suited society vampires, hanging upside down like bats in a foul cave, above a green woman in an open coffin. With his *Self-Portrait in Tuxedo* (1927), the painter, hand on hip, drooping cigarette, confrontational gaze, has stepped back from Mabuse's card table with the challenging posture of one of Lang's interchangeable criminals and commissars.

The year of *M*, 1931, sees the publication of *Berlin Alexanderplatz* by Alfred Döblin, an urban masterpiece in which Lang's themes are given epic extension. The fictional Franz Biberkopf, who has beaten his mistress to death, is released from Tegel Prison, at the very moment when the hunt begins for Peter Lorre's M, the childlike killer of children. Döblin makes great play of newspaper headlines, statistics, the trophies of crime. Reflections in the windows of department stores. Political debates in beer halls. Woodland, beside a shimmering lake on the edge of the city, is where the police search for bodies in book and film. In another comfortable weekend property at Wannsee, a few years later, party bureaucrats discuss the Final Solution to the Jewish 'problem'. It is at the exiled Döblin's house in Hollywood that Lang meets Brecht, to initiate their troubled collaboration on *Hangmen Also Die!* (1943), a propaganda piece built around assassination and treachery.

The original *Mörder unter uns* title had been revised, but the premise of *M* was unchanged: the belief that a malignant virus had invaded society. That murder, as a karmic act, informed the nature of the city, a necessary perversion. Death is an unholy fool, whistling Grieg's 'Hall of the Mountain King' and crunching apples as he drifts aimlessly down studio streets more hauntingly real than the real thing, waiting for the next victim to introduce herself. Lorre pouts, simpers, pleads; a carnival grotesque allowing his shadow to fall across the reward poster, the publication of his crimes. The cruel expressionism of Murnau's *Nosferatu* (1922) has been domesticated. A clerk's soft hat instead of vampire's claws crawling across the landscape.

Navigating by the pull of a warped eroticism, the child murderer is shocked by his own reflection trapped within a diamond of kitchen knives, the tarot of consumer goods. He thinks of himself as a genuine benefactor, bringing gifts to the children of the underclass, kindness before killing. They bob and curtsy.

Before the final amnesia of the unwitnessed attack, the balloon caught in telegraph wires. "I have to roam the streets, endlessly, always sensing that someone is following me," the monster whimpers, pleading with the court of thieves. "I'm stalking myself. And with me run the ghosts of the mothers and children."

Lang's phantom Berlin is photographed through discriminations of smoke. Steaming pots rattle on the stove. No-neck, shaven-headed toad merchants, out of Beckmann or George Grosz, nuzzle wet cigars while they argue at round tables. Ariston butts, scattered within 150 metres of the latest victim, are a significant clue. All those maps and compasses. The word 'Alex' is whispered again and again, calling up not only Döblin's novel, but the police station in Alexanderplatz where Lang had access to friendly detectives and informants. Serial killings have their lineage, their honoured models: in England. In Thomas De Quincey, Jack the Ripper. And the yellow-back sensationalism of Edgar Wallace.

Lang travels to London. He boasts of visiting Scotland Yard, dipping into the Black Museum, investigating asylums. The notion of the city as an incubator of violence travels with him. Railway murders in the smog and bistre of Sickert afternoons, in shrouded Whitechapel alleys. Hitchcock, serving his apprenticeship at the UFA studios in Potsdam in the mid 1920s, was an observer on the set when Lang was shooting *Metropolis*. Hitchcock borrowed the camera angles, the clocks, the architecture of a controlled city in which you make your own weather. When he came back to London from Hollywood, for *Frenzy* in 1972, he dealt, as English directors tend to do, with locality: Covent Garden Market at the point of disappearance. A damaged fighter pilot in an overambitious jacket. A psycho strangler who gives himself away, in the Peter Lorre fashion, by munching apples.

Lang's hierarchic city of bloodless aristocrats, snarling politicians, policemen behind vast desks, thieves in leather coats, beggars and cripples, is never taken on, in its entirety, in English films. They steal sequences and move them into actual streets, losing the integrity of Lang's obsessive vision. In 1965, Sidney J. Furie, in lifting the car assassination from *Das Testament des Dr. Mabuse* for *The Ipcress File*, misses the paranoia, the troubling intimations of a surveillance society, political apparatchiks as the murderers among us.

A serial-killer film like Richard Fleischer's *10 Rillington Place* (1971), by using the actual house where the murders took place, and the bodies

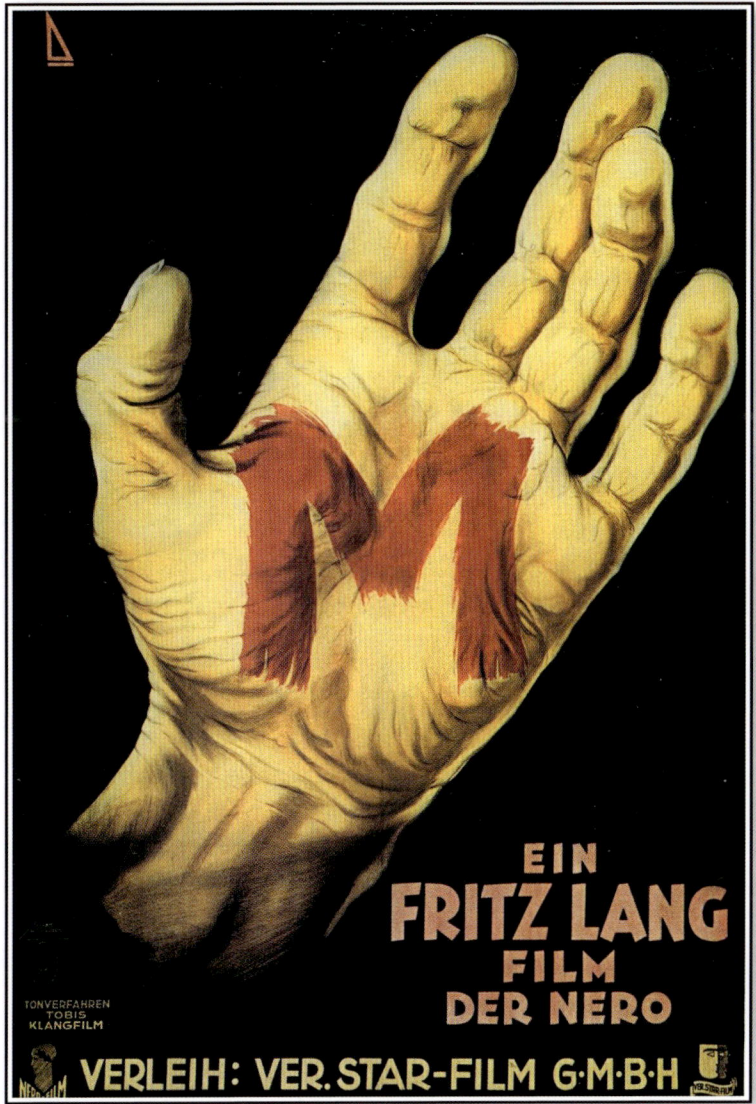

were buried, suffocates in spoiled authenticity. It becomes unwatchable as Richard Attenborough gets the bald wig right and underplays dialogue retrieved from police records. Crime is an artwork with rope deckchair and rubber tubes for lethal gas: ennui curdling into timid fetishism. Caught in this chamber of horrors, the playwright Clive Exton, through his screenplay, runs a toxic version of *The Caretaker*. Welsh fantasy from John Hurt, as Timothy Evans; arias borrowed from Pinter's tramp, Davies. Attenborough delivers sinister Joe Orton dialogue: "Terminations, we call them. I had to learn about that in the police." Endless cups of tea are pissed from black pots. When the shoot was over, and the house was finally demolished, crowds drawn in by the vans and lights made off with the bricks as souvenirs. *This article was originally published in the April 2010 issue of Sight & Sound magazine.*

(Above)
The striking original 1931 German theatrical release poster for Fritz Lang's seminal serial killer classic M.

CAN YOU TRUST YOURSELF?

CAN YOU TRUST YOUR PERCEPTIONS?

TROUBLE IN MIND: THRILLERS OF UNCERTAINTY

BY DAVID THOMSON

"I too often feel like a person I know nothing about." – John Ashbery

Look at it this way: you're lonely, unfulfilled, bored – maybe a touch depressed – your computer has gone haywire; it wants to lead you into a maelstrom. Is it talking to you? Are you more disturbed than you thought? Do you want to go to a movie? Won't that take you out of yourself?

Are you a Jekyll waiting to Hyde? Or are you Frank Sinatra in *The Manchurian Candidate* (1962) hoping to resolve your turmoil of reality and nightmare? Are you Julia in Joseph H. Lewis's *My Name Is Julia Ross* (1945), sucked into a malign conspiracy where you are told you are someone else and begin to doubt your own sanity? In Nina Foch's performance, Julia is a real, lonely person who has wandered into an insanely organised movie. Are you Guy Pearce's amnesiac in *Memento* (2000), so trapped in the immediate moment that you cannot establish the shape of your own experience? Or are you Edward Norton in *Fight Club* (1999) whose depression may be settled in a wild adventure in which you imagine your other self is Brad Pitt?

Thrillers time and again are drawn to an amnesiac condition in which the protagonist is uncertain what he has done, or what kind of person he is. In Hitchcock's *Spellbound* (1945) – a half-crazy recommendation for psychoanalysis – Dr Edwardes (Gregory Peck) believes he may have killed someone in the past. Jason Bourne is trying to regain his lost memory and to understand his phenomenal, lethal skill at disposing of enemies. The success of the Bourne movies surely touches on a smothered urge in all of us to explode, to wreak havoc in the dumb world, and even to kill. Suppose Jason Bourne was once a serial killer. It fits.

Out there in the dark

So what can *we*, the audience, trust? Aren't there movies that test our confidence in seeing, no matter that we are sitting in a warm dark place that seems so much more secure than Bourne's sense of being? For as long as movies have been made, we've had guardians, owners, producers and even directors who cried out, "Everything has to be clear! Those dopes who pay their hard-earned money want to follow what is happening. Keep it in order! You gotta hold your audience."

All this is understandable. The disturbed do hope for balance; the viewer wants to cling to the story. A movie is an information delivery system, theorists tell us – so be sure two and two come out as four. Make the process tidy!

But isn't there something inherent in film that wants to keep us in the dark? Aren't we sitting there watching so closely because we love the thrill of suspense? Sometimes we are nerve-wracked, yet we don't mind that too much. Part of the thrill in thrillers is not knowing.

Example? It seems to me the high point of Otto Preminger's *Laura* (1944) comes quite early on. The rather shabby detective (Dana Andrews) is on the case of whoever murdered the beautiful Laura Hunt. He thinks he'll spend the night in her apartment, soaking up the atmosphere and the information, just to get a better idea of why she died. It's a ravishing sequence as he looks at her clothes and her letters; he cannot escape the lush portrait of her on the wall. We may say he begins to fall in love with the dead woman. He sits in a chair and drifts into sleep. So it's like his dream or fantasy when the outside door opens and a woman enters – it's Gene Tierney, and it's Laura, too.

I love the whole *Laura* every time I see it. But nothing shakes my feeling that her arrival is the moment at which mystery becomes enchanting. I wonder if *Laura* should stop there, without a word between these two people. Maybe you like thrillers where the whole thing is worked out to everyone's satisfaction. But I wait for those moments of exquisite uncertainty. So many thrillers and mysteries are beaten into submission by the scenes where Hercule Poirot, or some know-all, takes ten drab minutes to explain what we just saw.

An example of that is the Simon Oakland scene in *Psycho* (1960). So after all the hurly-burly, when we've had a chance to see Mother restored to Normal, the surviving cast members gather in a room and in comes the psychiatrist (Oakland) who has the whole far-fetched backstory in the palm of his hand. He's got enough to publish a paper in a learned journal. Hitchcock had dreaded that scene; he relished a cruel uncertainty that afflicted his characters, and us. There's a story that he embraced Oakland after the scene was shot and told the actor he had saved the picture. Thus, the audiences who had been in tatters of dread throughout *Psycho* could compose themselves and walk out into the night, believing that everything was in order now. So, yes, there may be a psychotic killer living

(Right)
Dana Andrews can't believe his eyes when he wakes from his sleep and sees Gene Tierney, in *Laura* (1944).

(Top)
Amnesiac Jason Bourne
(Matt Damon) tries
to discover his true
identity in *The Bourne
Ultimatum* (2007).

(Middle)
Edward Norton with
his imagined other
self, Tyler Durden (Brad
Pitt), in David Fincher's
Fight Club (1999).

(Bottom)
Disturbed, uncertain
personalities are a
hallmark of Roman
Polanski's films, such
as *The Tenant* (1976).

next door to you, but if he kills you it will be satisfactorily explained. The droning caption for what happened is a tide that comes in to cover or absolve the rocks of agonised apprehension. But it's not the solution to *Psycho* that we treasure.

Don't we realise that we go to the pictures to be in the dark? Can't we see how often it is suspended certainty that is most seductive in a film? Back in the 60s, there was a woman at the National Film Theatre in London who regularly quit five or so minutes before the end of the film. She couldn't stand the explanations. Isn't it the case that the most memorable parts of thrillers come early on as we watch the private eye exploring the case but still unaware of the plot? No one could complain at the shocking end to Roman Polanski's *Chinatown* (1974), but I prefer the scenes where the cocksure Jake Gittes comes to realise that the intrigue is beyond his grasp as he tries to track water in the burned hills to the north of Los Angeles.

Look at Polanski more closely, and you appreciate how far he believes in uncertainty. *The Tenant* (1976) is another picture in which a disturbed sensibility dominates. Polanski's faith in unease makes a fascinating contrast with Hitchcock who regularly pursued disorder (with acute insight), but who believes in a final restoration of order. In that sense, Hitch was a company man, anxious to send the customers home reassured.

Hitchcock's brilliance hides in his instinct for having characters waver over trusting what they saw just as we are striving to make sense of visibility. But Hitch was a very commercially minded creator who believed in the strictures about being clear. From *The 39 Steps* (1935) to *The Wrong Man* (1956) he examined threatened belief, or the idea of a character whose insistence on something is betrayed by happenstance. In *The Wrong Man* Manny Balestrero (Henry Fonda) is a humble bass-player getting along as best he can until a web of plot descends on him.

The pressure on Manny's stability shows Hitch's quest for a hero having a crack-up. What the film does – and it is as remorseless as it is insightful – is to have Manny's wife (Vera MIles) begin to break down instead. So Manny is freed at the end, but maybe a part of his life is lost. *The Wrong Man* was too dark and afraid to be a big hit, but over 70 years later it feels prescient about a society in which trust in ourselves is waning.

The classic instance in Hitchcock of a character who is not believed is Jimmy Stewart in *Rear Window* (1954). But isn't there something so secure and attractive in Stewart and Grace

Kelly that lets us feel they must be right? Life in their courtyard will get organised (with all the windowed stories settled) until they do at last get married, and she moves him to the Upper East Side. That fate awaits him.

Rear Window nags at uneasiness, for Stewart's character does not quite want to be married, or settle down. He exists for the sensation and risk of journalistic photography and staying unattached. The more I see Rear Window, the more I imagine a reworking of the story where Stewart is on the edge of sanity. Maybe he has imagined a lurid melodrama in Lars Thorwald's apartment across the way – and got it wrong. Could those two men then share distress and reluctance at the idea of marriage? Hitch would have scoffed and said he couldn't do that and keep a large audience. But the possibility lurks in the film, and four years later Stewart played a complete neurotic ruined by what he thought he had seen. That's Vertigo (1958), so painful and disconcerting it was not a hit.

Withholding a sense of control in mainstream movies is a tricky thing – and it may lead to bad business. But Otto Preminger's interest in vulnerable belief didn't stop with Laura. He pursued scenarios where confidence was in jeopardy. That's evident in Angel Face (1953) and Exodus (1960), and it is the engine of Anatomy of a Murder (1959), in which we have no more surety about what the Ben Gazzara character felt and did than does his lawyer (Jimmy Stewart again). Stewart defends a man whose 'innocence' never convinces us. The insolent ending of the film, with a woman's broken shoe hooked on a trash can with a laconic note about an "irresistible impulse" (the defence strategy that got Gazzara off), lives up to the brazen alienation in the actor's performance, and the overall realisation that in legal cases you seldom rely on truth. Settle for a verdict. As the son of an important lawyer, Preminger had grown up knowing that testimony is not always reliable.

The movies are full of characters we know not to trust – they range from Joe Brody (Louis Jean Heydt) in The Big Sleep (1946) to just about everyone in American Hustle (2013). But the films establish those people early on, in terms of situation and acting. We don't trust them but we are so on guard we feel secure. Many stories of apparent delusion end very comfortably. There's a nice little *noir* from 1949, *The Window*, that's also based on Cornell Woolrich, the author of the story that made *Rear Window*. It has the inventive Bobby Driscoll as a kid who is always making stuff up, so when he sees a murder no one will believe him. It all works out in the end, and the kid is able to say he has learned his lesson. He's going to be a good boy from now on.

In practice, reform is not that easy. Some kids lie, and never stop. You could say that the greatest damage in Donald Trump is not his stupidity or bigotry but the ease with which he is turning lies into an orthodoxy. The consequent dismay is alarming; it's why so many people in America feel worn out and ill these days. Forget the harm to the Constitution, it is the dissolution of credibility that is Donald's psychic need. It's the air on which a fantasist soars. He's a moviegoer.

If you call that alienation, then film can come close to a modern sensibility in which fewer people trust the news, the ads or conventional sources of information. But in movie narrative that can be tough and restrictive. Hitchcock met that problem in *Stage Fright* (1950) where Richard Todd's character talks a lot of information into the film that proves to be misleading.

But as movies slipped into being so much less of a mainstream entertainment, so ambiguity and unreliability found ways of breathing that played well with our love of suspended moments. Antonioni is not really regarded as a director of thrillers, but he was fond of incidents that probed existential insecurity. In *L'avventura* (1960), a young woman vanishes on a trip to an offshore island. She seemed restless with her love affair, but

Antonioni does not bother with her motivation or her fate. She disappears and in the search her lover and her best friend become romantically involved. The woman, Anna (Lea Massari), is never found, and the film does not indulge that common trait of the thriller – the search for lost people.

A few years later, *Blow-Up* (1966) was a mystery movie, albeit with more amusement than was common in the genre. So Thomas the photographer (David Hemmings) thinks he has seen a murder. The lengthy sequence in which he constructs this plot with still photographs he has taken is the equal of Dana Andrews suspended in the apartment in *Laura*. Moreover, *Blow-Up* ends on a note of ironic resignation as if to warn a photographer not to trust what he has 'taken'. But it is part of human experience to look at things in life and be fooled. Does that drive us mad, provide for tragedy, or school us in silent laughter?

For Antonioni, the climactic work (or dead end) along these lines was *The Passenger* (1975), in which a journalist (Jack Nicholson) has so lost belief in himself that he tries to become someone else, or a shadow self. He's then caught up in an intrigue that will require his murder. That fate is undeserved, but the film's cool death scene is famously beautiful. It hovers over Antonioni's steady doubt as to whether the central character's abdication from life is the result of dismay at his job, from being badly married – or is it just that he was unluckily granted existence?

So movies have developed a form that is a metaphor for our wish to face danger while staying safe. Maybe you're saying, "What's this all about? I see a lot of movies and I'm OK, no screws loose. I'll admit it, I get blue sometimes, and I know what solitude is. Depressed? That never occurred to me."

You'll get over that. Take a movie before retiring.

ANATOMY OF A SCENE
BLOW-UP (1966)

1. Walking in a London park, photographer Thomas shoots a couple arguing. Back at his studio, he notices something unusual in one of his shots.

2. We're shown Thomas's view as he studies the photograph. The woman appears to look anxiously to her left – but at what?

3. Zooming in on the area to the woman's left, Thomas notices what appears to be a figure beyond the fence, almost obscured by trees.

4. Cropping in closer, the situation seems still more sinister. Is that a gun, pointed at the man? Has Thomas photographed a murder?

CAN YOU TRUST THE FACTS?
DOCUMENTARY AND THE THRILLER

BY ERIC HYNES

Edward Snowden in Laura Poitras's nail-biting 'Citizenfour' (2014)

So much cinema revolves around the withholding (and eventual revealing) of information. In many works of suspense, information is withheld from characters, fostering an anxiety of identification in an audience aware of what lurks around the corner. In other works, information is withheld from the audience – we're plunged into partial or obscured understanding while the characters are ennobled and empowered in knowing themselves better than we do. The latter is not exclusive to thrillers, and in fact is a favoured tactic of contemporary drama, imbuing even a quotidian scenario with a sense of suspense – think of films as disparate as *Manchester by the Sea* (2016), with its delayed reveal of why Casey Affleck's character is so damaged, and M. Night Shyamalan's twists in *The Sixth Sense* (1999) and *The Village* (2004).

Analogues to these tactics are both available and exploited by documentary filmmakers, who construct narratives as carefully and strategically as their fictional colleagues. Historical and archival films often utilise the former,

asking us to revisit events and lives about which we know (or could easily reference) the outcome. When you watch the Amy Winehouse documentary *Amy* (2015), you do so with a sense of dread and foreknowledge that the subject of the film doesn't have. Meanwhile in films such as *Searching for Sugar Man* (2012) and *Dealt* (2017), essential biographical information (such as whether the subject is living, or able-bodied) is kept under wraps until a dramatically advantageous unveiling. And though chronologically arranged courthouse crime films such as *Making a Murderer* (2015) are less overt in their string pulling, they still practise a delayed reveal, stretching a story to 10 or 12 hours, delaying and doling out every revelation and unanswered question.

Inherent in all of these examples is that there's a filmmaker (or team of filmmakers) choosing when and how the audience learns and experiences information. It's all about fostering suspense, managing effects. Whatever the film's source material, be it fictional, based on a true story, or tracking a true

story, the filmmaker already knows the information – the question is what she'll choose to share with the audience, and when. Yet with documentary film, there's also a third way. What if the filmmaker herself doesn't know what's going on? What if the ship is allowed to list, veer and bob?

This third way engenders a thriller native to documentary. It's an approach that's not only unrelated to and free from the tactics of fiction, but has the potential to be more suspenseful and unsettling than works of fiction. If the artist doesn't know where this is going, doesn't have greater access to information than we do, it's storytelling without a net, a rollercoaster without rails and without foresight. At some point in production, most documentaries concerned with present-day events encounter moments of such uncertainty, but it's less common to share that uncertainty with the audience. It's the difference between the externalised construction of a thriller and the internal experience of one. It's also the difference between a film that attempts to persuade the viewer of its handle on knowledge, and one willing to let go of that handle.

Exemplary of this kind of thriller are the films of Laura Poitras's post-9/11 trilogy – *The Oath* (2010), *Citizenfour* (2014) and *Risk* (2016). While the director stylistically summons elements of a fictional thriller – via moments of information-winnowing shallow-focus, and disquieting, slow-burn music – each film veers far off the map when it comes to what happens, when it happens, and even who and what we're following. In *The Oath*, an exposé of lives destroyed by US detentions in Guantánamo Bay leads the director to Abu Jandal, a free man in Yemen whose politics and past as Osama bin Laden's bodyguard are harder to reconcile than that of his imprisoned brother-in-law, Salim Ahmed Hamdan. Being alone in a room with Abu Jandal, who always seems camped on the border between welcoming and banishing Poitras, makes for deeply and complexly thrilling cinema. We never know what we're about to learn, or if we're even prepared to hear it, and we're also caught in a geometry of identification and sympathy, knowing the danger confronting Poitras as a reporter in the field, and also knowing the danger Abu Jandal has put himself in by talking to Poitras.

That sense of danger is only heightened in *Citizenfour*, which puts Poitras in a Hong Kong hotel room with Edward Snowden before anyone knew who or where the whistleblower was. Though the film came out well after Snowden went public, Poitras's footage retains a nail-biting tension, a live-wire quality as if everything could go wrong at any moment. We enter a private, secret space and are allowed to dwell in the present tense, making every turn in the conversation, every gesture, seem revelatory. Poitras so successfully establishes that we're in uncharted territory that Snowden watching cable television becomes riveting, vital cinema. These scenes and sequences are shaped in the edit, as they always are, but the shaping here is less leading, less sequential. We don't know what's going to be said or done next, and we're also persuaded that the filmmaker doesn't either. That's due to the unprecedented nature of the circumstances, of course, but also thanks to the filmmaker's decision to stay in these moments, to avoid putting the footage to work demonstratively. What might be banal

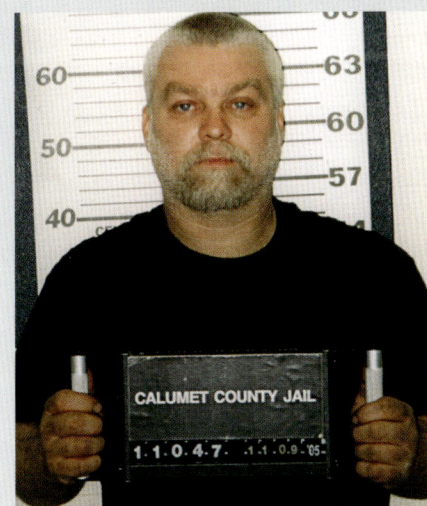

'*Making a Murderer*' (2015)

in real life – simply letting a moment or action play out – can be thrilling in nonfiction film. Snowden styles his hair in the mirror. The Rolling Stones sit around listening to the playback of 'Wild Horses' in *Gimme Shelter* (1970). A GoPro camera crashes into and out of the sea in *Leviathan* (2014). What happens next becomes less important than the fact that what happens next hasn't been predetermined.

In *Risk*, not knowing extends beyond present-tense moments – many of them just as intense as those in her previous films – to years of uncertainty over what to make of WikiLeaks and Julian Assange. For years, the filmmaker sat on enviable footage of Assange and his associates, uncertain of what film to make out of it, and uncertain of what she felt about it. In the end, she didn't adapt that footage to pre-existing genre boxes – whether a work of activism, a political thriller or, most tempting, a documentary profile. Instead she let the ambiguities fester. She questions her own intentions and involvement, and invites the viewer to question

them as well. Information arrives, but larger questions persist. We're left without familiar beats with which to synchronise the information. The film eventually just... ends after we've caught up on recent developments in the WikiLeaks saga, and the lack of resolution winds up being more jarring, and more meaningful, than the furtive, supposed scoop that ends *Citizenfour*.

Revelations in thrillers often function, at least in hindsight, as missing pieces being snapped into place. Whereas documentaries don't need to have a place for anything, at least in theory. The piece can be ill-fitting. Or stray beyond the frame. Or belong to a different picture altogether. In Jesse Moss's *The Overnighters* (2014), a pastor's efforts at housing itinerant workers in his church suddenly become muddled by a personal scandal. And in Peter Nicks's *The Force* (2017), a sincere attempt to represent the Oakland Police Department's sincere attempts at reform gets utterly derailed by a shocking series of officer scandals. Neither filmmaker seems to have foreseen these turns. Where Moss chooses to foreshadow the revelation in his final edit, Nicks doesn't. It's a choice that opens him up to allegations of naivete, or wilful ignorance of the officers' behavior. But it's also a choice that allows us to feel the full force of the whiplash, and the attendant emotional fallout. We think we're progressing one way, and then something knocks us completely off line. The subject falls apart, and the film follows suit. The big reveal in these films doesn't answer a question, or even necessarily pose a new one. But it does reinforce that there's nothing as jarring, or as terrifying, as being confronted with the fact that we often don't know, or understand, anything at all.

CAN YOU TRUST YOUR WITS?

KEEP ON RUNNING: THE CHASE THRILLER

BY NICK JAMES

Cops in black uniform fan out on the moors; their whistles explode the birds from the trees. Down in the hollows, light catches on a man's cheekbones. That hunted look on a handsome face, looking back, alarmed but capable. He might be an escaped prisoner from Dartmoor, such as the convict in *The Hound of the Baskervilles*, or perhaps the lovelorn escapee of Anthony Asquith's film *A Cottage on Dartmoor* (1929), but not so – those men-on-the-run are from the wrong class.

The scurrying owner of the kind of face I'm referring to knows his *veldcraft* – his hunting skills – from Africa (in the novels at least), just as the storycraft that created him is out of older Africa fantasies such as *King Solomon's Mines*. Whether he's Richard Hannay on the run in the novel *The Thirty-Nine Steps*, as adapted by Hitchcock, or the unnamed 'sportsman' hunter of *Rogue Male*, best portrayed by Peter O'Toole in the Clive Donner BBC movie in 1976, the skills of these heroes 'in country' are drawn from a time of colonial supremacy and adventure, a time of 'derring-do'. They're a cut above and not easily caught.

Like the Victorian author H. Rider Haggard, who, out of several real-life adventurers, created Allan Quartermain – the hero of *King Solomon's Mines* – John Buchan, the author of *The Thirty-Nine Steps*, had been a government administrator in South Africa. Geoffrey Household, the writer of *Rogue Male*, had been a marketing executive in Bucharest, Spain and the USA and would go on to work for British Intelligence in World War II. For these worldly writers, steeped in British establishment culture, hunting big game and/or fighting natives in Southern Africa were the best and most vivid kinds of backstory to give tough men of a certain class who find themselves on the run in the Empire's home country. Hannay is running because he's been framed for the murder of a foreign spy working for the British; Sir Robert Hunter (as Household's unnamed hero becomes in Donner's film) has to flee Germany after nearly assassinating an important Nazi and surviving the attempted reprisal. Stalked by Nazi agents, one of whom is as English as him, he is as much a fugitive at home as he was in the Bavarian forest.

Buchan's tale was written in 1914, before the full horror of the Great War became apparent; Household's in 1939, when World War II was imminent. As well as being great 'entertainments' – as Graham Greene would have called them – these novels are warnings of the coming threat, and of how bravery will be required of everyone. What also binds these key works together is the similarity of their heroes. Hannay and Hunter are two survivalist archetypes, figures to whom

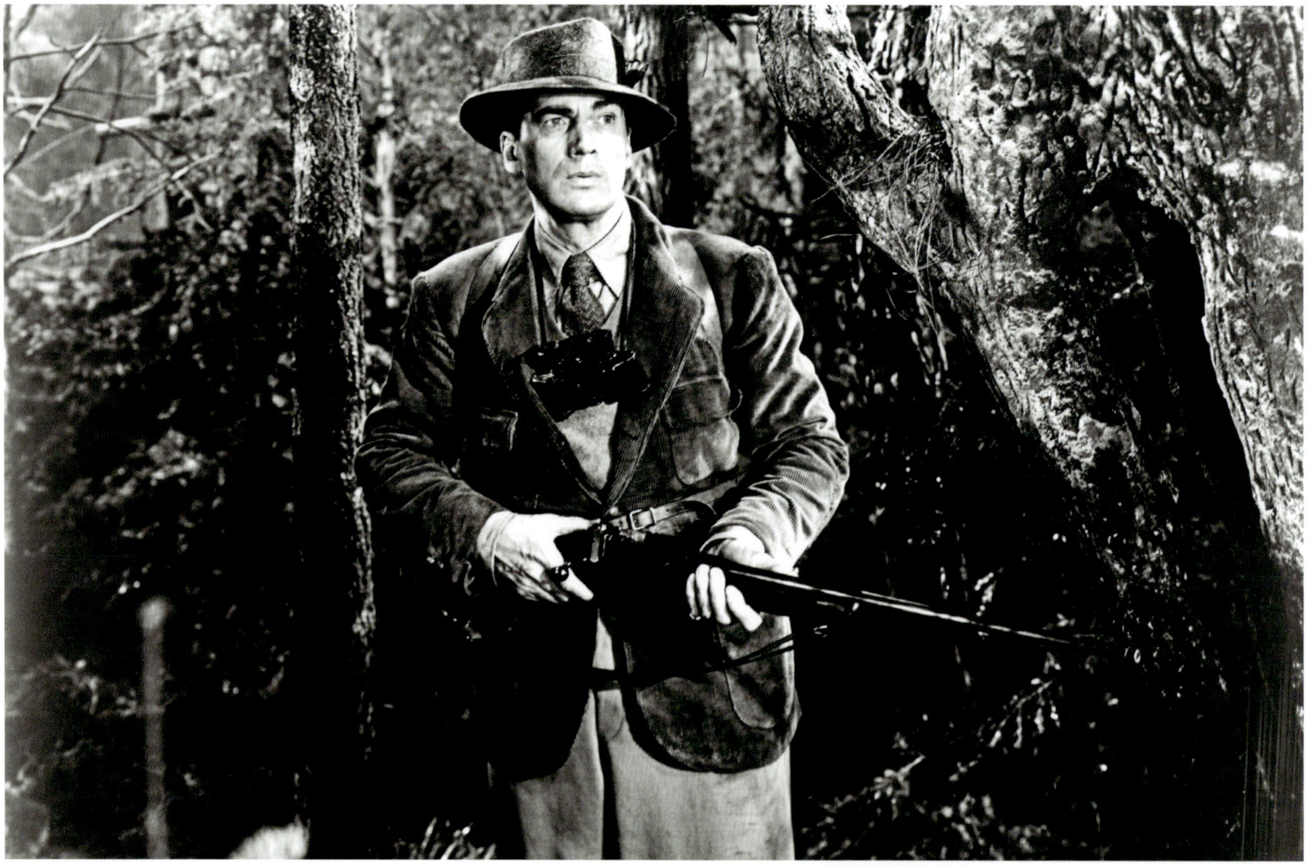

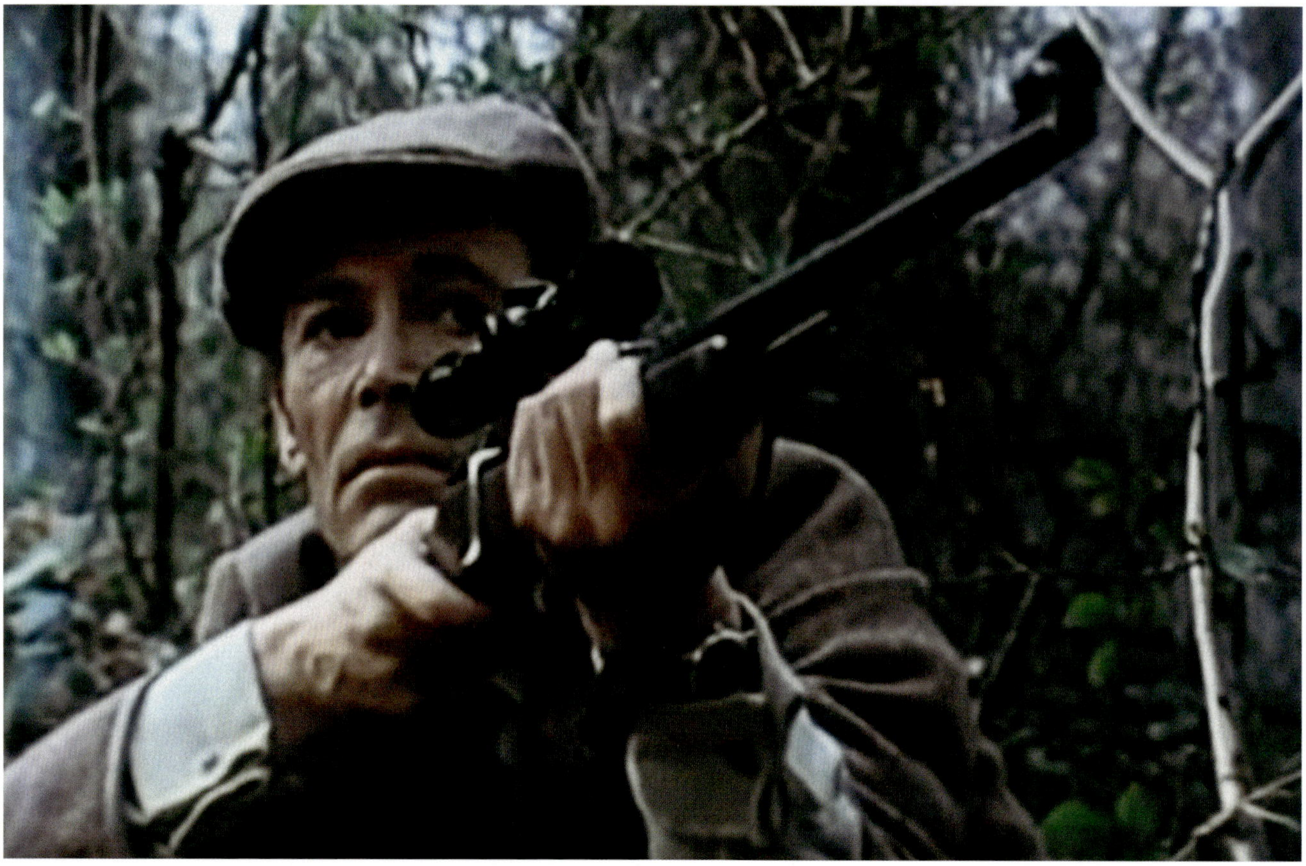

Bear Grylls and Ray Mears owe some of their TV appeal – they are resourceful men, out on their own, living for a while off the land.

But in the screen adaptations of these novels, as we shall see, women become essential, if only (as in the case of *Rogue Male*) in dreams. How trust and reliability are established in these fictions, how it is decided who is a real 'sport', and whether that figure should be identifiably upper class is a measure both of the way attitudes shift as the 20th century progresses and an indicator of the personal priorities the writers and filmmakers have. Differences between the books and their film adaptations are still more indicative in terms of racial attitudes and the continuing construction of the British hero.

Hitchcock's 1935 film *The 39 Steps* (a substantial makeover of the novel's story, scripted by Charles Bennett) is so archetypal that all the subsequent adaptations – including Ralph Thomas's of 1959, and Don Sharp's of 1978 – pale into insignificance. Donner's *Rogue Male* – scripted by Frederic Raphael – is superior to Fritz Lang's original 1941 adaptation *Man Hunt*, and much more faithful to the novel. But it cannot be said to be iconic in the way that Hitchcock's film is. There are key incidents in man-on-the-run thrillers that tend to be repeated. Jean-Pierre Melville said that there were 19 variations within his beloved world of cops and robbers and that John Huston's *The Asphalt Jungle* (1950) used all of them. Hitchcock's *The 39 Steps* is the equivalent for the man-on-the-run model, and the idea of the double chase, in which an innocent hero is being pursued while he pursues the real perpetrators of a crime, remained a constant source of inspiration for the director. Here are a few of the situations from *The 39 Steps*, with just one or two echoing examples in each case:

'The Implicating Crime': a knife in the back of a spy found in his flat sends Richard Hannay running. Leering, cocky handyman Hick (yes, really) is similarly knifed in Ralph Thomas's *The Clouded Yellow* (1950) sending the framed and psychologically delicate Susan Hayward on the run with her protector Trevor Howard. A thrown knife kills UN diplomat Townsend in Hitchcock's *North by Northwest* (1959), implicating advertising executive Roger Thornhill (Cary Grant), sending him on the run.

'The Spectacular Escape': Hannay's, famously, is from The Flying Scotsman travelling across the Forth Bridge; *Rogue Male*'s hero is forced off a cliff but lands in a life-saving bog. Harrison Ford's Dr Richard Kimble in *The Fugitive* (1993) does a high dive off a huge dam.

'The Threatening Formal Gathering': Hannay goes to an address given to him by the murdered spy. He's welcomed into a cocktail party by a Professor Jordan and introduced to the guests. Of course the professor is a German agent. Hitchcock has fun with a similar idea in *Young and Innocent* (1937), in which the on-the-run-couple are obliged to take part in a ghastly children's party while the suspicious aunt of the young woman, Erica (Nova Pilbeam), is trying to puzzle out what their relationship is.

'Obliged to the Podium': Hannay is mistaken for a politician and gives a rabble-rousing speech as the baddies close in. Graham Greene stole this idea for Holly Martins, the writer of westerns, in *The Third Man* (1949), whom the expat British in Vienna have mistaken for a serious writer.

'The Rescue Women': Hannay imposes himself on Madeleine Carroll's Pamela to keep her quiet and dodge the police. Donner's *Rogue Male* has Sir Robert constantly being inspired to revenge by his executed lover. In *Young and Innocent*, policeman's daughter Erica finds that murder suspect Robert (Derrick De Marney) has hitched a ride aboard her old jalopy, and soon finds it hard to believe he could be a murderer.

To make a definitive adaptation such as *The 39 Steps* you need a fan with a deep vein of irreverence. "I had been wanting to turn John Buchan's novel into a film for over 15 years," said Hitchcock in 1935. He had read it in 1919 or 1920, by which time, with the Great War just ended, it might have seemed naive. But Hitchcock, aged only 20 at the time, had been excused from frontline military service, and the novel thrilled him. As Charles Barr argues in his book *English Hitchcock*, Buchan remained a major influence on Hitchcock's idea of the perfect ripping yarn. When Hitchcock finally got the chance to film *The 39 Steps*, however, he and Bennett found that the characters, basic plot and locations were all that could be retained. Instead, they saw the opportunity to create a film that would follow the novel's basic shape but mildly send up its heroics. Hitchcock – the son of grocer – wasn't having any of the imperial snobbery. He starts the film in that cockpit of mockery, a music hall, and his first figure of fun is Mr Memory, a rather tragic clown of intellectual achievement.

Hitchcock's Hannay is sceptical too. He's from Canada rather than South Africa, and more of an outcast dreamer. Something about the character of Robert Donat, a major star of the mid-1930s, made him ideal. "He's blazingly ambitious, but difficult to satisfy," said Hitchcock, "a queer combination

(Above)
Jean Simmons and
Trevor Howard flee
across the Lake District
in Ralph Thomas's *The
Clouded Yellow* (1950).

(Below)
Harrison Ford as
Richard Kimble, the
doctor framed for the
murder of his wife in
The Fugitive (1993).

of determination and uncertainty." Who better
then to play someone relaxed under pressure
but cynical of his own chances of surviving the
spies on his tail. The Hitchcock/Donat Hannay
is as resourceful as Buchan's but more of a
pretender, a shape-shifter. He also needed to be
an everyman to appeal to the American market.

The best invention that Hitchcock, Bennett and
Alma Reville – Hitchcock's wife and ever-present
professional partner – bring to *The 39 Steps* is, of
course, the idea of Hannay getting handcuffed to
Pamela, the woman he initially imposes himself
upon with a kiss in the railway carriage of the
Flying Scotsman so as to avoid the police. Her
part, according to Hitchcock, was "built up" on
set during the shooting. In a reversal of what he
would later try to do to Tippi Hedren for *The Birds*
(1963) and *Marnie* (1964), he wanted to de-ice
Carroll's onscreen image as a self-conscious
and humourless figure. "Why not put yourself
on screen and cash in on your own personality,"
he told her. "It's a bright and likeable one." This
entailed a certain amount of rough treatment
from Donat and Hitchcock, but Carroll responded
in kind, matching the actor all the way for wit
and pretence. The play on marriage imagery –
not least the handcuffs – which, as Barr notes,
recurs throughout, also undermines Buchan's
idea of the man surviving on his wits alone.

Looking at *The 39 Steps* again, it's strange how
significant the 'in country' aspects remain in one's
memory given that they are extremely curtailed
compared with those in the novel. It seems a
general rule that directors of man-on-the-run
films don't dwell on the gone-to-ground aspects
of these thrillers for long. Once they've captured
set-up shots of moors, waterfalls, abandoned
barns and dugouts, they nearly all seem anxious
to get the story back to the city. In *The Clouded
Yellow*, for instance – scripted by thriller author
Eric Ambler and playwright Janet Green – in
which washed-up British Agent Somers (Trevor
Howard) goes on the run to protect his innocent
companion 'The Butterfly Girl' (Jean Simmons)
from being framed, they're in the Lake District for
around 15 minutes of a 90-minute film. The most
memorable moments in *The Clouded Yellow* are
those on the steps under the Tyne Bridge (which
echoes the Forth Bridge in design). The idea of
the urban jungle, the concrete labyrinth, which
animates so much of *film noir* from Fritz Lang's *M*
(1931) onwards, proves more easily and reliably
cinematic than woods, lanes and hedgerows.

Lang's *Man Hunt*, a 1941 Twentieth Century-
Fox project originally lined up for John Ford,

is similarly reductive of the gone-to-ground element – the very thing that nowadays draws new readers to *Rogue Male*. Made just before the USA entered the war, Lang's film is simple propaganda, aimed at the domestic market. Like Bennett, Lang's screenwriter Dudley Nichols kept little of the original and introduced a love affair. Walter Pidgeon plays a spectacularly arrogant version the Hunter, here named Captain Alan Thorndike. Lang gives Thorndike a similarly imperious enemy in George Sanders, who plays Major Quive-Smith, the English Nazi agent who pursues him to England. The scenes of pursuit around the London docks are the best in the film. But it's when Joan Bennett's street girl Jenny saves Thorndike from the agents stalking him by lending him money that his excruciatingly patronising attitude (to modern ears at least) begins to wreck the film.

Jenny being not only a woman, but also one of dubious morals and from a lower class (a prostitute in the script, but a seamstress in the studio-censored outcome), Thorndike treats her as stupid, naive and incompetent. Bennett, though apparently coached by a London music hall veteran, gives her a cockney accent almost as bad as Dick Van Dyke's in *Mary Poppins* (1964), outdoing Pidgeon's mid-Atlantic burr for annoyance. Thorndike later regrets his behaviour

towards Jenny but it is never even a possibility that they could be together. In the moral codes of the time, since she poses as a street girl to get a policeman to leave Thorndike alone – spoiler alert – you know she must die. This shabby romantic revision of a lone male adventure enables Lang to minimise the major aspect of the novel – how the hunter goes to ground in the Dorset countryside and how Quive-Smith finds and imprisons him – to a few final scenes.

Thorndike's smug urbanity points the way towards his near namesake, Cary Grant's Roger O. Thornhill in Hitchcock's *North by Northwest*, though of course there's nothing annoying about Grant playing an advertising executive at first kidnapped by spies in a case of mistaken identity and then framed for a murder he did not commit. In essence, Thornhill is an American update of Hannay a quarter-century on. There's nothing colonial or class-ridden about him; he's the very epitome of the Madison Avenue Mad Men who had destroyed all that with their own imperious visions, but he has almost exactly that mildly comical, mildly jaundiced view of the world that Donat embodied so well, and his character is sent up by Hitchcock as ruthlessly as ever. And if you want to solve the problem of filming in country, how about the Midwestern plains, where, ironically,

(Above)
An awkward moment as Hannay (Robert Donat) is handcuffed to Pamela (Madeleine Carroll) in *The 39 Steps*.

there's almost nowhere to hide? Hence the early helicopter one sees searching above the moors in *The 39 Steps* becomes the famous crop-dusting plane that, absurdly but just about plausibly, attacks Thornhill while he's on the ground.

If Hitchcock makes Hannay and Thornhill democratic figures, and Lang makes Thorndike the patrician opposite, Donner and Raphael's Sir Robert Hunter in the 1976 *Rogue Male* is a pleasingly quasi-liberal update, albeit riven with contradictions. To read deeply in 1930s British crime fiction is to often encounter off-the-cuff anti-Semitism – although not in Household. In any case Raphael and Donner are having none of that. Our hero's solicitor gets a Jewish surname, Abrahams, and is played by Harold Pinter. In the novel, Household is coy about his hero's lost love as a motive for the assassination he attempted. Donner's film shows her quite early on in flashbacks, clearly signalled as Jewish and played by Cyd Hayman, whose most famous role had been Nina, a half-Jewish agent in occupied France, in the 1970 TV series *Manhunt* (no relation to Lang's film).

The film's attitude to class and race also takes its cue from a speech Hunter makes in the novel. Household's hero is clearly a man of means with all the accoutrements of the 1930s gentleman, yet he talks about what he calls 'Class X', which is itself a confused category, something like a 'gent' but not quite. "I say Class X because there's no definition of it," he says. "I should like some socialist pundit to explain to me why it is that in England a man can be a member of the proletariat by every definition… and yet obviously belong to Class X, and why another can be a bulging capitalist or cabinet minister or both and never get nearer to Class X than being

directed to the Saloon Bar if he enters the Public."

But, alongside this noble inclusiveness, summed up perhaps by Hunter's remark in the novel that "natural leaders don't have any will to power", Donner's film is happy to enjoy the fetishism of the equipment of the classic English gentleman of the colonial era, not least his 'Bond Street rifle' – the inscription on the makers' nameplate is lingered over lovingly (in Lang's film the rifle is seen sticking ignominiously upright out of a swamp). Descriptions of necessary survival kit are given on several occasions. Thus the film looks in two directions: nostalgically to the colonial era of the 'true sportsman', the English amateur, and progressively forwards to the liberal mores of the decade in which it was made.

I have said that there's a better *Rogue Male* adaptation to be made. Interest in the novel has been revived by the current nature writing boom, epitomised not least by the 'in country' writings of Robert Macfarlane, who has described trying to find the location of the Hunter's hide deep in a Dorset Holloway. If the film were down to me I'd make of it a kind of slow, suspenseful anti-thriller, combine some of the love of landscape in the Russian cinema of Tarkovsky and Sukorov with a greater focus on the physical toll of survival. The only close example I can think of is Jerzy Skolimowski's *Essential Killing* (2010), in which Vincent Gallo's escaped terrorist is reduced to a kind of animal surviving in a freezing Polish forest. But that film left me rather cold. Any grimness in a new *Rogue Male* would need to be leavened with more than a modicum of humour. It would need to see its hero as a figure not only of determination but also of mild fun and amusement. "I always look for a subject that has plenty of action," said Hitchcock. "I introduce the comedy myself."

ANATOMY OF A SCENE
THE 39 STEPS (1935)

1. After a spy is killed in his flat, Richard Hannay flees on a train, but his name is in the papers, and people eye him with suspicion.

2. Police are scouring the train, and to evade capture he enters a compartment, kissing a woman to hide his face. But she gives him up.

3. Desperate, Hannay distracts the police and opens the train compartment door, daringly hanging to the side of the fast moving train.

4. As the train comes to a stop, Hannay manages to evade capture by hiding behind the truss on the Forth Bridge, before fleeing again.

CAN YOU TRUST YOUR DESIRES?

CRIMES OF PASSION: THE EROTIC THRILLER

BY ANNA BOGUTSKAYA

There was a brief period in American cinema that conjures images of a very particular brand of cinematic sleaze: soft-lit sex scenes; promotional posters with ass-grabbing and faces contorted in ecstasy; expensively suited priapic men prowling through luxury modernist appartments… If you think of early to mid-1990s American cinema, chances are it's such tropes of the erotic thriller that come to mind.

A descendant of *film noir*, the erotic thriller made the implicit sexual appeal of those earlier films explicit. *Noir* had always sold itself on the seductive allure of untrustworthy characters, on the trade-off between sexual excitement and danger; but the erotic thriller promised a lingering look at what classic *noir* could only hint at. Here you would find all the suspense of a classic thriller, but with the guarantee of sex and nudity. Taboos, social or sexual, would be broken. Like *noir*, erotic thrillers warned us of the risk in following our desires, and asked whether that risk was a price worth paying.

There had been forebears to the 90s wave in the form of sexed-up neo-*noirs* such as *Body Heat* (1981) and *The Postman Always Rings Twice* (1981), Adrian Lyne's glossy, racy tales of destructive relationships *9½ Weeks* (1986) and *Fatal Attraction* (1987), and Brian De Palma's postmodern, sexually explicit riffs on Hitchcock *Dressed to Kill* (1980) and *Body Double* (1984) – to say nothing of Italian *gialli* or the Gallic *amour fou* tradition exemplified in such Claude Chabrol films as *La femme infidèle* (1969) and *Juste avant la nuit* (1971). But it was only in the late 1980s that the term 'erotic' started routinely to appear in descriptors alongside 'thriller', and the genre's heyday truly began.

The boom owed everything to the dominance of the VHS format and the video store at the time – a moment when form and format were fused harmoniously. As scholar Linda Ruth Williams writes in *The Erotic Thriller in Contemporary Cinema*, "The sexual potential of home viewing (you could watch whatever you wanted with whoever you wanted, in privacy) and the increasing sexual explicitness of the erotic thriller, met and married, all the better to exploit each other as far as sex and sales would take them."

Home video meant that everything from the most cinematic A-list Hollywood feature to the most transparently exploitative quasi-soft-porn titles might appear side by side on the video-store shelf. Film titles at either end of the scale were typically short – two words was ideal – and suggestive of sex and death in a vague, interchangeable sort of way: *Lady Beware* (1987), *Fatal Exposure* (1989), *Night Eyes* (1990), *Body*

Chemistry (1990), *Love Crimes* (1992)… Throughout the 1990s, direct-to-video erotic thrillers were a thriving industry, with their own network of directors (such as Mike Sedan and Jim Wynorski), producers (such as Andrew Stevens) and stars (such as Shannon Tweed and Tanya Roberts).

But much as the straight-to-video industry provided a below-the-critical-radar bedrock, it was the major studio production *Basic Instinct* (1992) that came to define the genre. Based on a much-touted script by Joe Eszterhas that had attracted controversy before filming even began, Paul Verhoeven's hit wasn't the first erotic thriller of the 1990s cycle, but its huge success, and the way that it so centrally promoted its sexual explicitness, took the form squarely into the Hollywood mainstream. The film became a cultural phenomenon, spawning a run of imitators.

The essential ingredients of sex and death are intertwined in *Basic Instinct* right from the famous opening scene, in which a couple writhe vigorously beneath a mirrored ceiling before the unidentified blonde woman stabs the man repeatedly with an ice-pick at the point of orgasm – he defenceless because his hands are tied to the bed by a white silk scarf. In symbolism you hardly needed Dr Freud to decode, for the rest of the film the prospect of being penetrated by an ice-pick mid-coitus becomes a recurring danger.

The plot follows the police investigation of that first murder, led by detective Nick Curran (Michael Douglas, an actor who epitomised the erotic thriller leading man). Curran suspects that the victim's sometime girlfriend – smart, sexy, rich, bisexual crime novelist Catherine Tramell (Sharon Stone) – might be involved, for her novel *Love Hurts* describes a man being killed in precisely the same way. In the role that will forever define her, Stone completely stole the film from her male co-star, despite Douglas's name being the only one 'above the title' on the film's promotional posters.

Basic Instinct perfected the formula that everyone, including its own creative team, would soon attempt to replicate. Coming out only a year later, *Sliver* (1993) again paired Eszterhas and Stone, but this time made her the potential victim rather than the black widow figure. Stone plays a book editor who moves into a hyper-modern, phalically high-rise tower in which several women have recently been killed, and begins an affair with the building's owner (Billy Baldwin), who, unbeknown to her, has installed cameras throughout and can watch her every move. The film teased the audience for its own voyeurism, its tagline asking: "You like to watch, don't you?"

The most high-profile global female sexual icon of the early 1990s was undoubtedly Madonna, whose 1992 *Erotica* album and *Sex* book chimed with the heyday of the erotic thriller and its foregrounding of sex as provocation and selling point. A year after *Basic Instinct*, the singer took the leading role in the markedly similar, if entirely inferior, *Body of Evidence*. A sexed-up procedural/courtroom thriller, the film co-starred Willem Dafoe as an attorney tasked with defending the seductive Rebecca Carlson (Madonna), who may or may not be killing off wealthy older men by having intense sex with them and causing them to have heart attacks. Spoiler alert: she is. Although it suffers from less-than-inspired performances and stale courtroom scenes, and the undeniably preposterous central conceit, *Body of Evidence* nonetheless remains interesting for the way it quite literally weaponises the female body. Carlson herself is the murder weapon.

Where *Body of Evidence* used sex to spice up what would otherwise have been a pretty bog-standard courtroom drama, Barry Levinson's *Disclosure* (1994) did something similar for the corporate thriller, while also reflecting an underlying contemporary male anxiety about the rise of women in the corporate world (a theme that also informed 1993's *The Temp*, starring Lara Flynn Boyle). Tom Sanders (Michael Douglas, once again) is overlooked for a promotion at a tech company in favour of Meredith Johnson (Demi Moore), a rising star in the office and an ex-girlfriend. Ballsy and direct, Meredith makes a pass at Tom when they are both working late one night at the office, and later accuses him of sexual harrassment. What starts off as an erotic thriller investigating the intersections of greed, sex and the balance of power between men and women in corporate America eventually becomes an akward cyber-thriller. As with Rebecca in *Body of Evidence*, Meredith is upfront and unapologetic about her sexual appetites, but is ultimately undone by her greedy pursuit of power. In a way, she is really punished for attempting to break up the all-American family unit.

It's not until John Dahl's *The Last Seduction* (1994) that the erotic thriller got a truly remorseless femme fatale for the ages in the shape of Linda Fiorentino's Bridget Gregory. After stealing a large sum of money from a one-time drug deal by her hapless husband Clay (Bill Pullman), Bridget stops off in the small town of Beston, where she wastes no time picking up local good guy Mike (Peter Berg), who she quickly susses as the perfect patsy for her schemes.

Fiorentino's entrance into the bar in Beston is pure character gold: she strides into a room full of plaid shirts, all sharp angles in her black-and-white suit, and barks at the bartender for a Manhattan, who pointedly ignores her. "Who's a girl got to suck around here to get a drink?" she mutters. Heads are turned. "City trash," Mike's friend calls her. She's rude and vulgar, but Mike is instantly smitten, projecting his own unfulfilled dreams of escaping to a bigger town on to her. His attempts at charm are pitiful, and only when he tells Bridget he is "hung like a horse; think about it", does she look up – promptly testing the merchandise before taking him to an alley out back for unceremonious sex.

Bridget is the perfect erotic thriller villain: confident, unrepentant, self-aware and cruel. But she is also liberating. She knows exactly who she is, what she wants and how to use sex to manipulate people into getting it. "You're my designated fuck," she tells Mike at one point. Bridget Gregory is to femmes fatales what Gordon Gekko is to yuppie men. While *Basic Instinct* plays around with the did-she-didn't-she mystery, baiting us with shots of ice picks, and *Body of Evidence* tries for the most part to convince us that Rebecca is just kinky, not really evil, *The Last Seduction* makes no such apologies for Bridget. She's rotten to the core – and we love her for it.

Teenage daydreams

If the titles above mostly offered calculating, mature female characters in cool command of their sexuality, another trope that became a mainstay of erotic thrillers, especially in the later 90s and noughties, was the 'teen temptress'

(Opposite, top)
Linda Fiorentino as rotten-to-the-core Bridget Gregory in John Stahl's neo-*noir The Last Seduction* (1994).

(Opposite, bottom)
Demi Moore and Michael Douglas in an after hours office tryst in Barry Levinson's *Disclosure* (1994).

(Below)
The pre-eminent female sexual icon of the 90s, Madonna, starred in erotic thriller *Body of Evidence* (1992).

figure. Many of these films barely rose above the level of a highly questionable male fantasy – for instance, such Alicia Silverstone vehicles as *The Crush* (1993) or *The Babysitter* (1995), or the Julia Stiles-starring *Wicked* (1998), or even *Wild Things* (1998), which came out during the tail-end of the peak erotic thriller period, and merged the teen temptress with the social climber in its pitting of blue-collar gym teacher Sam Lombardo (Matt Dillon) and investigating officer Sergeant Ray Duquette (Kevin Bacon) against savvy teens Suzie (Neve Campbell) and Kelly (Denise Richards).

Within this strain of films, Katt Shea's *Poison Ivy* (1992) stands out as something more interesting. Arriving the same year as *Basic Instinct*, *Poison Ivy* had a stealthier impact, more in line with the direct-to-video titles of the genre. After screening at the Sundance Film Festival, and following an unsuccessful limited theatrical release, Shea's film belatedly found an audience on video and cable TV, spawning three lesser sequels that continued the murderous teen sexpot plotline without the charm of the original.

The first time we see the eponymous Ivy (Drew Barrymore), she is being watched by well-off but rebellious teen Sylvie Cooper (Sara Gilbert), and we see the things that make her so alluring through Sylvie's teenage eyes. The camera focuses first on her rebel girl signifiers – the short skirt, boots, tattoo, leather jacket – before finally revealing her face. "Obviously, big problems," Sylvie says in an awe-stricken voiceover. In the very next scene, Ivy puts an injured dog out of its misery by mercy-killing it with a shovel. Sylvie and Ivy exchange a look. A kinship is born. It's sex and death, on the nose.

Poison Ivy is as much an exploration of intense teenage friendship, class and female sexuality as it is an eroticised fantasy of a sexy young teenager seducing her way into a wealthy family. What sets it apart is how we look at the deep sadness of the Ivy character. Ivy isn't even her real name: she's christened that by Sylvie after she realises she had never even learned Ivy's name in all the time she had been watching her from a distance. Ivy becomes whatever she needs to be to succeed. Sylvie needs her to be the alpha to her beta, a best friend who will give her the confidence she lacks to be herself. For Sylvie's father (Tom Skerritt), Ivy acts as a sexual surrogate for his sick wife, much to Sylvie's horror. Ivy struggles to balance both of those projections, and the film finally does end up conforming to the suburban norms that Sylvie is supposedly trying to escape – Ivy is punished, order is restored.

Poison Ivy is one of relatively few erotic thrillers to have been directed by a woman, sitting alongside titles such as Karen Arthur's *Lady Beware* and Lizzie Borden's *Love Crimes*. A female perspective behind the lens can bring different aspects to the fore, and though the marketing for most erotic thrillers clearly assumed a straight male audience, the genre can be a fantasy space for us all to indulge in our darkest desires. Jane Campion's masterful, dreamy *In the Cut* (2003) recognises this well. Frannie (Meg Ryan) is a mild-mannered English teacher drawn to the darkness. Her desire is unspoken. We first encounter it when she spies on a man getting a blow job in a New York bar, and later with her obvious attraction to the brash detective investigating a murder to which she's unwittingly connected. "I can be whatever you want me to be," says Detective Malloy (Mark Ruffalo). The seducers in erotic thrillers are chameleons, channelling the insecurities of both men and women to create the perfect object of their desires, whether explicit or not. Sometimes, these seductions are a means to an end: Catherine Trammell wants a better character for her new novel, Rebecca wants to win the court case, Meredith wants to climb the career ladder, Ivy wants a more comfortable life. And then again, sometimes they're just contrivances to expose more flesh on screen…

The morning after

As the turn of the millennium faded from view, it became clear that the heyday of the erotic thriller had passed. In part it was surely the opening of the Pandora's box that is the internet that signalled how things would change – the ready availability of any and all erotic fixes online sating audience desires. But there has been an afterlife. The steady stream of straight-to-video movies may have slowed to more of a trickle, but it lives on all the same. And every now and then a title crops up that brings new life and fresh dimensions to the classic formula, away from Hollywood – think of French director François Ozon's *Swimming Pool* (2003), Taiwanese Ang Lee's *Lust, Caution* (2007), Armenian-Canadian Atom Egoyan's *Chloe* (2009), or French filmmaker Alain Guiraudie's *Stranger by the Lake* (2013), a rare case of a gay-themed erotic thriller reaching a wider audience. More recently still there is South Korean Park Chan-wook's *The Handmaiden* (2016), the box-office success of which has shown that audiences are clearly still drawn to films whose illicit thrills and seductive suspense ask them anew if they're really ready to trust their desires.

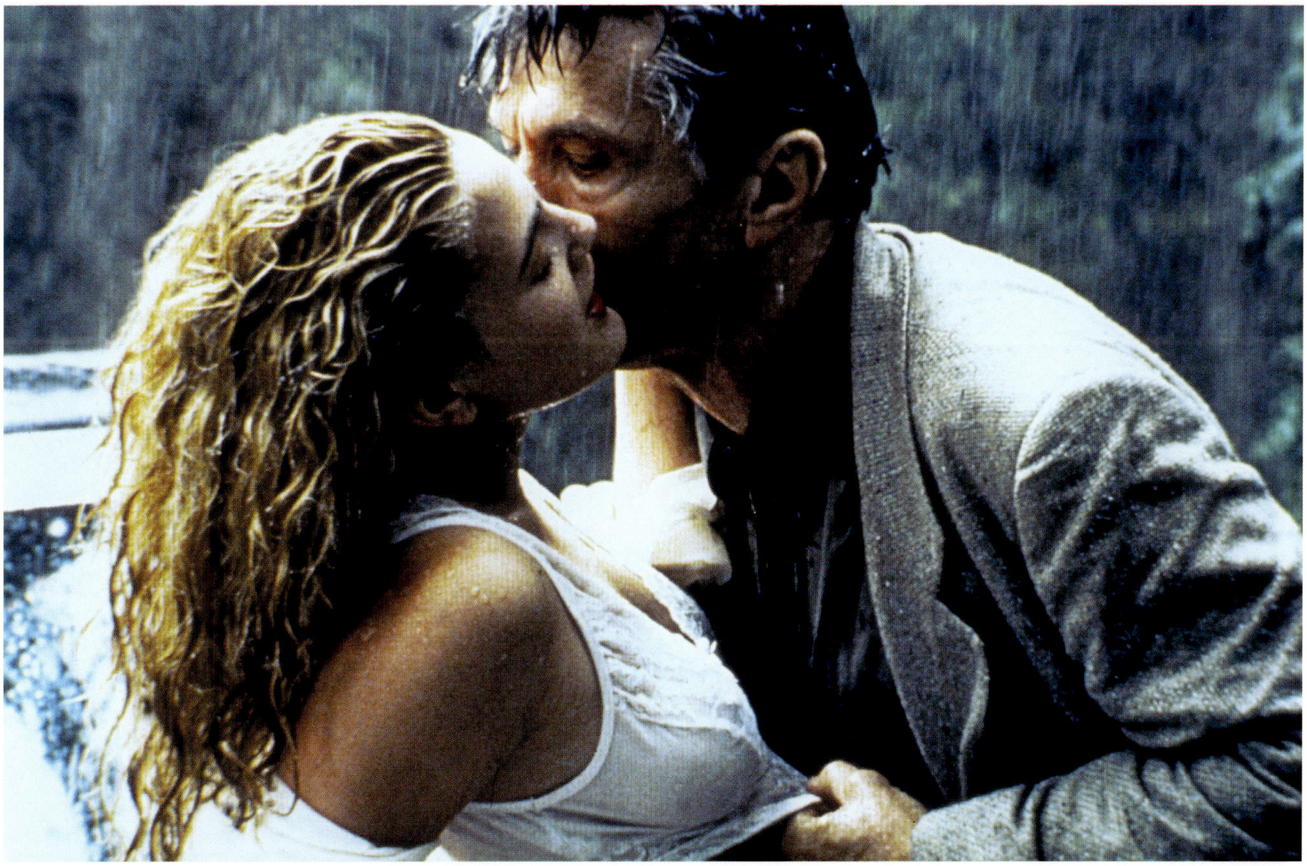

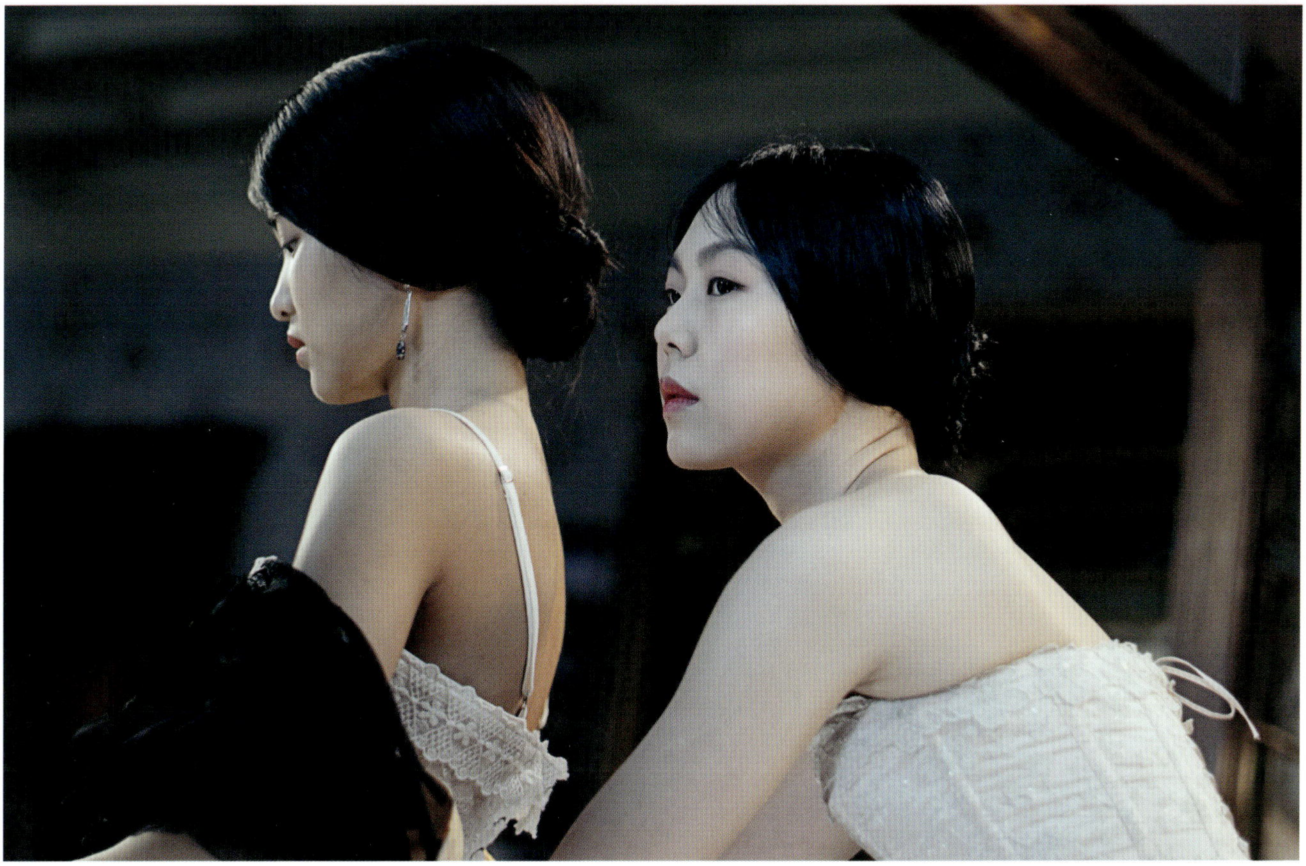

FILM INDEX

CONTRIBUTORS

Jake Arnott's novels include *The Long Firm*, *He Kills Coppers*, *The Devil's Paintbrush* and *Johnny Come Home*. His latest novel is *The Fatal Tree* (Sceptre).

James Bell is features editor at *Sight & Sound* magazine, and is series editor of the BFI Compendium books.

Anna Bogutskaya is events programmer at BFI Southbank, programme director of the Underwire Film Festival, and one half of The Final Girls, a programming collective that explores the intersection between horror film and feminism.

Josephine Botting is a curator at the BFI National Archive and programmes regular archive screenings at BFI Southbank. She recently completed a doctorate in British cinema of the 1920s.

Lee Child is author of the bestselling Jack Reacher series of novels and short stories.

Mar Diestro-Dópido is a film critic based in London. She is a researcher and regular contributor to *Sight & Sound* as well as an experienced arts and media translator. She currently holds the post of BFI Sight & Sound postdoctoral research fellow at the Royal Central School of Speech and Drama (CSSD). Her book publications include a BFI Modern Classic on Guillermo del Toro's *Pan's Labyrinth* and a forthcoming book on film festivals.

Bryony Dixon is curator of silent film at the BFI National Archive. She specialises in British silent cinema, is the author of the BFI screenguide *100 Silent Films*, and is currently working on a book on Victorian-era film.

Mark Duguid is a senior curator at the BFI National Archive and oversees the presentation of archive material on BFI Player and other platforms. He writes on British television and film and is the author of the BFI TV Classic on *Cracker* (Palgrave/BFI TV Classics, 2010), and co-editor of *Ealing Revisited* (Palgrave/BFI, 2012).

Robert Hanks is a freelance writer, editor and broadcaster based in Cambridge.

Pamela Hutchinson is a freelance writer and film critic, who contributes to *Sight & Sound*, Radio 4 and the *Guardian*. She is the editor of the silent cinema website SilentLondon.co.uk and the author of the BFI Film Classic on *Pandora's Box*.

Eric Hynes is associate curator of film at Museum of the Moving Image, New York. He writes a regular column about the art of documentary for *Film Comment* magazine, and has written for publications including the *New York Times*, *Rolling Stone*, *Slate*, the *Village Voice* and *Sight & Sound*.

Alexander Jacoby lectures on Japanese film, manga and anime, and world cinema at Oxford Brookes University. He has curated or co-curated film programmes at the BFI, Il Cinema Ritrovato in Bologna, and the Museum of Modern Art in New York and MoMA Tokyo. He is a frequent writer for *Sight & Sound* and the author of *A Critical Handbook of Japanese Film Directors* and a forthcoming monograph on Hirokazu Koreeda.

Nick James is editor of *Sight & Sound* magazine, and author of the BFI Modern Classic on Michael Mann's *Heat*.

Richard T. Kelly's most recent novel is the political thriller *The Knives* (2016). He is also the author of the novels *Crusaders* (2008) and *The Possessions of Doctor Forrest* (2011). He has written several studies of filmmakers: *Alan Clarke* (1998), *The Name of this Book Is Dogme 95* (2000) and the authorised biography *Sean Penn: His Life and Times* (2004).

Philip Kemp is a freelance reviewer and film historian, writing regularly for *Sight & Sound* and *Total Film*, and edited *Cinema: The Whole Story* (Thames & Hudson, 2011). He's a visiting lecturer in film journalism at the University of Leicester.

Simon McCallum is archive projects curator at the BFI, programming across the organisation's digital platforms and working with filmmakers drawing on the BFI National Archive. In 2017 he curated the BFI Southbank season 'Gross Indecency: Queer Lives Before & After the '67 Act'.

Hannah McGill is a writer and critic based in Edinburgh, and is a former artistic director of the Edinburgh International Film Festival. She is currently undertaking doctoral research at Queen Margaret University, Edinburgh

Kim Newman's most recent novel is *Anno Dracula: One Thousand Monsters*. His other fiction includes *The Hound of the D'Urbervilles* and the *Anno Dracula* novels; his nonfiction includes *Nightmare Movies* and the BFI Classics *Cat People* and *Doctor Who*. He writes for *Sight & Sound* and *Empire*.

Nick Pinkerton is a Cincinnati-born, Queens-based writer. His writing appears regularly in *Artforum*, *Film Comment*, *Sight & Sound*, *Frieze*, *Reverse Shot*, and sundry other publications, and in areas of interest, he covers the waterfront.

Vic Pratt is a film archivist, writer, historian, Blu-ray and DVD producer. One of the co-founders of BFI Flipside, he has written on British and international film and television history for a wide range of books, magazines, websites and DVD releases. He has curated seasons of vintage British B Pictures at BFI Southbank, and is currently co-authoring a book on British cinema and television history.

Iain Sinclair's latest book is *The Last London: True Fictions from an Unreal City*.

Imogen Sara Smith is the author of *In Lonely Places: Film Noir Beyond the City* and *Buster Keaton: The Persistence of Comedy*. She has written for *Sight & Sound*, The Criterion Collection, *Film Quarterly*, *Reverse Shot* and many other publications.

David Thomson is a film critic and historian. His many books on cinema include *The New Biographical Dictionary of Film*, *The Big Screen: The Story of the Movies and What They Did to Us*, *Have You Seen...?: A Personal Introduction to 1,000 Films*, *The Whole Equation: A History of Hollywood*, and *Warner Bros: The Making of an American Movie Studio*.

Sarah Weinman is the editor of *Troubled Daughters, Twisted Wives: Stories from the Trailblazers of Domestic Suspense* (Penguin) and *Women Crime Writers: Eight Suspense Novels of the 1940s & 50s* (Library of America). She publishes the weekly newsletter *The Crime Lady*.

Kelli Weston is studying for a PhD at Birkbeck, University of London, and is a regular contributor to *Sight & Sound*. Her doctoral research project is 'The 'Other' Women: Representations of Women of Colour in Female Gothic Cinema'.

Andy Willis is reader in film studies at the University of Salford, Manchester. He is currently senior visiting curator (Film) at HOME, Manchester. He is co-editor (with Felicia Chan) of *Chinese Cinemas: International Perspectives*, and co-editor (with Wing-Fai Leung) of *East Asian Film Stars*.

PICTURE CREDITS

All images courtesy of BFI National Archive/Special Collections except: p33, 38 (top), 55, 56, 80 (bottom), 100 (bottom), 105, 113, 144, 149, 150 (top) Ronald Grant Archive; p13 Paramount/Kobal/REX/Shutterstock, p36 (top) Moviestore Collection/REX/Shutterstock, p50 (bottom) ITV/REX/Shutterstock, p89 RKO/Kobal/REX/Shutterstock, p90 Paramount/Kobal/REX/Shutterstock; p153 (top) Moviestore/REX/Shutterstock; p103 Everett Collection Inc / Alamy Stock Photo

ACKNOWLEDGEMENTS

Thank you to all of the writers who contributed to this volume. Thanks for their advice and assistance to BFI colleagues Nigel Arthur, Aga Baranowska, Anna Bogutskaya, Stewart Brown, David Edgar, Gaylene Gould, Justin Johnson, Tim Platt, Heather Stewart, Douglas Weir, Rob Winter and Darren Wood. Special thanks to Rhidian Davis, to Nick James, as always to Lisa Kerrigan, to Jamie McLeish for proofreading, and to Christopher Brawn, this book's designer.

ALSO IN THE BFI COMPENDIUM SERIES

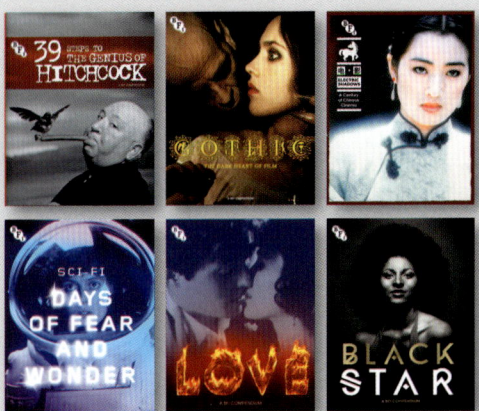

1903

The Edison Company produces *The Great Train Robbery*, directed by Edwin S. Porter. The film pioneers the use of cross-cutting to build suspense.

1912

D.W. Griffith makes *The Girl and Her Trust*, about a girl who finds herself threatened by two vagrants who are trying to steal her money.

1913

Lois Weber directs *Suspense*, which shows a woman home alone with her baby being terrorised by a vagrant as her husband races to rescue her. In France, Louis Feuillade directs several films in the *Fantômas* serial, about the exploits of a master criminal. The series pioneers the 'cliff-hanger' at the end of each episode.

1915

John Buchan's influential spy novel *The Thirty-Nine Steps* is published.

1922

In Germany, Fritz Lang makes the two-part crime epic about a master criminal, *Dr. Mabuse: The Gambler*.

1923

Harold Lloyd dangles precariously from a clock on the edge of a building in the comedy/action thriller *Safety Last!*

1926

In Britain, Alfred Hitchcock directs his breakthrough silent thriller *The Lodger*, adapted from a novel by Marie Belloc Lowndes and inspired in part by the Jack the Ripper case.

1928

Fritz Lang makes the stylish, groundbreaking spy thriller *Spione*.

1929

Hitchcock's *Blackmail*, starring Anny Ondra as a woman who kills a man who tries to attack her, becomes one of the earliest 'all-talkie' features made in Britain. A silent version is also produced.

1931

Peter Lorre gives a magnificent performance as a child killer in Fritz Lang's *M*. The film will have a huge

Alain Delon as Tom Ripley in René Clément's *Plein soleil* (1960)

influence on the serial-killer thriller subgenre, and captures the sense of dread felt in Germany at the time – something felt even more in Lang's next film *Das Testament des Dr Mabuse*, released shortly after Hitler had been appointed chancellor in 1933.

1935

Hitchcock makes the archetypal innocent-on-the-run thriller, *The 39 Steps*, adapted from John Buchan's book.

1941

Humphrey Bogart and Mary Astor star in John Huston's *The Maltese Falcon*, based on the novel by Dashiell Hammett.

1944

Barbara Stanwyck plays the scheming femme fatale Phyllis Dietrichson in Billy Wilder's classic *film noir Double Indemnity*, written by Raymond Chandler and based on a novel by James M. Cain. Gene Tierney plays a woman whose murder Dana Andrews investigates in Otto Preminger's mystery thriller *Laura*. Ingrid Bergman plays a wife driven to the edge of madness by her husband in George Cukor's adaptation of Patrick Hamilton's play *Gaslight*.

1945

Edgar G. Ulmer makes his ingenious, low-budget B-thriller masterpiece *Detour*, starring Tom Neal and Ann Savage. Nina Foch plays a woman pushed to doubt her identity after a malign plot in Joseph H. Lewis's *My Name Is Julia Ross*.

1946

Jane Greer and Robert Mitchum star in Jacques Tourneur's *Out of the Past*.

1947

James Mason plays an IRA man on the run in Carol Reed's *Odd Man Out*. Sympathetic portraits of criminals are found in two British thrillers: Alberto Cavalcanti's *They Made Me a Fugitive*, and Robert Hamer's *It Always Rains on Sunday*. Criminals are seen as more of a blight on society in Roy Boulting's adaptation of Graham Greene's *Brighton Rock*, starring Richard Attenborough.

1948

Hitchcock's *Rope* implies that its two coolly intellectual killers are gay.

1949

Joseph Cotten and Orson Welles star in *The Third Man*, Carol Reed's classic film set in post-war Vienna,

written by Graham Greene.
Max Ophuls makes the domestic suspense thriller *The Reckless Moment*.

1950

Anxieties about the atomic age underpin Roy Boulting's *Seven Days to Noon*.
American-born Jules Dassin makes the seedy London-set *noir Night and the City*, starring Richard Widmark.
Joseph H. Lewis makes his B-movie masterpiece *Gun Crazy*.
Gloria Grahame fears her lover Humphrey Bogart may be a killer in Nicholas Ray's *In a Lonely Place*, adapted from Dorothy B. Hughes's novel.

1951

Hitchcock adapts Patricia Highsmith's classic thriller of 'exchanged murders', *Strangers on a Train*.
Earl Cameron stars in Basil Dearden's *Pool of London*, the first British film to hint at romance between a black man and a white woman.

1953

Sam Fuller makes the anti-communist espionage thriller *Pickup on South Street*.
Fritz Lang spotlights police corruption in his crime thriller *The Big Heat*.
Henri-Georges Clouzot makes the classic action suspense film *The Wages of Fear*.

1954

James Stewart and Grace Kelly believe they have seen a murder in Hitchcock's ingenious mystery thriller *Rear Window*.

1955

Ralph Meeker stars as detective Mike Hammer in Robert Aldrich's adaptation of writer Mickey Spillane's hardboiled tale of Cold War paranoia, *Kiss Me Deadly*.
Simone Simon and Véra Clouzot conspire to murder the latter's abusive husband in Henri-Georges Clouzot's *Les Diaboliques*, set in small French town.
Jules Dassin directs *Rififi*. The French *noir* is celebrated for its extended heist sequence, shot entirely without dialogue.

1959

The man-on-the-run archetype is given a comic spin in Hitchcock's *North by Northwest*, starring Cary Grant.

Britain's fading claims to world power-status are spoofed in Carol Reed's *Our Man in Havana*.

1960

Two thrillers about highly disturbed killers are released: Michael Powell's *Peeping Tom* and Hitchcock's *Psycho*. Both push the envelope in their depiction of onscreen violence.
Alain Delon stars in *Plein soleil*, René Clément's adaptation of Patricia Highsmith's *The Talented Mr. Ripley*.

1962

Cold War-era fears of Soviet infiltration are captured in John Frankenheimer's *The Manchurian Candidate*, in which a US soldier is brainwashed into becoming a communist assassin.

1963

Toshiro Mifune stars in Akira Kurosawa's kidnap thriller *High and Low*.

1964

Post-Cuban Missile Crisis anxieties about the possibility of nuclear war surface in Sidney Lumet's *Fail Safe* and Stanley Kubrick's *Dr Strangelove or: How I Learned to Stop Worrying and Love the Bomb*.

1965

Richard Burton stars as a British spy in Martin Ritt's *The Spy Who Came in from the Cold*, adapted from John le Carré's novel.
Michael Caine gets one of his iconic roles as spy Harry Palmer in *The Ipcress File*.

1966

David Hemmings plays a photographer who may have photographed a murder in Michelangelo Antonioni's modernist thriller set in Swinging London, *Blow-Up*.

***The Day of the Jackal* (1973)**

George Segal plays an American agent in Berlin in Michael Anderson's *The Quiller Memorandum*, written by Harold Pinter.

1967

Audrey Hepburn plays a blind woman whose New York home is invaded by criminals in *Wait Until Dark*.

1969

Costa-Gavras captures the mood of the times in his classic political thriller *Z*.

1970

Stéphane Audran fears her boyfriend is a killer in Claude Chabrol's *Le Boucher*.

1971

A young Steven Spielberg directs the cat-and-mouse thriller *Duel*, in which Dennis Weaver's car driver is pursued by a truck.
Jane Fonda plays a prostitute stalked by an ex-client in Alan J. Pakula's *Klute*.
Right-wing ideas about policing are felt in two gritty cop thrillers: Don Siegel's *Dirty Harry* and William Friedkin's *The French Connection*.

1973

Al Pacino stars as a New York cop who uncovers corruption within his force in Sidney Lumet's *Serpico*.
Edward Fox plays an assassin in Fred Zinneman's *The Day of the Jackal*, adapted from Frederick Forsyth's novel.

1974

A woman finds her life picked apart by police and the media in Volker Schlöndorff and Margarethe von Trotta's *The Lost Honour of Katharina Blum*.
The post-Watergate mood is captured in Francis Ford Coppola's *The Conversation*, starring Gene Hackman, and Pakula's *The Parallax View*, starring Warren Beatty.

1975

Robert Redford is a CIA agent targeted by his own side in Sidney Lumet's *Three Days of the Condor*.
In Italy, Francesco Rosi makes *Illustrious Corpses*, starring Lino Ventura.

1976

Robert Redford and Dustin Hoffman star as journalists Bob Woodward and Carl Bernstein in Pakula's Watergate-exposé *All the President's Men*.

1979
Alec Guinness is George Smiley in the BBC's classic series adapted from John le Carré's book *Tinker Tailor Soldier Spy*.

1980
Al Pacino plays a cop who goes undercover in New York's gay leather bars in William Friedkin's *Cruising*. Brian De Palma makes *Dressed to Kill*.

1981
The 1969 Chappaquidick incident is referenced in Brian De Palma's *Blow Out*. Kathleen Turner is the femme fatale in Lawrence Kasdan's neo-*noir Body Heat*.

1984
The Coen brothers make their neo-*noir* debut feature *Blood Simple*.

1985
Bob Peck and Joanne Whalley star in Troy Kennedy Martin's classic BBC conspiracy miniseries *Edge of Darkness*.

1986
Rutger Hauer's psycopathic drifter torments C. Thomas Howell in Robert Harmon's *The Hitcher*.

1987
Michael Douglas and Glenn Close star in Adrian Lyne's hit yuppie nightmare thriller *Fatal Attraction*.

1988
George Sluizer makes the terrifying kidnap thriller *The Vanishing* (*Spoorloos*).

Sofie Grabøl in *The Killing* (2007-12)

1991
Jodie Foster stars in Jonathan Demme's *The Silence of the Lambs*. Rebecca De Mornay plays a venegeful nanny in *The Hand that Rocks the Cradle*. Helen Mirren plays DCI Jane Tennison in the first series of *Prime Suspect* on UK TV.

1992
Jennifer Jason Leigh is Bridget Fonda's flatmate from hell in *Single White Female*.

1993
Basic Instinct marks the highpoint of the 90s erotic thriller. Harrison Ford stars in *The Fugitive*.

1994
Linda Fiorentino updates the femme fatale in John Dahl's *The Last Seduction*. Danny Boyle makes *Shallow Grave*.

1995
Sandrine Bonnaire and Isabelle Huppert play partners in crime in Chabrol's Ruth Rendell adaptation *La Cérémonie*. Brad Pitt, Morgan Freeman and Kevin Spacey star in David Fincher's *Se7en*.

1997
Stellan Skarsgård plays a sleep-deprived detective in the Norwegian film *Insomnia*.

2000
Guy Pearce plays an amnesiac in Christopher Nolan's *Memento*.

2001
The tense post-9/11 mood is felt in the TV series 24, starring Kiefer Sutherland.

2003
Jane Campion puts her spin on the erotic thriller with *In the Cut*, with Meg Ryan. Korean director Bong Joon-ho makes the police procedural *Memories of Murder*.

2005
Michael Haneke makes the arthouse mystery thriller *Hidden*.

2006
The Lives of Others explores Stasi surveillance in 1970s East Germany.

2007
David Fincher's *Zodiac* details the still unsolved manhunt for the 'Zodiac killer'. Sofie Grabøl stars as Inspector Sarah Lund in the Danish TV series *The Killing*, a key entry in the 'Nordic noir' boom.

2008
Liam Neeson deploys his particular set of skills to find his daughter in *Taken*.

2013
Alain Guiraudie's *Stranger by the Lake* references and subverts many of the clichés of gay characters in thrillers.

2014
David Fincher directs *Gone Girl*, adapted from Gillian Flynn's bestselling novel.

2017
Jordan Peele's directorial debut *Get Out* uses the form of the social thriller to explore racism and black anxiety.

Bong Joon-ho's *Memories of Murder* (2003)